FAIRIES IN CABS

COMIC AND CURIOUS CLIPPINGS FROM
THE LEGENDARY THEATRICAL PAPER

THE ERA
1890 – 1900

COMPILED BY

JULIA D ATKINSON

Copyright © 2017 Julia D Atkinson

All rights reserved.

ISBN: 978-1-9997610-0-4
ISBN-13: 1-9997610-0-6

Dedicated to my parents, Wendy (1936-1988) and Brian Atkinson

AT the New Theatre Royal, Croydon, on Thursday evening, an accident occurred owing to some of the scenery giving way, several of the ladies representing fairies in the Palace scene in *Aladdin* falling from a considerable height on to the stage. Some of the principals fainted and five of the fairies were sent in cabs to Croydon Hospital to be treated for sprains and bruises, two being seriously injured.

The Era, 20th January 1900

CONTENTS

ACKNOWLEDGEMENTS......ii

INTRODUCTION.....1

1 – 1890: MR WILBERFORCE'S PAROXYSMS.....3

2 – 1891: A STORM OF MOCK OSCULATION.....10

3 – 1892: VERY INTRICATE WHIRLS.....18

4 – 1893: THE STUFFED BABY HAS WON THE DAY.....34

5 – 1894: THE BEAUTIES OF HER INCOMPARABLE BUST.....46

6 – 1895: THE PEA-SHELLING PRIMA-DONNA.....58

7 – 1896: A POUND OF SAUSAGES ENCLOSED IN A DAINTY BOX.....74

8 – 1897: THE WAY IN WHICH IBSEN ARRANGES HIS HAIR.....90

9 – 1898: THE PATENT PNEUMATIC TAIL.....102

10 – 1899: MR SHAW'S EXTRAORDINARY JOCULARITY.....114

11 – 1900: THE EXPLODING BOER.....125

INDEX.....143

ABOUT THE AUTHOR.....149

Acknowledgements

Many thanks to the British Newspaper Archive for making *The Era*, and many other fascinating vintage newspapers, available online.

The cover was designed by Maduranga Sampath of MSN Art Studio.

The image on the back cover is a poster from the Library of Congress' Print and Photographs Division (dig. ID var. 1360). Dated 1900, this work is in the public domain in the United States because it was published (or registered with the U.S. Copyright Office) before January 1, 1923.

Introduction

First published in 1838, *The Era* started out as a journal owned by, and dedicated to the interests of, members of the public-house business. After a shaky start the the paper passed into the ownership of of Frederick Ledger, who edited *The Era* for three decades and expanded its coverage to include Freemasonry, sport, and – above all – the theatre, music hall and popular entertainment in general. Between the 1850s and the beginning of the First World War *The Era* was required reading for actors, music hall artistes, musicians and indeed everyone connected with the theatrical profession (the paper lingered on until 1939 as a shadow of its former self). Performers used its columns to find work and companies to find theatres; reviews and gossip columns helped members of the public to find sources of entertainment and keep abreast of the doings of their favourite stars.

1
1890
MR WILBERFORCE'S PAROXYSMS

THE Marquis de Leuville appeared to a summons at the Marlborough Street Police Court, on Wednesday, to answer a charge of having incited and procured various persons to create a disturbance at the Princess's Theatre, on the occasion of the production of a piece called *The Gold Craze*, on Nov. 13th. It was alleged that the defendant, believing he was to be caricatured or held up to opprobrium in the character of the Baron De Fleurville, played by Mr Barnes, commissioned his man-servant Vincent to engage men to go to the theatre and hiss the piece. Some eighteen or twenty men performed this service, and created so much uproar that the actors were not able to make themselves heard. It was also given in evidence that a number of men were engaged nightly to go to the Empire Theatre to applaud a song called "Samoa," written by the defendant. The hearing was adjourned.
4/1/1890

MR SEYMOUR HICKS, the youthful juvenile of the Kendals' company in America, has been the subject of an amusing correspondence in the American papers relative to his age. His versatility led one American critic to complain of a middle-aged man like Mr Seymour Hicks playing the boy's part in *The Scrap of Paper*. As Mr Hicks is only eighteen years old the correspondence has afforded vast amusement to the company, with whom Mr Hicks is a great favourite.
11/1/1890

WE have to announce the death, on Sunday, at the age of seventy-four, of Mrs FitzGeorge, wife of his Royal Highness the Duke of Cambridge*. Mrs FitzGeorge, before her marriage, was a Miss Farebrother [*sic*], and in her early days was known as an accomplished actress. She appeared at the Lyceum Theatre on Jan. 23rd, 1848, under the Mathews-Vestris management, in the character of Transimenus, an Arcadian Prince, in Planche's extravaganza *The Golden Branch*; and her refined style and graceful and finished dancing captivated both the critics and the public. She was considered the most lovely woman of her time. It is stated that in the course of Mrs FitzGeorge's long and painful illness the Queen has sent to make frequent inquiries at her residence in Queen Street, Mayfair. Mrs FitzGeorge was buried at Kensal Green Cemetery on Thursday afternoon. The funeral was attended by a large number of distinguished and titled personages.
*Prince George, Duke of Cambridge, was a grandson of King George III. His marriage to Sarah Fairbrother took place without Queen Victoria's consent and therefore was not recognised under the Royal Marriages Act of 1772, hence Mrs FitzGeorge's lack of a title. The marriage was not, as is sometimes claimed, a morganatic one.

AT the Hastings Pier Pavilion, during the progress of the pantomime *Jack and the Beanstalk* on Tuesday, a curious accident occurred. About fifteen of the ladies of the ballet, dressed as peasants, had formed a ring by joining hands, and were engaged in dancing round and round at a rapid rate, when

suddenly one of the dancers, quitting her hold of her companions' hands, was hurled outwards by the centrifugal momentum that she had acquired with such force as to snap asunder the guard protecting the footlights. She fell across the back of a chair, on which an astonished pianist was sitting in the orchestra, and finally was found reclining at the conductor's feet. Though a little surprised and shaken, the young lady, Miss Bessie Barham, took her place on the stage again later in the evening.
18/1/1890

MISS MARIE LOFTUS'S landlady in Glasgow two weeks ago engaged a servant from an industrial school, where she must have been taught that a theatre was the house of the devil. Miss Loftus takes her dinner in the dressing-room on Saturdays in consequence of the morning performance. Her landlady last Saturday sent the new girl with the dinner. When at the back of the stage she saw the supers all made up, and the pantomime properties and the glittering scenery, she dropped the basket of food and rushed from the place, shouting "The de'ils house! The de'ils house!" She sent to the landlady for her box next day, and had not been heard of since.

WANTED, Artistes to Send 3s. and Cabinet or C. de V., and I will send them Fifty Miniature Photographs perforated and gummed like postage stamps, for sticking on envelopes, cards, &c. *The Era* says: Artistically got up, invaluable to all who wish to make themselves known to Proprietors. W. FRANCIS, 104, Mallinson Road, Wandsworth Common, London.
1/2/1890

ON the 31st ult. a dressy young woman named Emily Knight was remanded by a stipendiary at Wolverhampton on a charge of stealing £30 belonging to an old man named Robert Anslow, with whom she had lived as housekeeper. The old man having no faith in banks kept his money in a hole in the stairs. The prisoner, by accident, discovered his hoard, stole the whole of it, and eloped with a clog dancer. The clog dancer lived with the woman until the money was nearly all dissipated, when, hearing that a detective was on their track, he robbed the girl of the few pounds she had left, and basely deserted her.
8/2/1890

TO THE EDITOR OF THE ERA.
Dear Sir, – Different customs prevail in different countries, and I have every reason to believe that in the Empire on which the sun never sets it is not considered ill-bred for one man to display the sole of his foot to another. I have frequently seen in this country an individual reclining at full length along the seat of a railway carriage, and presenting two upturned soles to the disgusted gaze of his fellow-traveller in the opposite corner. In the presence of ladies, too, the elegant custom prevails of resting an ankle on a knee, and thus displaying a well-developed, fine, flat sole to the members of the fair sex assembled. Such things, Sir, are not permitted on the Continent, but here they are looked upon as good, or at least tolerable, manners; and as one of the main objects of the modern stage is to reflect the manners of the time, it is pardonable in our actors that they should seize each frequent opportunity of crossing their legs.

It is, however, with their manner of dressing these crossable legs, and more especially the feet attached, that I have to find fault. In this respect our players are careless to a degree. I have a bad offender in my mind's eye at this moment in the form of a young and promising actor at present engaged at the Court Theatre. In the first act he has to sit on a chair facing the audience. To do this he pulls up a good foot of wide trouser, and then crosses one leg over the other, displaying to the astonished eyes of the audience a large patent leather boot, *shod with a broad white sole*, and surmounted with an ample quantity of loose and untidy red sock. This gentleman is supposed to be enacting, and generally accepted to give a fair impersonation of, a courtesy lord!

Sir, the offence is as easily remedied as it is easily committed. Let actors have boots made which fit, let them have black soles to their boots, let them wear tight-fitting socks and trousers, which do not require an effort of tugging when the wearer sit down in them, and then they will be able to indulge to their hearts' content in the national custom of crossing the legs, without offending the eyes of those who have paid to see them act.

I should also like to take this opportunity of pointing out to the clever young actor who plays the title-role at the Avenue Theatre that two buttons of his right boot and one of the left are hardly sufficient to fasten when setting out on a visit to the police-station, especially when the weather is such as to necessitate the constant wearing of a fur-lined coat.

Your obedient servant, A. TEIXEIRADE MATTOS*. *Arts and Letters Club.*
**The journalist and translator Teixeirade de Mattos is probably best remembered as the second husband of Lily Wilde, the widow of Oscar Wilde's brother Willie.*

MR JAMES M. CHUTE, who, we are pleased to say, is now quite recovered from his late severe illness, gave a tea on Saturday last, between the two performances, at the Prince's Theatre, Bristol, to the thirty-two children who appear in the pantomime. The little ones seemed heartily to enjoy the good things provided, and one sturdy little chap, in answer to a question put to him by a member of the company, remarked, "I never had so much to eat in my life; I've been sick twice."
22/2/1890

THE demon of discord played an important part in the pantomime of *Aladdin* at the Theatre Royal, Birmingham, on Saturday night. It is a matter of common gossip that it has for weeks past been lurking in out of the way corners behind the scenes, but until Thursday, 20th ult. – the occasion of Miss Jenny Hill's benefit – it was not allowed to present itself to the public. On that night the pantomime was abruptly terminated because of Miss Shirley's absence from the stage. On Friday night the performance passed off quietly, and to all outward appearance the the demon had been ruthlessly exorcised.

It was not so. On Saturday it again put in an appearance, and the large audience which had assembled to wish *Aladdin* farewell was treated to an exhibition of temper. When the second scene of the pantomime was reached, it seemed as if the artists were bent on infusing additional mirth and merriment into the performance by introducing funny and unexpected "business." Wigs were exchanged and various "make-ups" were indulged in, and the ludicrous effect produced by these innovations were heartily appreciated by the large audience. The performance, brisk, bright, and funnier than ever, ran with exceeding smoothness until about half-past nine. It then became evident from several ill-natured "gags" introduced by one or two of the artists that some difference of opinion had taken place behind the scenes.

The announcement made by advertisement on Saturday that Miss Madeline Shirley had been adjudged the winner of the prize for the most talented lady in the pantomime, presented by the proprietor of a weekly journal, was the subject of much unpleasant comment by the artists while on the stage. Those of the spectators, and they were few, who understood what was meant evidently did not appreciate the introduction of personalities, and every now and then hisses from the audience betokened how strong was its disapproval of them.

In the sixth scene Mr Rock, the Abanazar of the cast, and Mr Rich, the Benzine, presented Miss Shirley, in complimentary terms, with a small birthday cake. At the sides of the stage the ballet ladies and choristers had ranged themselves, and, contrary to every known stage custom, indulged in hand-clapping and cheering, a fact which showed strongly how matters stood. After the presentation Miss Shirley sang "The song that reached my heart" with excellent effect, and was honoured with three recalls. She repeated the last verse twice, and an excited admirer threw to the fair singer a handsome bouquet. By accident it fell on the footlights. In a second the paper surrounding the flowers was alight. Miss Shirley, with much presence of mind, promptly rescued the bouquet. She extinguished the flame with her hand and continued the song. But just before concluding she was made aware by the presence of extreme heat that the paper attached to the bouquet was still smouldering, and with a sudden movement she tore the paper off and trampled it on the stage. Of course, the incident heightened the excitement prevailing amongst the audience.

The enthusiasm which had been aroused by Miss Shirley evidently reached the hearts of some of the other artistes. The next scene – Aladdin's Palace – was characterised by disorderly confusion. While Miss Hill and Miss Shirley were on the stage a bun was thrown from the dress circle and fell at the feet of the artistes. This was evidently intended as a satire upon the "cake" incident of the preceding scene, but, if so, it failed in its object. Miss Shirley left the stage almost before the presence of the bun could be remarked, and Miss Hill was left to deal with it. This she did in indiscreet fashion. Miss Hill proceeded with her song, "Bai Jove." In answer to a recall, she walked to the front of the stage and requested to be allowed to make a few remarks, in consequence of "a malicious and slanderous statement which had been in circulation behind the scenes." There were cries of "No" and "Yes" from the audience, and Miss Hill, who was labouring under exceptional excitement, proceeded to deliver herself of a speech. She had, she averred, been accused of securing some person to present Miss Shirley with an explosive bouquet, for the purpose of injuring that lady. It was a wicked and dastardly untruth. She had been before the public for twenty-eight years, and "was it to be expected that from her high pedestal she would stoop to do a degrading and unwomanly act?" Of course the spectators who had witnessed the accident to the bouquet which had been presented to Miss Shirley were aware that Miss Hill, by no stretch of the imagination, could be charged with having thrown the bouquet, which, of course, everyone knew was not filled with explosive material. Cries of "Go on with the pantomime" became general, and then, as Miss Hill persisted in continuing her harangue, complaining bitterly of the manner in which the ballet ladies and choristers had assembled at the "wings" and applauded Miss Shirley, a storm of hisses burst forth from the audience.

Just then Miss Shirley appeared on the stage. She managed to say in tremulous tones that Miss Hill was making a great mistake, and added, "You have made a terrible error, Miss Hill, in mentioning such a thing before the public." Miss Hill retorted that Mrs Keene and Miss Jongmans had told her that a bouquet had been thrown to Miss Shirley which had exploded in her hand and nearly set her on fire. The audience laughed loudly at this. Miss Shirley – I think the people saw what happened. Miss Hill – You and I have never had any quarrels. Miss Shirley – No. Miss Hill then offered her hand to Miss Shirley, and together they left the stage amid the laughter of the audience.

In the Eiffel Tower scene Miss Hill appeared in her "'Arry" costume, but instead of singing that well-known song she rushed suddenly from the stage. She appeared again with tear-dimmed eyes in the "tag" scene, where Miss Shirley, as Aladdin's bride, ought to grasp Miss Hill's arms. Miss Hill refused to allow her to do so, and with an impetuous shake of the head again left the stage, and the other artistes had to bring the pantomime to a close. Some slight mark of sympathy with Miss Shirley was given by a crowd of people who assembled at the stage door, and who followed the cab in which she was seated as it drove to the hotel, at one of the windows of which building Miss Shirley was compelled to appear to bow her acknowledgements to the few hundred people who had assembled below.
1/3/1890

MR J.W. MATHEWS' dog Dougal (a large, rough-coated St Bernard), which has been appearing for the last eighteen months in *The Real Little Lord Fauntleroy,* had a narrow escape from death last Saturday evening. The company left Manchester by the 11.55 p.m., for London, Dougal, as usual, being chained in the guard's van. On arrival at Leicester he was missing, but had left a small portion of chain. The telegraph wires were set in motion, and on Sunday it was ascertained that he had made his way to Loughborough, after having jumped through the window on to the line whilst the train was running at the rate of forty miles an hour. Remarkable to relate, beyond a slight shaking, he is none the worse for his adventure. *29/3/1890*

THE Whereabouts Required of WILLIAM FLYNN, an American, on Tour in Colonies with Midgets. Deserted his Five Children, who are now in Tonbridge Union Workhouse. No remittances sent by Flynn. Information required as to Tour and places to be visited. Address, CLERK TO GUARDIANS, Tunbridge Wells, England.
3/5/1890

ON Sunday afternoon last Captain H. Pomeroy Gilbert's *Still Alarm* company were the innocent means of delaying for ten minutes or more the 3.10 train from Brighton to London. The scenery had been evidently somewhat insecurely packed on the luggage van at the rear of the train, and a sudden gust of wind getting under the flats packed on the top had the effect of lifting them like kites and finally deposited them some distance behind the train on the metals. The guard very soon discovered what had happened, and the train was brought to a standstill at Purley to the evident disquietude of one or two nervous passengers, whose "alarm," however, on looking out of the carriage window was quickly "stilled" by seeing two officials toiling down the line with a portion of "the Central Fire Brigade Station, New York," on their shoulders.
17/5/1890

A STREET MINSTREL IN TROUBLE.
AT the Marlborough Street Police Court, on Tuesday, Albert Kirby, aged twenty-one, a musician, of York Street, Lower Marsh, Lambeth, was charged with having violently assaulted Walter Hollings, an errand boy, of Market Place, Oxford Circus.

The evidence of the prosecutor, whose left arm and head were bandaged, and a companion was that about ten o'clock on Monday evening they were standing in a crowd in Vigo Street watching a band of "niggers." The prisoner, who was one of them, was singing "The Marquis of Camberwell Green," when a number of boys took up the chorus of the song and refused to be quiet. At length Kirby went up to the boys and remonstrated with them, and then crossing the road to where Hollings was standing knocked him down with his banjo and struck him on the arm while he was down. Hollings's head was severely cut and the drum of the prisoner's banjo broken from the force of the blows. Just as the prisoner was about to deliver a third blow, Police-constable 421 C came up and took him into custody, while he sent the boy to the Middlesex Hospital in the care of another constable.

For the defence several members of the troupe were called. They said that they were mobbed by about fifty boys, who refused to keep silence, and that the prisoner only struck out with his banjo in self-defence.

Mr Hannay remarked that he had yet to learn that street musicians had the right to enforce silence upon those who did not wish to hear them. He considered that the prisoner had committed a serious assault, and sentenced him to one months' imprisonment with hard labour.
19/7/1890

CURIOUS errors are occasionally made in telegraphing to managers. Mr Horace Lingard, the well-known opera bouffe manager, has recently had some droll experiences in this direction. It is the practice of acting-managers to send each evening a cipher telegram in words giving the receipts of the house, the first letter in each word representing a figure, and if anything else is required it is usually added in the same telegram. Judge, then, of Mr Lingard's surprise on receiving one as follows from his acting-manager: "Naughty Miss Collier wants white tights," the explanation of this being NM, the letters denoting the receipts, and Collier (the wardrobe mistress) wants white tights. Mr Lockwood, wishing to augment the company, through three ladies leaving, at the reopening of the New Middlesbrough Theatre, the other day, wired Mr Lingard, "Must have three more girls in chorus, and if Faithfull goes four." Miss Beatrice Faithfull had to rejoin the *Old Guard* company at the Grand Theatre, Leeds. The

message was received as follows: "Must have three more girls in chorus, and if faithful ones four." Mr Lingard was also astonished a few months ago to receive a wire saying, "Mr ---- (a new member of the company) has filled his pants well." "Pants," of course, should have read "parts."
9/8/1890

A MEMBER of Mr Wilson Barrett's company, recently returned from his American tour, tells the following amusing story: – At a theatre in Philadelphia several watches, belonging to members of the company, mysteriously disappeared, and, while everything was being turned upside down in the endeavour to find them, a solution to the mystery came by post to the super master. It was a short epistle from an absent super, and it ran thus: – "Dear Gus, I return the pawn tickets of the watches I stole. I was jolly hard up. Please excuse."

DURING a performance of *The Slave of Drink* at the Grand Theatre, Nottingham, this week, Mr Fred. Wilberforce, the representative of Jackson, had no less than five epileptic fits, one of such duration that the curtain had to be lowered, and an apology made to the audience for the delay. In spite of these embarrassing attacks, Mr Wilberforce bravely went on with his part, which he sustained until the end of the performance. Curiously enough, the flute player of the orchestra had two fits during the evening. Before actually leaving the theatre, the number of Mr Wilberforce's paroxysms amounted to ten in all.
23/8/1890

MR CHARLES COBURN has had an amusing experience with the phonograph. At a recent display of Mr Edison's instrument at Edinburgh, he sang the foreign choruses to "Two lovely black eyes," but when he came to the Greek one he found it had entirely slipped his memory. An awkward pause was put an end to by one of the lady operatives bringing a cylinder, upon which the singer had impressed the chorus some time before. He had therefore the peculiar experience of being prompted by his own voice. No wonder Mr Coburn styles the phonograph "an uncanny thing," and declares that he would be afraid to be left in the same room with it.
13/9/1890

FEW actors have had to die upon the stage as often as Mr William Terriss has had to do under Mr Henry Irving's management. In the realistic duel in *The Corsican Brothers* Mr Terriss was killed some two hundred times in succession; in *The Cup* he departed his stage life about a hundred; as Mercutio he was two hundred times run through the body; in *Hamlet* he likewise met a violent end; as Romeo he perished on two hundred nights at the Lyceum; and now, as Bucklaw, in *Ravenswood*, he falls nightly by the "Master's" sword. The boards of the Lyceum have evidently a deadly influence on Mr Terriss, who may be calculated to have expired on them on very nearly one thousand occasions. We sincerely trust, however, that it will be many years before so admirable and popular an actor will receive his last thrust.
On 16th December 1897 William Terriss was stabbed to death by Richard Archer Prince, a mentally unstable fellow-actor, at the stage door of the Adelphi Theatre.
18/10/1890

A NEW YORK telegram says: The Duke and Duchess of Marlborough occupied the upper proscenium box at the Lyceum Theatre on Wednesday night, where *The Maister of Woodbarrow* was being played. They were the guests of Mr Henry Clews, the banker. Soon after taking his seat, his Grace began talking in such a loud voice that he disturbed the actors and actresses, and attracted the attention of the audience. During the second act, notwithstanding the angry looks from the stage and orchestra seats, the conversation in the box continued, and, finally, some of the occupants of the front row loudly hissed. Mr E.C.H. Sothern, who was the leading actor on stage, said, after the performance, that had the talking not ceased when it did he would have stopped the piece and rung down the curtain.
25/10/1890

THE performance of *Darry the Dauntless* at the Theatre Royal, Leamington, on Monday, was somewhat interrupted by several ill-mannered racing men, who amused themselves by mimicking Miss Nellie Sheffield's very creditable efforts to please. When this had gone on for some time, Miss Lizzie Wentworth interpolated in the speech which she was delivering as the "good fairy" of the play, "Gentlemen, you ought to be ashamed of yourselves to mimic a child who is doing her best to entertain you." The rebuke had the desired effect. Miss Sheffield was not again interrupted, and the more noisy members of the sporting fraternity shortly afterwards left the theatre.

WANTED, Cheap Lot of Hand Grenades. Address, Oswald Stoll, Empire Theatre, Cardiff.
22/11/1890

TO THE EDITOR OF THE ERA.
Sir, – Whilst so much correspondence is flying about re dressing-rooms in provincial theatres, we feel it is our duty to expose the disgraceful state of a "Theatre Royal" up in the north of England. The theatre is leased by managers, themselves touring actors, and therefore one would expect a little courtesy and consideration from them. So as to encroach as little as possible on your space we will briefly expose the arrangements for the comfort of their breadwinners. The entrance to the stage-door is through a stable-yard, in which are urinals and w.c.'s for the hotel adjoining the theatre (no endeavour being made to mask them in). During the week we were there, this horrible yard was never lighted, although a gas lamp was there for that purpose, and the ladies of the company had nightly to pick their way through to get to the stage.

The ladies' dressing-rooms are right in front of the house, they having to pass along the corridor (used by the circle and boxes) to and from the stage, more than once during the week being spoken to by would-be mashers. Under the stage are two dressing-rooms, reached by almost perpendicular ladders, which you have to climb with the assistance of a rope. The room on the O.P. side we will describe. A stone floor, bare walls, crumbling and dirty, and on one side streaming with water, a small fireplace without bars to the grate, the stairs on this side coming down into the room from the stage, and used by the artists wishing to get across when the stage is set, as well as all the stage hands, carpenter, gas-man, and night-man. One gas burner lights this cellar by night, and a small window with the glass knocked out admits daylight, rain, and wind in about equal proportions.

We have no doubt that members of the profession will recognise the theatre from our description, and if managers would only before booking a theatre sign their contracts subject to clean, healthy, and convenient dressing-rooms being provided for their companies, this disgraceful state of affairs could not long exist. Thanking you for insertion, we are, sir, yours truly,
THE MEMBERS OF THE CO.

AT the Princess's Theatre, the other night, in the last act of *Antony and Cleopatra*, where the Queen in the monument is surprised by a party of Roman guards, a gentleman in the gallery, very much excited, called out, "Look out, Missus, the swaddies are coming down the stairs." This completely upset the gravity of the house, and the action was interrupted by general laughter.
13/12/1890

2
1891
A STORM OF MOCK OSCULATION

MR ARTHUR BOURCHIER met with a somewhat unexpected mishap on Saturday last, at the conclusion of his night's work at the Criterion Theatre. As he was dressing, somewhat leisurely, for a supper party, the electric light in his room suddenly went out, and his servant discovered that the hall-porter, supposing all the company had gone – it being about 11.45 – had locked up for the night, and left them in darkness to find their way out as best they might. This proved to be no easy task. Groping their way to the stage, they soon discovered by the solitary gaslight that all the officials in front had also gone, and that they were, therefore, imprisoned in the subterranean theatre. With the aid of matches, they arrived at a window overlooking Jermyn Street, and at about 12.30 engaged the sympathy of a passing policeman, whose only consolation was that at the end of his "beat" he could knock up a neighbouring ironmonger. Ultimately, at about four o'clock on Sunday morning, Mr Bourchier and his servant were liberated from their predicament. Whether the door-keeper has evaded the "wrath to come" we know not.
3/1/1891

WANTED, Everyone to Know P.W. O'Brian, Talking, Singing, and Dancing Clown, is beating his own record, Crouste's Circus, Wakefield. Now raising the dead to life. That's better than killing them. Hundreds of undertakers emigrating. Pirates beware. Oh, give over.
31/1/1891

WE have eccentric comedians, Glasgow-Irish comedians, true Irish comedians, Cockney comedians, quaint comedians, coster comedians, melancholy comedians, mimicking comedians, knockabout comedians, acrobatic comedians, topical comedians, and to this list we must now add the expectorating comedian. In this last line of business it is thought funny to force from the mouth either a stream of water "pouched" for the purpose or the natural saliva. We noted two instances only this week, and another gentleman (?) evidently thought it extremely funny to stroke his nostrils with his fingers and then wipe his hands on his hair. True humour can surely never be linked with such disgusting vulgarity.
14/2/1891

THE famous theatrical horse Victoria died this week, its last appearance being in the play of *Antony and Cleopatra* at the Princess's Theatre. The owner, Mr Hales, theatrical jeweller, has handed the hoofs to Mr Rowland Ward, F.Z.S., for the purpose of mounting. The body has been sent to the Royal Veterinary College, and will be interesting on account of its indefinite sex.
28/2/1891

IMPERSONATING AN ACTRESS.

AT the Worcester City Police Court, on Wednesday, Mary Elizabeth Eastman, aged sixteen, described as a servant, of 54, Wood Lane, Treetop, near Rotherham, was charged with stealing a black dress and a small silver brooch, value 18s., the property of John Hill, at Little Southfield Street, Worcester, on January 30th. The Chief Constable stated that the case was a curious one. The prisoner went in the first place to Mr Gomersal, the lessee of the Theatre Royal, and told him that she was a daughter of Mr T.C. King, the tragedian, a former lessee of the theatre. Mr Gomersal did not comply with her request to engage her for the pantomime, and she then went to the house of the prosecutrix, who took in lodgers, and said that she was Miss Maude Stafford, the actress, who was then playing in the pantomime of *Red Riding Hood*, at the theatre. She took a bedroom and sitting-room at Mrs Hill's at the rate of 7s. 6d. a week, and, to keep up the fiction, she used to stay out at night during the time the performance was on at the theatre. Prisoner bore no resemblance to Miss Stafford. Prosecutrix did not receive payment from the prisoner, and on making inquiries found that she was not Miss Maude Stafford. She then told prisoner that she had discovered her deception, and that she must leave the house. Prisoner left, and prosecutrix missed the articles which formed the subject of the charge. The prisoner had also deceived her mother by telling her that she was engaged to a Gerald Lloyd, who had died and was to be buried at Worcester. Her mother went to Worcester, and the prisoner left her by some pretence at the station, and did not return, but took with her some things, which she pawned. She was arrested in the gallery of the theatre on Tuesday night.

Mrs Hill, the prosecutrix, proved the first part of this statement, and added that when she told prisoner she had discovered that she was not Miss Maude Stafford, the actress, prisoner declared that she was, and said she would fetch Mrs Gomersal.

Prisoner's mother, Mrs Mary Howell, appeared, and said the prisoner was sixteen years of age. In September last she left home, and went into service at Armley, near Leeds. In about a month she was told that her daughter was not at Armley, but was at Rotherham with a theatrical company (Arthur Lloyd's company), and witness went to Rotherham and took her daughter home. Whilst at home her daughter represented that she received letters from Arthur Lloyd's brother (Gerald Lloyd), and she showed witness letters which she believed to come from that gentleman, but, as she was "no scholar," she could not tell. The letters purported to tell the prisoner that she was to go to Worcester to join the company, but witness now believed that they were written by the prisoner herself. She still believed, however, that her daughter had been with the company. She afterwards received a letter from her daughter saying that Gerald Lloyd was dead and was to be buried at Worcester, where the letter was written from. Witness found that this was untrue. The prisoner said she and Gerald Lloyd were to be married at Easter. When a child the prisoner fell from the table and hurt her head, and a doctor had said that her brain was affected. Witness had had a great deal of trouble with her.

Prisoner, in reply to the charge, said she did not know what possessed her to take the dress, which she pawned for 2s. She must have been out of her mind, and she knew that she had a weak brain.

The mother was at first reluctant to take the prisoner back home, saying that she would "get up to some more wickedness;" but, after some persuasion from the magistrates, she consented to do so, and she and prisoner were bound over in £5 for the prisoner to come up if called upon.

ON Monday last Captain Fisher, the tattooed man and Indian club manipulator, visited the ancient Parish Church of Kidwelly, Wales (of which town his parents were natives), in search of records of his family. He was accompanied by a young lady, and the natives seeing both in company with the vicar entering the sacred edifice, at once concluded that a wedding was about to come off. Several persons hastily got rice and ropes, and as the party left the church they were met by showers of the former edible, and their progress was barred by by ropes stretched across the gates. (It is the custom in Wales to thus bar the progress of wedding parties until a sum of money is given by the bridegroom.) The captain expostulated, and tried to explain that no wedding had taken place at all, but all to no purpose, those holding the ropes

seeming to know better. At last the captain got out of temper, launched out his good right arm, and levelled one of his assailants with the ground. This seemed to convince the others that something was wrong, and they slunk away sadder if not wiser men.
7/3/1891

A REMARKABLE incident occurred at Her Majesty's Theatre, Carlisle, on Saturday night last, during the performance of *Macbeth* by Mr Osmond Tearle and company. Between the first and second acts Mr Tearle appeared before the curtain, and was greeted with loud cheers, the "gods," who were present in force, apparently expecting that he was going to make a speech. The actor, however, soon showed that his purpose was not so amiable. He said that he regarded the action of "that gentleman in the boxes who was continually reading a paper as an insult," adding that it was a pity the offender had paid his money to come there and read while the company was doing their best to amuse him. The speech evoked yells of "Turn him out!" and similar expressions from the gallery, by whom this unexpected feature of the entertainment appeared to be much relished.

MR HENRY HAYES, a leading baritone in Mr Arthur Rousbey's English opera company, who have this week been fulfilling a three nights' engagement in Perth, on Wednesday last fell over the cliffs at Kinnoull Hill, in the neighbourhood of that city, and sustained such serious injuries that he died in Perth Infirmary a few hours after the accident. Mr Hayes, accompanied by Mr Albert Broadbent, another member of the company, ascended Kinnoull Hill, and the two gentlemen wandered about till they reached a ruined tower, where they began to scramble along the cliff. Mr Hayes fell suddenly, and became suspended head downwards in the fork of a tree, about 150 feet below. With assistance summoned he was extricated from his perilous position, and conveyed to Perth Infirmary, where it was found that he had sustained severe internal injuries. He died the same evening, without having recovered consciousness. Mr Hayes was a native of Birkenhead, and was about twenty-eight years of age.
21/3/1891

THE Anglo-French telephone line has been the subject of an experiment. About eight p.m. the other evening five telephone receivers were connected to the new line in Room 90 of the Post Office, and the electricians there distinctly heard the music of the Grand Opéra in Paris. The orchestra sounded so clearly that the piccolo could be plainly heard joining in. The voices of the singers were also wonderfully well heard. In a duet the two voices could be separated by the ear. There was no confusion of voices, even in the chorus. The applause of the audience and the cries of "Bis" were also heard by the listeners. The transmitters were microphones placed on the stage of the Opera House.
28/3/1891

MR TONY BENSON, of Elliott and Benson, died suddenly in an epileptic fit at Halifax on Wednesday last. Our Barnsley correspondent says it is rather a remarkable coincidence that poor Benson had a mock funeral at Bradford, on Feb. 16th. The Theatre Royal and Prince's Theatre pantomime companies had a football match for the benefit of the local charities. During the match Benson, for a joke, pretended to be killed. His remains were paraded round the ground, a pit was dug, and a mock burial took place with musical honours. A splendid wreath was placed at his head, with a bottle of spirits and some cake. Needless to say, the corpse came round, devoured the cake, emptied the bottle, and appeared at night on the Royal stage with the wreath around his neck.
4/4/1891

WHILST a troupe of Japanese jugglers were giving a performance at the Alhambra, West Hartlepool, on Monday night, one of the knives they were throwing flew into the orchestra and struck a violinist on the head. He was obliged to retire, with blood flowing freely from a scalp wound, and it was some time ere he could return.

WANTED, Leading Lady and Useful Gent., who are not taken ill at the last moment and afraid of Runcorn. Sobriety in all cases. Terms, J.W. SNAPE, Britannia Theatre (Portable), Runcorn; after Tuesday, Nantwich, Cheshire.
11/4/1891

ON Monday, on the occasion of the revival of *Hamlet*, while Mr Wilson Barrett as Hamlet was listening to the Ghost, a limelight man suddenly had a fainting-fit, and fell a distance of ten or twelve feet. There was a loud crash, a shriek of pain, and then the performance went on as if nothing had happened, the Ghost raising his voice to drown the sufferer's cries. The poor fellow was conveyed to the hospital, where it was ascertained that no bones were broken, but that he was bruised, and had badly bitten his tongue.
18/4/1891

WANTED, Re-engagement by Young Lady (Creole), age Twenty, in good Dramatic Company, Stock or Tour. Had some good experience. Willing to give time in genuine concern. Tragic, Pathetic, or Foreign Parts preferred. Address, NYDIA, Tavistock Terrace, Upper Holloway, N.

WANTED, a Woman to Clean Heavy Weights, Cannons and Real Chains. Same must be a little up in Club Swinging. Terms, £5 weekly. Address, VICTORINA, the Strongest Lady on Earth, Quinette's Circus, Southport.
25/4/1891

WANTED, a Sterling Character Actor. Must create Tears and Laughter in Speech of Four Lines, or useless for the Part. Address, SIDNEY COOPER, 7, Church Street, Leamington.
23/5/1891

DURING the performance of *The Diver's Luck* at the Theatre Royal, West Hartlepool, the other evening, a "gentleman" entered the dress circle, and after quietly watching for some time the progress of the piece, suddenly burst into loud and ironical laughter at one of Mr Fred. Cooke's jokes, which, it is presumed, he recognised as an old familiar friend. No notice was taken of the interruption from the stage, though several people in the auditorium turned and looked in the direction from which the unusual noise came. Mr Cooke, however, in his part of Big Barney, has a good many of these wheezes to crack, and almost every one of them appeared to excite the gentleman in the circle. "Oh! Oh! Ah! Ah!" he repeatedly shouted at the top of his voice, varying his reception of the joke by an occasional cry of "Chestnut, chestnut!" Presently Mr Cooke stepped down to the footlights, and, casting a withering glance at the occupant of the dress circle, exclaimed "This is not a pantomime, nor is the performance for children." "Hear, hear," shouted the audience. "Oh, I'm sorry I spoke," responded the "gentleman," and no doubt he was, for he did not attempt to interrupt the performance again.
30/5/1891

MR AUGUSTUS YORKE, son of Mr Reginald Yorke, who, under the stage name of A. Danemore, has been appearing in *A Pantomime Rehearsal* at Terry's Theatre, has met with a painful and shocking death. While he was asleep the covering of the dressing table in his room took fire, and Mr Danemore, awaking, tried to put out the flames. In the attempt his nightshirt became ignited, and he rushed out into the street. Here a working man wrapped him in his jacket and smothered the flames; but Mr Danemore was terribly burned, and died in St George's Hospital from shock to the system.
4/7/1891

ON Monday night, at the Grand Theatre, Nottingham, a female occupant of the gallery had secured a front seat. The comic policeman in *East Lynne* tickled this good lady's sense of humour to such an extent that she abandoned herself to mirth and forgot her false and insecurely fastened teeth. The silver palate plate with several molars attached dropped from their appropriate resting-place and took a front seat in the circle. After a hunt the missing molars were restored to the anxious owner.
11/7/1891

WHAT would an English audience say to a play in which a great man of less than thirty years ago was brought upon the stage as the hero, the protagonist, and in which, moreover, questions that were burning in our younger days – the boyhood of men yet under fifty – were reopened, and the feelings of people yet alive, famous and respected, were sorely outraged? Suppose Prince Albert, or Lord Palmerston, or Lord Beaconsfield, were made the hero of a melodrama, what should we in London think of the taste and good feeling of its author? If we condemned him, we must surely condemn, even more strongly, the American playwright who proposes shortly to produce a drama which shall deal with the life of Abraham Lincoln, and shall end with his assassination by Booth. Yet Messrs McKee Rankin and Archibald Gordon have written such a drama, and intend, it is said, to produce it early this autumn at Indianapolis, and take it on tour through the West; though the brother of John Wilkes Booth is yet one of the most eminent and most respected of American actors, and though no one is ignorant of his extreme and most natural sensitiveness on the subject – nor, we may add, of the way in which unprincipled enemies have used this foul weapon against him. Nearly thirty years after his brother's crime, Mr Edwin Booth might fairly have supposed that at all events a brother actor would have refrained from pillorying that unhappy man on the stage whose disgrace he was; while that the length of time has not blunted the keenness of Mr Booth's own feelings on the subject is shown by his continued refusal to act in the town in which the deed was done.

Open for Engagements in England, Oct. 1st. 1891. Three Great Troupes Consolidated – Three.
Show No. 1, Wm. Foote and Co.'s Afric-American Character Concerts.
Show No. 2, Wm. Foote and Co.'s Original "Uncle Tom's Cabin" Minstrels and Afric-American Native Choir.
Show No. 3, Wm. Foote and Co.'s Crescent City Creole Company (from New Orleans, La., U.S.A.)
All now Combined and Concentrated in One Superbly Unique Entertainment for the present Tour of the World, preliminary to filling an extended Engagement at World's Fair, Chicago, in 1893.
A Bevy of Brilliant Black Beauties, a Mammoth Afric-American Native Choir, a Challenge Corps of Coloured Creole Ladies, a Host of Happy Hottentots, Thirty Genuine Negro Artists. No Burnt Cork. No Imitations.
N.B. – Every person, Man, Woman, or Child, taking part in this Entertainment is a genuine "person of colour," and Member of Native Afric-American Choirs. Positively the offspring of Savages and Slaves. They have progressed during the present Half Century from Savage to Slave, Soldier to Citizen. The combined Entertainments portray vividly every phase of Negro life, showing the advantages of education, the fruits of emancipation and march of human civilisation through the medium of Mirth, Music, and Mimicry.
Managers having Open Dates (Weeks only) will please send terms immediately, as our time in England is limited. Address, WM. FOOTE, care of "The Era" Office.
8/8/1891

A JEALOUS CONJUROR.
AT the Westminster Police-court, on Tuesday, a well-dressed young man named Albert Stanton, described as a conjuror, of 14, Ashburnham Road, Chelsea, appeared to a summons before Mr De Rutzen for using threats to Mr William Henry Jones, builder, &c., of Basuta Road, Parson's Green. Mr

Duerdin Dutton appeared for the complainant, and the defendant conducted his own case in an excitable and declamatory style, which occasioned much amusement and laughter.

Mr Dutton said the defendant's wife was housekeeper to a lady living in Cheyne Row, Chelsea, and she had been greatly inconvenienced by her husband's jealous disposition. His latest suspicion was directed against the complainant, who had been at work in the house where Mrs Stanton was in service, and going there the defendant created a great disturbance and threatened to knife Mr Jones, who, being alarmed, escaped by a back door.

The complainant gave evidence in support of Mr Dutton's statement, and said the offence for which he had obtained the summons was committed last Bank Holiday. There was no truth in the allegations made that he had had relations with Mrs Stanton of an improper character.

The Defendant – If you are supposed to have work at the place you would not be there till half-past ten at night, your worship. I have been there at that time, and when my wife opened the door she looked uncomfortably surprised. She asked me what I wanted. I said, "Well, that's very peculiar. You usually say, 'Come inside, dear.'" She did eventually ask me into the dining-room instead of into the kitchen. But I walked downstairs, and found this gentleman (the complainant) there. What occasion had he to be there at half-past ten? He was not decorating then.

Mr De Rutzen – What time was it when he found you downstairs? The complainant – About seven or eight in the evening. I was only doing up the kitchen.

The Defendant – How can you stand there and say it. You are the "gentleman" who sent away the little boy who cleans the knives, so that you could be alone with my wife – I know – d'you see.

The Complainant – Nothing of the kind.

The Defendant – I found you there, and you had no occasion to be there. Your worship, I hardly like mentioning it in public, but what do you think I found? When my wife was undressing a card fell out of her stocking. And that card, sir, was Mr Jones's card. I have the card now. Now, I can't see the reason why my wife should keep a gentleman's card in her stocking – can you? Nor why a master painter should keep in the kitchen till 10.30, and send the boy away. Very likely I did catch hold of "the gentleman" (scornfully said) and threaten to break his neck. But that's all. And what would you do under the circumstances, sir, I ask you? Is my wife's stocking a proper case for Mr Jones's cards?

A gardener employed at the house in Cheyne Walk said that the defendant came there most excitedly on Bank Holiday and hammered at the door. He said he would shoot Jones, and if one barrel would not do he would fire twice.

Mr Dutton said nothing was worse than a jealous man like the defendant, who had been sent to prison for two months before for wilful damage at the house and annoying his wife.

The Defendant – Yes. Committed through perjury, sir.

Mr De Rutzen – The way you have been going on makes me think at first you were not right. It is impossible to say what a man suffering from a fit of jealousy like you might do, and therefore you will have to enter into your recognisances in £10 and find a surety as well to be of good behaviour and keep the peace for two months, or go to gaol for fourteen days.

The Defendant (waving his hand) – Thank you, sir. I shall do the fourteen days.

He was removed to the cells.

A SHOWMAN'S TRAGEDY.

IT is a common idea with many good people that a showman's life is a mean and sordid one, and that his existence is passed amid surroundings that give no opportunity or occasion for the exercise of truth, or patience, or faithfulness. A pitiful tragedy which occurred in Glasgow at the beginning of the week might be taken as a text from which to demolish this notion of a showman's life.

A Negro "Fire King" had married a Scotchwoman of more than passing comeliness, and, despite the difference in colour, they seemed to have led a happy and contented life, he following his vocation as a showman, while his wife managed a shooting saloon. The "Fire King" lived a somewhat migratory

existence, travelling from place to place as the exigencies of his calling demanded, while his wife remained at home to look after the shooting saloon. During one of her husband's absences, a stranger was attracted by her good looks, and a relationship was formed which did no credit to either of them. After the intimacy had lasted a few months, the man, who was a farmer in British Columbia, returned to that country, sold out his farm, and transferred his belongings to Canada. During his stay in Canada he corresponded with the showman's wife, but about six months ago he made over his farm to his eldest son and came to Scotland, which was his native country, for good – or rather evil, as it ultimately turned out. He renewed his acquaintanceship with his mistress, and they met frequently by appointment. They passed last Saturday night in each other's company, and on Sunday they were seen in the streets of Maryhill, an outlying suburb of Glasgow. There they quarrelled, for the man suddenly whipped a revolver from his trouser pocket, fired a bullet in the woman's back, gazed on her a few moments as she lay bleeding on the footpath, and then, placing the pistol to his head, blew out his brains. He died almost immediately afterwards, but the woman's injuries have not proved fatal. The most pathetic circumstance in this sad tragedy, however, is the attitude of the woman's dusky husband on her faithlessness. "Nawful business," said he, in response to certain queries, "don't know if I shall ever get over it, and can't say if she'll get over it. Hope she will, poor dear. I've nothin' agin her, not I. She was a good-natured little girl, and a big help to me, by Jove, she was, an' I hope she'll be spared to be so again. Dat skunk's gone, now, an' if Nelly recovers we may be happy again." He is a big burly fellow, who describes himself as "Fire King of the World and Champion American Quoit Player;" but he is not built like Othello, for evidently his philosophy is liberal enough and catholic enough to enable him to forgive and love the wife who has so greatly wronged him.
The victim's surname is elsewhere given as Murray or Gabriel.

WANTED, to Sell, Curiosity, Balloon-Headed Male Child, Petrified, Perfect Condition, with Hair, Hands, Feet, Nails, &c. Loose in Coffin, £5. Also Live Animal, known as "Churchyard Devil" (in Cage). Recently captured in a vault in Tredworth Cemetery, Gloucester. £5. PROPRIETOR, Victoria Hall, Cheltenham.
15/8/1891

PROVINCIAL audiences, especially in Scotland, are not too considerate in their treatment of actors. The other evening a performance of *The Merchant of Venice* was being given at Motherwell, near Glasgow, and the company suffered considerable annoyance from the constant interruptions. In the first scene of a short sketch which followed *The Merchant* a storm of mock osculation was raised upon the hero kissing and hugging the heroine. Thereupon the said hero, with a scornful glance to the front, left the stage, and allowed the lady to inform the audience that he had felt so insulted that he refused to return. The band played "God Save the Queen," and the performance terminated. Loud demonstrations are not uncommon in Scotch theatres, but they are usually taken in good part by the actors.
19/9/1891

A MOST amusing incident occurred at the Theatre Royal, Rochdale, on Thursday, 17th inst. The play was *Men of Metal*, performed by Mr T. Morton Powell's company. During act three – Cobham Junction – the London train steams out of the station, and passes behind the window of the waiting room, the effect being produced by a profile engine and train, which of course must be lighted, this being done by the property-man running behind the train with a pan of red fire. On this particular evening, however, from some unexplained cause, the property-man was not there, and the duty was entrusted to his sister, a little girl of some ten summers, who, not having seen it done before, was rather late, and, to the amazement of the audience and the uncontrollable laughter of the actors, the train went across, and about two yards behind it, running along, was seen a little girl with a pan of red fire in her hand.
26/9/1891

TO THE EDITOR OF THE ERA.
Sir, – I beg to draw the attention of your readers to the disgraceful state of the Theatre Royal, ------. So great is the stench that none of the artists dare venture on the stage except holding a handkerchief saturated with perfume, or as the majority of the company are doing, holding big pieces of camphor in their hands. In the dressing-rooms things are just as bad, the only difference is that the higher the dressing-rooms are, the less they smell. But the artists with all the hard work and quick changes must necessarily dress in the rooms nearest the stage, and they are consequently in this frightful atmosphere from 6.30 to 11.30. I do not exaggerate when I say that one gentleman was so overcome while on stage by the effluvium that he could scarcely go on with his part. Added to this, the dressing-rooms are so fearfully damp that dresses cannot possibly be hung near the walls. Yours faithfully, ALICE KINGSLEY. *The present state of the law of libel compels us to suppress the name of the theatre, but Miss Kingsley will doubtless furnish the Actors' Association with full particulars [ED.]*
24/10/1891

TO LET, Best Novelty in England, for the Christmas Pantomime, the Trained STAGS and HOUNDS in the great scene of the "Stag Hunt," the same beautiful Stags and Hounds that was the great attraction of Olympia, London. These animals are most docile, and will Leap Gates across the Stage 7ft. high, and over Water Jumps 9ft. wide. The scene is the most novel and exciting, and can be fitted in any Pantomime. At the end of the Hunt the Stags and Hounds clear the Water Jump, a Canvas Tank to hold about Twenty Buckets of Water. The Comic Man, Woman and Fat Policeman get drowned, while the Clown and Pantaloon save their lives. Reference, Crystal Palace Theatre, Birmingham Theatre, &c. Splendid and Magnificent Posters and Cuts – these alone a great attraction. The Stag Hunt, as performed by these Trained Stags and Hounds, would make a splendid Novelty for a Touring Company, to write a Drama (Sporting), to finish with the Stag Hunt. On arrival in each town, to parade in their van, followed by the Hounds, Huntsmen blowing their Horns, &c. The Stags and Hounds travel in one van together. Address, F. GINNETT, Circus, Brighton.
21/11/1891

A SERIOUS disturbance took place on the evening of the 20th inst. in the People's Music Hall, Lower Mosley Street, Manchester, resulting in considerable damage to the interior of the building. The frequenters of this place of amusement were given to understand that the entertainment was to include a clog-dance contest, in which prizes were to be offered. This announcement appears to have attracted a large audience, and great was the disappointment when, at 10.30, the performance terminated without this particular feature of the programme. The occupants of the gallery at once showed their dissatisfaction in a most marked and riotous manner. They picked up seats and threw them into the pit, broke the windows, turned out the lights, and did other damage. Many other persons in the body of the hall also behaved in a most reckless manner, and hurled all kind of missiles on to the stage. Those in charge of the building were unable to quell the disturbance, and it was only when the rowdy visitors learnt that the police had put in an appearance that they lost no time in getting into the street. A large crowd of persons collected outside, some of whom threw stones at the windows, and in this way caused much damage.
28/11/1891

WANTED, to Sell, Mighty Kamchatka Owl, with immense Horns, Eyes like Oranges; stretches 8ft. 6in.; carries off sheep. £21 10s. 9d. BLAKE, Book Publishers, Portsea.

WANTED, Conqueror to send Doddie safe Address. Post-office preferred. Advantageous offering. Strict confidence. Refresh memory for solution of names.
26/12/1891

3
1892
VERY INTRICATE WHIRLS

SHOCKING THEATRICAL DISASTER.
A serious disaster occurred at Gateshead on Saturday evening, when, at the Theatre Royal, a panic resulted in the death of ten people. Mr Turner and Mr Bacon, lessees of the Gateshead Theatre Royal, had on Christmas Eve produced their third pantomime, on the subject of *Aladdin*. On the night of Boxing Day a holiday audience, numbering twelve hundred, assembled, filling the spacious gallery and pit to overflowing, whilst the other parts of the house were numerously occupied. The theatre has two tiers, the lower being divided into circle and side balcony seats, the higher being the gallery, wherein accommodation is provided for seven or eight hundred spectators. The whole of the ground floor is devoted to the pit.

As the performance progressed on Saturday the greatest good humour prevailed in the house, and it was on the opening of the last scene – the Great Wall of China – that the incident occurred which was fraught with such terrible consequences. In the lower circle on the left-hand side facing the stage a woman, who was attended by her husband, dropped either a scarf-pin or a florin on the floor. Without thinking that any danger might be caused by the act, the man struck a match and looked for the missing article. By this means a piece of paper on the floor caught fire, and the paper and sawdust smouldering together caused a flame which, though slight, was sufficient to alarm the woman, who called out "Fire, fire." A hand was put across her mouth to prevent a repetition of the words; but, as a volume of smoke was now curling upwards, the alarm spread at once, and the audience started to its feet and made straightway for the exits from the stage.

Mr Turner and his company, realising at once the dreadful nature of the rush, and also the smallness of the fire, called on the audience to keep their places or go out in order. Their appeals were, however, unheeded, and as some of the pit occupants went back to the ordinary exits, crowds tore down the orchestra partition and, clambering to the stage, swarmed out at the narrow private staircase. From the lower circle the people got out safely, but numbers preferred to lower themselves or jump to the pit; whilst from the gallery at the edge nearest the stage the more venturesome jumped direct to the stage. In the meantime, the bulk of the gallery audience made its way to the one exit, the door of which was bolted. Foster, the check-taker in charge, managed eventually to draw the bolt, thus releasing the door; but the act cost him his life, for before he could leave the place the weight of the surging crowd forced him down three stairs to a landing on the way to the main staircase. In their haste to leave the theatre, those who pressed onwards stumbled down the three stairs, and were fallen upon by the mass behind, and the means of egress thus became greatly impeded, though hundreds found their way down to the street without injury.

When the people ceased to pour down the stairs it was assumed by the excited populace in the streets surrounding the Theatre Royal that all had emerged; but as Thomas Butler and James Gordon were ascending the gallery stairs they were terrified to find a heap of living and dead people five deep, whilst, behind them, there still struggled those who had not been able to proceed further. With assistance they pulled out men, lads, women, and girls, most of them suffering from shock, whilst others were more dead than alive, and did not long survive when carried out to the neighbouring houses. A door at the top of the gallery stairs was then opened, and numbers passed through in safety, and windows were broken to admit fresh air. One little lad was held back just as he was on the point of jumping down to the hard surface of Nelson Square from a height of about 70ft. Inside the theatre, other parts of the house were cleared in good time, and when it was discovered that there was a stoppage at the gallery door, long benches were raised from the pit to the gallery balcony, and down these a great number of people reached the floor in safety, thence making their way to the street, where the news of a panic spreading quickly attracted an enormous crowd, which increased as the victims were carried out to the surrounding houses for medical treatment. It was about half-past ten o'clock when the catastrophe took place, and in a few minutes the fire had been extinguished with the aid of a few buckets of water. Before eleven o'clock death had ensued in several cases, and by midnight there had been ten deaths, whilst at the Newcastle Royal Infirmary several patients were admitted suffering from shock and bruises. Nine of the dead bodies were removed to the Temperance Hall.

On Monday an inquest was opened by Mr Coroner Graham, who remarked upon the necessity of people leaving places of amusement in a quiet and orderly manner when fear of danger arose. The jury had sufficient evidence placed before them to show that the fire had been a very trifling affair comparatively, and one which could have easily and speedily been extinguished without inconvenience to anyone in the building except those in the immediate vicinity. The inquiry was adjourned. Our correspondent, who was in the theatre, confirms the statement made by Mr Turner, who says: "There was really no fire at all; a little water soon quenched what there was, and when the seats were torn up on Monday morning we found that they were only scorched underneath, and the paper on the wall was not even burnt off." To Mr Turner and Mr Bacon, who retained their self-possession throughout, and did all that men could possibly do to prevent the panic, the greatest praise is due, and sympathy is expressed for them on every hand. The theatre remained closed on Monday and Tuesday, and reopened on Wednesday with the pantomime, when the entire proceeds were handed over to the widow of the deceased check-taker, Thomas Foster, who leaves a family of four children. The lessees also gave another benefit performance for the parents of the children who were killed. [...]

The members of the company all escaped unhurt, but several of them had not time to change their stage dresses for ordinary attire. Immediately on the panic becoming known a number of roughs broke into the theatre and fairly ransacked the dressing-rooms, taking with them most of the artists' clothes, and anything they could lay their hands on. This dastardly outrage has created great indignation in the town.

THE Countess of Clancarty, known to music hall patrons and theatre-goers who patronise burlesque as Belle Bilton, on Sunday last presented her noble lord and master with twins – both boys – who possibly may some day appear upon the scenes of mamma's vocal and Terpsichorean exploits as the Brothers Bilton.

WANTED, Doddie's Conqueror to understand. Presents ready. Alone with Joe on Christmas Day, remembering St George and Dragon. Forgave all. Refresh memory for names. Send Post-office address.
2/1/1892

AT the Marylebone Police Court, on Tuesday, John Brown, of Carlisle Street, Marylebone, was charged on remand with stealing by a trick sixpence from Lina Fuller, of Chichester Road, Kilburn.

The prosecutrix and a cousin went to the Marylebone Theatre to see the pantomime on Boxing Night. Seeing an announcement that early admission could be obtained by payment of an extra fee at the stage-door in Little Church Street, they went in the direction indicated. They came across the prisoner and another man who were standing at an open door, and not knowing the locality well they supposed that was the stage door. The men asked if they wanted the early admission door, and they replied that they did. The men then charged them sixpence, wrote something on a piece of paper, and directed them into the basement of the house. They followed the instructions and soon found themselves in the kitchen of a common lodging-house. The room was full of men who were smoking and talking, and when the young women asked if that was the way into the theatre the men laughed heartily and showed a disposition to play a practical joke, but the women quickly retreated and gave the prisoner into custody, the other man escaping.

The prisoner, in reply to the charge, said he was drunk at the time. He had no intention of taking the money. There were thirty or forty men in the kitchen. He gave the prosecutrix 5½d. out of his own pocket because she seemed upset.

Mr Montagu Williams – You were sober enough to commit a rather clever fraud on these young women.

The Prisoner – I was drunk. Drink got into my head. I've been in an asylum.

The Magistrate – Yes, and I understand you have been in an another asylum of a different sort.

The Prisoner – I've been in Colney Hatch, and my mind has been a little out of order.

The Magistrate – So I should think. Three months' imprisonment.

9/1/1892

DEATH OF MR AND MRS J.B. ASHLEY
(FROM OUR OWN CORRESPONDENT.)
SPENNYMOOR, JAN. 12. – I regret to have to record the death of that estimable lady and capable actress, Miss Evelyn Unsworth (Mrs J.B. Ashley), which took place at Spennymoor, county of Durham, on Saturday last. The deceased arrived at the town named on Monday, 4th inst., with her husband's company, of which she was leading lady. She was then suffering from a severe cold. After she had got into her lodgings she was unable to go to the theatre, and, getting worse, she was prematurely confined on Tuesday, the 5th. Influenza followed, and so acute did the complication become that the poor lady died on Saturday last, notwithstanding the unremitting attention of Dr O'Hanlon and his able assistant, and most careful nursing. Deceased was buried on Monday at St Paul's Churchyard, Spennymoor, the funeral being attended by Mr Ashley's company, and by that of Miss Claire Scott, who succeeded Mr Ashley's people at the theatre. The coffin was of polished pine, with brass fittings, and two beautiful floral wreaths were contributed by the company, and one by Miss Claire Scott and company. Deceased, who was twenty-six years of age, leaves a daughter four years of age. It is certain that the legion of friends whom Miss Unsworth had in the dramatic profession will be much moved to hear of her sad and sudden death. Miss Unsworth was the author of a piece, *For Queen and Country*, produced at Neath on Dec. 26th, 1890.

SPENNYMOOR, JAN 13. – Since writing the above Mr Ashley has died. His death took place at an early hour this morning. With his company last week he performed up to Friday night, but owing to the death of Mrs Ashley on Saturday, he did not act on that evening. On Sunday he was taken ill, and influenza supervened. On Monday deceased was so ill that he could not attend the funeral of his wife. Death followed as stated. Deceased was a native of Market Deeping, Northamptonshire, and was thirty-six years of age. […] The daughter on Monday was taken on to Seaham Harbour to fulfil the week's engagement. The little orphan is to be taken care of by Mr Fred. Everett, a great friend of both the deceased. Arrangements are being made for Mr Ashley's burial by Mr W. Green and Mr C. Johnson. The funeral is to take place at noon on Friday at St Paul's, where deceased will be laid by the side of his wife. *16/1/1892*

WANTED, Conqueror to answer soon. Is our friendship ended? Are we to be strangers? Let reply be honestly truthful; my future depends upon it; study self only; my happiness is small consideration. Your decision must be final. Have been ill. DODDIE.
23/1/1892

A TALL, thin individual, who stated that he was a Welsh schoolmaster, applied to Sir John Bridge at Bow Street, on the 22nd inst., for a warrant against a man for obtaining money by false pretences. Applicant described how, being allured by an advertisement in a daily paper, promising theatrical positions to all and sundry, he parted with £8 on the understanding that he was to be engaged at a liberal salary to appear on the stage. The person who engaged him afterwards stated that the Lord Chamberlain had put a stop to a projected performance at Camden Town, but that he had taken the Novelty Theatre, and further showed him "great big offices" in the Outer Temple, which he alleged were his. But the truth leaked out that he had never taken the Novelty, that the offices were really tenanted by a firm of solicitors, and that the promised salary of the applicant was scarcely likely to be forthcoming from a man who had abandoned his dwelling.

Sir John Bridge reminded the applicant of the adage that "No cobbler should go beyond his last," and suggested that in these days of extended education he would be better employed in teaching the young idea how to shoot than in strutting his little hour on the stage. However, inquiries should be made as to his statement.
30/1/1892

WANTED, Conqueror to be Human, and Answer Doddie's Questions in "The Era," Jan. 23rd. Suspense cruelly hard. Do write.
6/2/1892

WANTED, Known, Tony Baker's American Child Giantess was presented with a Magnificent Gold Ring at Leeds on Jan. 28th. Now holding Receptions daily at Fell's Paragon Waxworks, 101, Trongate, Glasgow. Enormous success. Premises packed daily to view this Mountain of Flesh. The Voice of the Public and Press is, "Have you seen the Fat Child at Fell's Waxworks?" Open for First-class Engagements. All communications to be made to TONY BAKER, as above.
13/2/1892

A PROPRIETOR in the East End was recently informed by a friendly inspector of police that a complaint had been made against his hall by an individual who expressed annoyance that the noise of the audience leaving the said house disturbed his rest. On making inquiries the proprietor found that the aggrieved individual was one of his late waiters, discharged as of no use owing to the fact of his being *stone deaf*.

AT Woolwich Police Court, on the 13th inst., Jeremiah Parker, chief mate of the steamship *Norway*, a Hartlepool collier, was charged with assaulting James Tees, surgeon, 144, High Street, Woolwich, who stated that on the previous night the prisoner came into the waiting-room of his surgery, and wanted to go upstairs. He said he wanted to go into the music hall. He was stopped, and told that there was the Mitre Music Hall next door. The prisoner then struck the witness a blow in the face, and the witness struck him back again. Police-constable Gatehouse, 42 R R, said that when he was called the doctor was bleeding from the face. Mr Marsham fined the prisoner 10s., or seven days imprisonment, just by way of helping Jeremiah Parker in the future to distinguish between a music hall and a doctor's shop.
20/2/1892

MISS JESSIE MILLWARD and her sister arrived safely in town on the 12th inst., after a most enjoyable holiday trip to the Canary Islands. On the outward voyage the surgeon was washed overboard in the Bay of Biscay. Miss Millward is again fully occupied with her theatrical preparations, but her sister is still resting.

AS Miss Nellie Korrie, the talented child pianist, daughter of the Musical Korries, was proceeding along St Mary Street, Southampton, a few days since, she was approached by two juvenile footpads, who attempted to steal a purse she was carrying. So stoutly did she defend herself, however, that whilst one of her assailants took to immediate flight, the other became so demoralised that she was able to hold him until assistance arrived in the shape of a policeman. This young lady is but seven years of age.
27/2/1892

MADAME WANDA ZALESKA, lessee of the Theatre Royal, Spennymoor, had a rather exciting adventure the other night. Hearing a suspicious commotion in the rear of her private residence, she rushed out, and, with revolver in hand, the courageous lady "went for" the intruders, who hurriedly made tracks. Later Madame Zaleska fired two shots in a melee, in which some unidentified ruffians were making an attack on one of the stage men, under the belief that the latter had the night's takings with him.

WANTED, Known, I, Professor Quickman, Siffleur and Mimic, am not and never have been Married as falsely reported. Nuff sed.
5/3/1892

MR J.W. HALL, the representative of Johnny Stout in the pantomime at Halifax, has been telling a local interviewer that during his career he had met some queer characters. "I was taking a benefit at Wigan one Friday," said he, "and was delivering my hand bills to a host of colliers who were just leaving the pit, when one of them came up to me and asked 'Ar't' ta him 'at sings "Silly Tommy?"' I said I was, and he then said, 'Well, I'm coming deawn ta neet, an' if tha does na sing it I shall put mi clog in thi ribs.' Of course I sang it."

ON the 4th inst., during the performance of *Dick Whittington* at the Prince of Wales's Theatre, Birmingham, the audience was somewhat startled by a man rising in the stalls of the theatre, and producing a revolver, at the same time shouting to Mr O'Gorman, of Messrs Tennyson and O'Gorman, who occupied the stage with Miss Louise Henschell, the Princess of the cast, that he would shoot him. Miss Henschell fainted, and Mr O'Gorman hurriedly left the stage, and refused to return until the individual who had threatened him had been ejected. As it was discovered the revolver was not loaded, no proceedings were taken by the police.

"THE MYSTERIOUS CROWLEY", who is still appearing at the Trocadero, is to the majority a mystery no longer, for he is boldly announced as "Mr Herbert Crowley, America's greatest lady impersonator." His make-up, however, is so artistic and so complete, and his imitation of the "little ways" of the weaker sex is so perfect, that we would still counsel him to make assurance of his masculine character doubly sure either by removing his wig or by making a little speech in his natural voice at the end. It is not well that any should go away with the belief that they have been listening to an indifferent vocalist of the female order.

WANTED, to Buy or Hire, Dog's Dress (Poodle's preferred). Fit Boy about Twelve. Must be in good condition. HEATH, Grand, Sheffield.
12/3/1892

TO THE EDITOR OF THE ERA.

Sir, – A most remarkable assault, I can't call it burglary, took place here last night. On going to the theatre this morning for rehearsal it was discovered that the place had been broken into. The box or basket of each member of the company had been forced, and the contents turned literally upside down; but, strangely enough, nothing seems to have been taken. In my room the scene that presented itself is impossible to describe, or, if it were possible, the description would not be believed. The contents of my box had been turned topsy-turvey, every package thrown open or torn to pieces; my grease paints, spirit gum, and powder, had been freely used to disfigure anything that caught the ruffians' eye, as being a little more artistic than the general surroundings. My clothes, papers, and props. in general were thrown here and there in the wildest confusion – packages, wig boxes, locks, literally torn to pieces. The same wanton destruction had taken place in every room, the ladies being great sufferers; their delicate stage costumes and packages of finery were found roughly thrown in all directions. The bar in the front of the house shared the same fate, and here is the only place that anything was missing, viz., three shillings or four shillings in coppers. The police up to now are utterly unable to account for such apparently meaningless perseverance. An amusing episode of the morning's investigation was the discovery of a strange coat in my room, the pocketings of which clearly showed the owner to be a worker in metal. The police attached great importance to their find, and an officer was gravely walking off with the coat, when it was discovered that a plumber had been at work on the water tap during the morning, and had left his coat while he went to have his eleven o'clock drink – this important clue therefore fell to the ground, and now nothing remains to point to the offenders.

Yours faithfully, ARTHUR BEARNE.

My Jack company, Theatre Royal, Coatbridge, March 17th.

WANTED, the African Pigmy Witch Finder and Vitreo, the Human Ostrich, to write in at once to FRANK ALLEN, Balfe House, South Shields.
19/3/1892

THERE was just a moment of awkward uncertainty at the Haymarket last Saturday night, when the least nervousness on the part of the actor, or the folly of one person in the audience, might have caused a panic. The torch that Hamlet uses had set fire to a small portion of the scenery, and Hamlet was soliloquising in blissful unconsciousness of this fact when a gentleman in the stalls said quietly, "There is a fire behind you, Mr Tree." With absolute tranquillity Hamlet turned and extinguished the flame, and then went on with the play, interrupted only by the round of applause in which the audience naturally expressed their thanks.

WANTED, Good Low Comedian. Must be Short. W.J. MACKAY, 133, Fentiman Road, S.W.
9/4/1892

THREATENING AN ACTRESS.

Alexander T. Thorpe appeared before Mr Vaughan, at the Bow Street Police Court, on Wednesday, to a summons charging him with making use of threats to Louie Pounds.

Mr Crashaw, who prosecuted, stated that prior to November, 1890, the plaintiff, who was now engaged at the Prince of Wales's Theatre, was a pupil at the Metropolitan School of Shorthand. The prisoner was also a pupil, and, after annoying her, he threatened her with a revolver, in consequence of which he was brought up at this court, and committed for trial. He was tried on November 24th, 1890, and sentenced to twelve months' imprisonment, and ordered to find sureties to be of good behaviour for a like period. He was still under these recognisances when he began to haunt the stage-door and to visit the theatre. He sent letters to her, to her brother, Mr Courtice Pounds, and also to Mr Sanguinetti. A postcard, addressed to the Prince of Wales's Theatre, and dated April 9th, read as follows:

I think you have not the common decency of a woman, let alone a lady, not to answer my letter nor grant me a fair hearing. I will humbug you more than ever, and after this year, if not before, I will ruin you, as you have ruined me, unless you forgive, you cruel, unforgiving creature. Forgive, either by writing or speaking, or you shall rue it to the day of your death, as you have no right to stop me from earning my living, or make my life a misery for ever. You would like to send me to the bad, I know, or even to hell, but you had better mind that you are not sent there first. Act as a lady, and I will [treat you] as one.

In a letter from Woodberry House, Oakleigh Park, Whetstone, dated May 9th, 1892, and addressed to C.H. Sanguinetti, Esq., the defendant wrote of "the threat which I still intend to carry out unless you can persuade Miss P. to forgive, nothing more." In this letter were the following passages:

Forgive she certainly shall, or I will make her by foul means, if she will not do it by fair, though I would much prefer to meet her as a lady, if she would but act as one. There is more than one revolver in the world, remember, besides vitriol, and the latter, if thrown into her face, would blind her for life, so now you know what she may expect after this year has expired. I may change my mind, and give her something which she will not at all relish if she is still determined to have me as an enemy – I am her bitterest, I know – instead of as an acquaintance. She shall pay dearly, some day, unless she will write.

In all some fourteen letters were written since February, which were a breach of his suretyship to keep the peace. There was no foundation for his annoying this lady, who from the first had refused to have anything to do with him. He had so harassed her that on one occasion she fainted in the theatre, and now went in fear of her life.

Miss Pounds said she lived at 17, Warwick Place, Kensington, and made the defendant's acquaintance three and a half years ago at the Metropolitan School of Shorthand. Up to November, 1890, he made attempts to speak to her. On November 4th she charged him at this court with attempting to shoot her with a revolver.

The prisoner, interrupting – No, no, not attempting; merely threatening.

Witness went on to say that he was convicted and sentenced at the Old Bailey. She had never since communicated with him. […] She had seen him outside the stage-door about twice, as she was going to the theatre. He did not see her. She saw him twice in the theatre, and was so overcome that she had to leave the stage. She was harassed in the performance of her duties and went in fear lest he should do her some harm.

The defendant sobbed and said – They would swear my life away.

Mr Vaughan remanded the defendant, and said he would take two sureties in £250 for his appearance. *It was eventually decided that Thorpe should be sent to Brazil, where he had a brother, in the hope that he would never return.*
23/4/1892

ON Monday night, after the performance of *The New Mazeppa* at the Theatre Royal, Leeds, by Mr Fred. Cooke's company, the horse used in the piece was being led out when the stage gave way, and the unfortunate animal was precipitated into the cellar. Fortunately Miss Burgoyne, who as Mazeppa had been strapped on the animal's back, had been released, or she would have undoubtedly sustained severe, if not fatal, injuries.

WHILE Mr Hubert O'Grady was admiring a new twelve-sheet portrait poster of himself in Limerick the other day an old woman stopped in front of him, and, looking up at the big head, exclaimed in a stage whisper, "Glory be to God. Shure there is no man that size."
7/5/1892

MR WYNN MILLER, having come to the conclusion that the title of *The Mouth of the Pit* is calculated to convey the erroneous impression that his drama treats mainly of colliery life, has altered the name to *Birds of Prey*, by which the piece will in future be known.
21/5/1892

AN aspiring young playwright introduced himself the other day to a provincial manager, and begged his attention to a new sensational drama which he said he had just finished, and which he believed would prove a big success from the fact that the hero was altogether an unconventional being. He had, in fact, provided him with a wooden leg, with which, at a convenient period of the drama, he disposed of the villain by firing a rifle which formed part of the artificial limb, and which exploded when acted upon by a spring at the top of the leg. The manager was struck with the novelty of the idea, but he has not yet decided to produce the piece.
28/5/1892

ABOUT midnight on Saturday the New Olympia Circus, which was opened only a few months ago in Overton Street, Liverpool, was destroyed by fire. Berry, the ex-hangman, had been fulfilling a lecturing engagement at the circus, but the audience had dispersed before the outbreak. The internal fittings being mostly of pitch-pine, the fire spread with such rapidity as to defy the efforts of the full strength of the fire brigade, who soon after the outbreak directed their attention to saving the adjoining property, the circus being in a thickly-populated area. In this the firemen were successful, although a number of people in a state of panic removed their furniture. Several horses which were in the circus stable were rescued. During the fire a large cylinder, containing oxyhydrogen, which was used by Berry in the lantern illustration of his lecture, exploded with a terrific report, and, going through the roof of the circus, fell into a neighbouring street, fortunately without injuring anyone, though thousands were attracted to the place. The circus seated over 2,000 people.

WANTED, to Sell, Beautiful, Intelligent, Rare Animal with Porcupine Quill Fur, each hair handsomely ringed in Red, White, Black, &c. Walks about free. Turns Somersaults, Performs, &c. Price 45s. BLAKE, Bookseller, Portsea.
4/6/1892

WANTED, Stuffed Monkeys for Riding on small Ponies. Address, E. Pinder Orde's Circus, Wednesday, Buckie; Thursday, Keith.

WILL any well-known London Actress Join Miss Ada Ward in a Month's Trip to Norway and Sweden, leaving London about 30th this month? A Good Horsewoman preferred, as many excursions will be done *a la cheval*. Address, Fernleigh, Victoria Grove, Southsea, Hants.
11/6/1892

MR AND MRS F.V. ST. CLAIR left London on Sunday last, and drove to their place in Yorkshire. Master Fred., nine years, did the journey on his bicycle. At one village inn where they put up for the night they were highly amused by the performance of a village comedian, who sang in broad Lincolnshire dialect Albert Chevalier's song, "Knocked 'em in the Old Kent Road." St Clair asked the vocalist where the Old Kent Road was. He said "he wasn't exactly certain, but he thought it was *somewhere in Scotland!*"

WANTED to Buy, Monkey Parachute, good condition. Address, with terms, E.F., Teatro Dal Verme, Circo Mariano, Milano, Italy.
25/6/1892

A WELL-KNOWN and popular actor, on a Sunday when the days were not so long as they are just now, gave a dinner party, but the fact that he was engaged for a new and important part in some measure interfered with the arrangements. Throughout the day the actor was engaged in hard and wearisome study. As the time for the assembling of the guests approached he was reminded by his better half that it was necessary to go upstairs and dress. The darkness of early night had come on; the gas had been lighted, and the actor, still thinking of his part, in quite a mechanical sort of way obeyed the wifely instruction and proceeded to his room. But having removed his morning costume he went to bed, and it was only when he was aroused by the violent ringing of the dinner bell that, awaking from his reverie over his author's lines, he became conscious that it was not exactly bedtime, and that he had hungry friends below eagerly awaiting his appearance.
2/7/1892

THERE died on Monday, at Hetton, County Durham, Mr E. Sheppard, an African Negro, who was well known in the north of England as an accomplished violinist, who had fulfilled engagements in many of the principal theatres and music halls of the northern circuit. Lately he had been settled at Hetton, and had devoted himself to teaching and playing at high-class concerts. He married an English lady some six years ago, and leaves several children. He is believed to have been the first pure-bred African Negro who has ever acquired proficiency on the violin, and his appearances in public never failed to attract.

WANTED, to Sell, a very Handsome Elephant Tricycle, in perfect working order. To be Sold cheap, cost £35, no reasonable offer refused, to clear. ATHERTON, 48, Reculver Road, Rotherhithe, London, S.E.
16/7/1892

SOME days since, a lady walking in Alpha Road suddenly saw before her on the pavement a singular object, which proved to be a small snake, wearing round its neck a ring studded with gems, to which was attached a slender gold chain ending in another jewelled ring. Startled at first, the lady, however, managed to capture the little animal in the folds of her umbrella, and immediately recognised that she had possessed herself of the asp of Cleopatra. Not knowing the exact address of Madame Sarah Bernhardt, she was about to ask a policeman, when the gates of a villa some yards off were flung open, disclosing the great tragedienne and her attendants frantically searching for the escaped snake. Her joy at having it restored was rapturous, her gratitude fervently expressed, and the caresses she showered on the truant were enthusiastic.

THIS is an age of rapid evolution – revolution, we might say. Dancers become countesses, and countesses dancers. The Countess of Orkney used to gaily skip in measured time; the Countess of Clancarty has learned all the mysteries attaching to the single and double shuffle; and the Countess Russell has lately taken to lifting the tempestuous petticoat in a dainty *pas*. If these ladies could only be persuaded to join forces and take an engagement at the halls, the fortunate proprietors securing their services would do prodigious business.
23/7/1892

THE following paragraph appeared in the Grand Theatre, Birmingham, programmes on Monday last: – "In consequence of the mysterious disappearance of Mr G.H. Fulford and Mr Frank Hammond, their parts will be played at very short notice by Mr F. Constable and Mr W. Ames." What can this possibly mean?

ON Wednesday, at Harrogate, Harry Fischer, comedian, of Holtham Road, London, was shot at by Violet Gordon, of Belgrave Road, St John's Wood. The bullet did not strike him, and he was unhurt. The shot was fired while Mr Victor Stevens's *Bonnie Boy Blue* company were on the station platform awaiting the train for Scarborough, where the company have been playing for the rest of the week. Gordon was brought before the magistrates on Wednesday morning, and remanded until Thursday. The event caused considerable excitement. Two of the actresses fainted, and the station platform was crowded. Gordon had no connection with Mr Stevens's company, but had followed it to several towns. Her professional name is Violet Hamilton.

At the magisterial inquiry on Thursday it appeared that the accused accosted Fischer and requested to have a word with him. He refused to speak to her and she retired, but came up again and renewed her request, saying "Won't you speak to me?" He said, "No," and Miss Gordon then fired a revolver, the bullet striking the platform. A scene of great excitement ensued, Mr Fischer seizing the woman's hand, and, a police-sergeant hurrying up, she was given in charge.

Before the Magistrates, Mr Fischer said he did not wish to press the charge. He admitted, in cross-examination, that the woman had lived with him, and whilst she lived with him he paid the bills. After she left him he allowed her £1 a week under an agreement, which was drawn up by Messrs Clark and Robson, solicitors, Newcastle-on-Tyne, prisoner covenanting not to molest him. She had written annoying letters and postcards anonymously to him, had gone round to landladies in Manchester, and had tried to ruin and disgrace him in every way. In consequence of this he stopped the £1 a week in February last. Mr Fischer also stated that, after firing the revolver, the prisoner said, "I've missed you this time, Harry Fischer, but I'll kill you yet." A revolver was taken from her pocket on a former occasion in the Crown Hotel, Newcastle. The accused, who appeared considerably agitated towards the close of the hearing, was committed for trial, the Bench offering to accept bail, two sureties in £20 each, and prisoner in £10. Prisoner's solicitor stated that she had friends in London and Bristol, and she was removed to the cells to await the result of her solicitor's communication with them.

TO THE EDITOR OF THE ERA.
Sir, – Will you kindly allow me to contradict the statement that Miss Nellie Herbert, sister to Miss Jenny Valmore, was married on the 13th inst., at St Luke's, Liverpool, to a gentleman called Ashton Potts, of Manchester. Allow me to say that I myself was not present at that interesting ceremony, and can only put the report down as a very bad joke of some ill-disposed person. Am still in single blessedness. Offers invited.
(Signed) NELLIE HERBERT.
Empire, Swansea, July 26th, 1892.

AT Leamington on Monday morning George Leslie Hacket and Andrew Hacket, midshipmen, were ordered to pay £40 8s. for disorderly conduct and wilful damage to the windows of four tradesmen. The accused returned from Birmingham in an intoxicated condition, and on the way home sang "Ta-ra-ra Boom-de-ay," accompanying each verse by smashing a window.

WANTED, a Black Boy as Page. Half-caste won't do. The Blacker the Better. One used to Horses preferred. About Fourteen to Sixteen Years of Age, respectable. HUBERT O'GRADY, Hubert Villa, Fairfield, Liverpool.
30/7/1892

AN amusing story is told of a provincial performance of *Jim the Penman*, in which the part of Percival was played by the late Mr Edmund Leathes. Mr Leathes had taken the part at short notice, and was quite conscious that he did not know too many of the words. So he made his first entrance nervously enough, and looked for inspiration to the gentleman who was playing James Ralston – the society forger, whose unmasking forms, it will be remembered, the entire subject of the later acts of the play. "What! My old friend, James Ralston!" These, or something like these, were the words he ought to have spoken. But he hesitated, and was lost – and with him was lost the entire plot of the play, for he began his scene by remarking, "What! My old friend, *Jim the Penman!*"

MR GEORGE ALEXANDER finished his season at the St James's Theatre on the evening of Friday, 29th ult., when *Lady Windermere's Fan* was played to a large audience. Mr Alexander briefly addressed his good friends in the front at the end of the performance, and began by saying he could not hope to rival Mr Oscar Wilde in speech-making, neither could he appear smoking a cigarette*, for the very sufficient reason that the last in the theatre had been used up at the end of the third act, when certain characters in the play converse upon various subjects, and solace themselves with tobacco.
On the first night of Lady Windermere's Fan *Wilde notoriously took his curtain call whilst smoking a cigarette.*

MISS ADA RUSSELL, by her expressive rendering of her pathetic song "Somebody's Mother," at the Star Music Hall, Bradford, last week, was the means of converting a man, who says in a letter to the vocalist: "I thought I had lost all such things as feelings, but your singing has made me feel really ashamed of my behaviour to my mother. I have been an awful scamp, and very unkind to her; but in future shall try to behave better." The incident proves that even the much-abused music hall ballad may be an instrument for good when rendered with real ability.
6/8/1892

AN opera company who paid a brief visit to an "off the map" town the other day had a rather lively experience. The theatre in which the performances were given had been in the hands of the Salvation Army, who had removed all the grooves on the stage, and thus rendered the working of the scenery a matter of no slight difficulty. There was no time to mend matters, and when the "flats" were pushed on, a stage man had to placed behind to hold them up. On the occasion under notice, *Sonnambula* was being performed. All went well until the scene in which Elvino plights his troth to Amina in the song, "Take now this ring," when by some dreadful mischance the stage man lost his hold of the "flats," which descended like an avalanche upon the heads of the unlucky vocalists. Fortunately for Elvino, his head came through the canvas, and he escaped comparatively uninjured, though the situation, as may be imagined, was exceedingly embarrassing for the principal tenor. Amina, however, was not so fortunate. She was borne down to the stage by the weight of the "flat," and, though not seriously hurt, was carried off in a fainting condition and a cloud of dust.

WE regret to learn that an accident happened to Miss Eliza Johnstone at the Opera House, Blackpool, on Thursday evening, during the performance of *Walker, London*. Miss Johnstone, it will be remembered, has to pretend to sleep in an armchair on the deck of the houseboat, when Mr Toole, to get rid of her, fastens the chair to a light crane and lowers her into a punt alongside. Just as the actress was being lowered a slip broke, and she fell about fourteen feet on to the stage. Medical assistance was obtained, but beyond a shaking and a bruised face she was nothing the worse for the fall.
13/8/1892

AT the Theatre Royal, Plymouth, the other night, a large bouquet was handed over the footlights to Mr C. Arnold's little girl during the performance of *Hans the Boatman*. With the bouquet was this letter: – "Aug. 13th 1892 This Bokie I have Presented your daughter hoping every success To you if you Wish To see me I ham in the Corner by the Drum Man I suppose you do not want a boy to mind your dog if you do I would like to Travel with you if you Want one Would you send Answer by a boy Around."

WANTED, Dates, Berry, Ex-Hangman, Lecturer. Strangest, Weirdest Show Extant. Scaffolds, Pinions, Caps, Ropes, Confessions, Death Warrants. Edwin Drew, 50, New Oxford Street.   *20/8/1892*

AN inquest was held at Birmingham, on the 23rd inst., on the body of Reynaud Cooper, thirty-five, actor. Last week the deceased and his brothers were engaged at the Grand Theatre, Birmingham, under the name of the Renads, and took part in *The Swiss Express*. He was staying with his wife at 21, Easy Row, and during the week enjoyed good health, but occasionally complained of a pain in the heart. His wife stated that on Saturday night he was cheerful enough. In the morning he seemed all right, and after rising he began to play with the children. He called witness's attention to a bottle on the table, and asked her to put it out of the reach of the children, as it was poison which he used for cleaning buttons on his theatrical costumes. Witness placed the bottle on the mantelshelf, and then left the room. Immediately afterwards deceased cried out, "Rosa, what have I taken?" Witness ran back into the room and said, "Why, it's the poison you told me to put away from the children." Deceased added, "Good God, I have taken some, then. Get me some milk." Witness hurried downstairs to comply with his request, and he followed. He made an attempt to open the door, but fell backwards. She caught him. She had never heard him threaten to take his life, and nothing had occurred which would give the faintest suggestion of self-destruction.

Howard Cooper, brother of the deceased, informed the jury that he was present just before the fatal act. They had mapped out their plans for the morning. There was not any idea of suicide. Witness had never seen deceased use poison for cleaning buttons. He had been accustomed to take a little lavender water. On the one side of the vase on the shelf was the bottle of poison, and on the other was a bottle of lavender water. Witness's impression that was while reaching the lavender water, deceased's attention was attracted by the children, and he picked up the wrong bottle.

Clara Hadden, the landlady, said that while staying at her place deceased and his wife were on the best of terms.

Charles Cooper explained that the custom was to clean the buttons with a powder, but about three weeks ago deceased said, "Oh, I've got a fine thing for my buttons. All you have to do is rub it on. I think it is an acid." Witness never saw bottle from which deceased drank.

The doctor who was called in told the court that when he arrived deceased was to all appearance dead. All efforts were in vain. A post-mortem examination revealed a distinct odour of prussic acid. The coats of the stomach were much congested, and gave all the evidences of poison. Witness saw the bottle from which deceased had drunk, and found it contained about four drachms of cyanide of potassium, which is a compound of potassium and prussic acid, which was a virulent and rapid poison. Such lotions were used for cleaning metals. Five grains of cyanide of potassium would kill in five or ten minutes, and much less would be a fatal dose of prussic acid, and it was from these two poisons that deceased had died.

The Coroner said the jury might put on one side any suspicion that the unfortunate man's death was contributed to by anyone around him. It was rather odd that the wife should be unaware of the presence of deadly poison in the house, but the evidence of the brother cleared up the possession of the bottle. How deceased took the poison no one could say, and he thought the better plan would be to record the fact that deceased poisoned himself, but why there was not sufficient evidence to show. That was tantamount to an open verdict. One of the jurymen enquired whether a taste would be sufficient to produce death. The doctor replied that less than half a teaspoonful would be fatal. The jury returned an open verdict. The funeral took place on Friday at the London Necropolis Cemetery at Brookwood.

IT has come to my knowledge that Certain People have been spreading a Report that my Wife and I are not Married, which I emphatically Contradict. Any one can satisfy themselves of the fact at the Registry Office, Brixton Road. Yours truly, ERNEST C. ALEXANDER, professionally known as Ernest A. Douglas.

27/8/1892

A rather amusing incident occurred at a North London theatre not many nights ago. A harrowing scene was in progress between the villain of the piece and the heroine, when suddenly a big black-and-white cat jumped upon the keys of the piano in the orchestra, and thence on to the stage. Pussy struck a solemn chord that came in very appropriately, seeing that the situation had reached its climax. The intruder gave a startled look at the villain, and then disappeared on the prompt side. The heroine had some difficulty in keeping her countenance.

WANTED, Mystic Muriel to Know if Things left at Sunderland are not Claimed by Sept. 30th they will be Sold to cover expenses.
3/9/1892

TO THE EDITOR OF THE ERA.
Sir, – In an article published in a morning contemporary, of Sept. 1st and 2nd, headed "A Girl's Escapade," it is stated that a girl calling herself Amy Augarde, and claiming to have lately played at the Gaiety Theatre, London, has been fruit picking in Kent, and while doing some high kicking in a lane was seen by a priest, who provided her with a lodging during the time that her friends should be communicated with, but she disappeared the following morning, taking with her sundry articles of clothing, &c., belonging to her landlady. It was also stated that the impression in theatrical circles was that this girl was my sister. I am glad to say that she is in no way connected with me or my family. I am, sir, faithfully yours, AMY AUGARDE.
Theatre Royal, Plymouth, Sept. 6th.
10/9/1892

WANTED, Known, Parker, Champion Jumper, made a big hit Last Week at Guernsey, when he Jumped over Twenty Chairs in Twenty Spring Jumps, clearing a distance of 200ft. Likewise Jumped over an Elephant to oblige Mr Claude Ginnett. Those who want a sure draw write, PARKER, Jumper, Circus, Cambridge.
17/9/1892

A SINGULAR mishap befell Mr Walter Casson on Monday night whilst playing Tony Faust in *My Sweetheart* at the Gaiety Theatre, West Hartlepool. Towards the close of the second act Tony was suddenly missed from the stage. There was an embarrassing wait of a few seconds, and as Mr Casson failed to appear the act was brought to a hasty close without him, and the curtain dropped. It was then ascertained that Mr Casson had lost his way in the labyrinth of passages leading from the dressing-rooms to the stage, and was unable to extricate himself in time to put in an appearance.

HER Imperial Highness Princess Eugenie Di Christafore Palæologæ-Nicephoræ-Comnenæ is announced to appear during the Subscription Musical Evenings at Leeds this season. This is the kind of name which, as the phrase goes, "would look well on the bills."
8/10/1892

AN amusing incident occurred last week at the Lyceum, Stafford. During the performance of *The Crimson Mask,* Miss Elsie Irving as Bertha Oldfield made her entrance in the Ranelagh Garden scene for a trying interview with Cargill (Mr S. Creagh Henry), and, on turning round, found to her surprise that a third party was present in the person of her dresser. This good soul, who had been manipulating the train of Miss Irving's dress in the wings, was told to follow to the entrance, and then let it go, but, owing to over-zeal or absence of mind, had marched studiously to the centre of the stage with all the assurance of an Elizabethan lady-in-waiting. When she realised the situation she beat a hasty retreat, to the evident amusement of both actors and auditors.

AT Marlborough Street PoliceCourt, on Monday, Mr William Taylor, conductor of the orchestra at the Pavilion Music Hall, was summoned before Mr Newton for having assaulted Mr A. Martini, pianist. Mr Crawshaw, solicitor, appeared for the defence.

The complainant said that till recently he had been employed as pianist at the Pavilion Music Hall. On the night of the 8th inst., after the performance, he went under the stage, when the defendant patted him on the shoulder and said, "In future don't come to business drunk." He told him that he was not, and Mr Taylor replied, "You are; you are not sober now." He retorted, "Well, that takes the cake," whereupon the defendant said, "If I have any more of your insults I will give you a good hiding," and struck him a blow in the eye, which was cut and blackened. In cross-examination, the complainant said it was not true that on the night in question he left the orchestra for half an hour and that when he returned he kept annoying the conductor by playing a lot of rubbish on the piano and trying to put the band out.

Mr George Wilks, a member of the orchestra, said the complainant was not sober on the night in question. Mr Crawshaw – Was the complainant frequently sounding the A? Mr Wilks – He did so now and then.

In defence Mr Crawshaw said that the complainant left the orchestra for half an hour, returned drunk, and kept sounding the A, which naturally annoyed Mr Taylor. After the performance the complainant went up to the defendant, put himself in a fighting attitude, lurched against him, and fell down. […]

Mr Newton said Mr Taylor had acted in a very cowardly way in striking a drunken man, and ordered him to pay a fine of 40s., with 42s. costs, or in default one months' imprisonment.

ON the 13th inst. considerable commotion was created in the neighbourhood of Lake Road, Landport, by an extraordinary escapade of the elephant Piccaninny, belonging to Mr Dan Sullivan, the "strong man" performing at the People's Hall of Varieties in that thoroughfare. The animal, which was stabled in a store behind some premises in Clarendon Street, belonging to Mr F. Pearce, the proprietor of the hall, escaped from the building by breaking open the door, and having found its way into an adjoining alley, abutting Timpson Street, entered the house of a man named Charles Hubbs, where it remained unobserved for a considerable time. Both Mr and Mrs Hubbs happened to be away from home when the animal gained admission by forcing open the front door. Finding no one to interfere with its diversions, it proceeded to demolish the contents of the two rooms on the ground floor.

Meanwhile its escape from the stable was discovered by the keeper, who, on going to the place for the purpose of feeding his "little pet," was dismayed to find the store unoccupied. A thorough search of the premises was followed by an inspection of the open ground adjoining, but no trace of the missing animal could be discovered, and the owner ultimately offered a reward of £1 to anyone who could give him information as to its whereabouts. Presently Mr Hubbs returned home, and noticed that some turf in front of his cottage had been torn up. This he attributed to mischievous boys, but on reaching the door he observed that the window blind downstairs had disappeared, and at the same moment heard a peculiar noise, apparently proceeding from the back of the premises. Peering through a back window, he was astonished to find the apartment tenanted by Piccaninny, of whose escape he had heard. The animal was playfully throwing some pictures about the room with his trunk. The keeper was soon brought upon the scene, and with some trouble the elephant was coaxed through the narrow passage, and led out of the house to safe quarters. Mr Hubbs estimates the damage resulting from Piccaninny's unwelcome visit at £10.
22/10/1892

THE second sensation* was the introduction on Thursday of a boxing kangaroo. This is Jack, who is three-and-a-half years old, 7ft. high, and a widower, his wife having committed suicide by jumping overboard on the voyage from Australia to fulfil the engagements made for them by H.J. Didcott and Co. The trainer of Jack is the gentleman who captured him. Professor Richard Landermann, who has certainly coached him well, not only in the "noble art of self-defence," but in the courtesies of that art,

for although Jack may knock his opponent down he is careful to "fight fair," and affords him plenty of opportunity for getting up again. Jack, of course, wears his "mitteuse" on his fore-paws, but occasionally supplements the blows they administer with others artfully delivered with the feet attached to the hind legs. It is said that he has taken some of the sauciness out of the once-great J.L. Sullivan, and that Madame Sarah Bernhardt, when in Australia, offered in vain as much as £1,000 for his possession. Altogether Jack and his trainer supply a clever and decidedly amusing show, about which, ere long, all London will be talking.
*At the Westminster Aquarium.

WANTED, by Prof. Morris and Miss Hall, King and Queen of the Sword, Cutting a Grape between the Lips, on the Throat; also other Fruits in various ways with the Sword. Zaro's Circus, Wakefield. 21st, Surrey Palace, Barnsley. Liberty Nov. 28th, Dec. 5th.
19/11/1892

AN amusing incident, illustrating the craving amongst a certain order of playgoers for strong dramatic fare, occurred the other night at West Hartlepool. Three solemn-looking seamen presented themselves at the pay-box of the Gaiety Theatre and enquired of the money-taker the name of the piece. "*Kindred Souls*, by the Milton-Rays," was the reply. "How many murders are there in it?" asked one of the men. "Not a single murder," responded the money-taker. "No murder!" exclaimed the man in surprise. "Then is there a suicide?" "No." The sailor turned to his companions, and, after holding a brief conference with them, remarked to the money-taker, "All right, mister; we'll not go in tonight."
26/11/1892

AN article in the new Australian magazine, *The Antipodean*, on the drama in Australia, opens with an amusing anecdote. It is that of an English actress of some celebrity, who was asked by an impertinent interviewer whether she considered that she had "improved artistically during her stay in the colonies." The lady contrived a look of keen amazement, and replied that she did not think so. "Actors don't come to Australia to improve themselves," she said; "they come to Australia to make money."

ON Monday last, during the performance of *The Young Recruit* at the Theatre Royal, Portsmouth, by Sir A. Harris's company, an accident happened to Miss Violet Malvern, the principal danseuse. In the third act, in ending her serpentine dance, in which she introduced some very intricate whirls, she lost her balance, and fell over the footlights into the orchestra. Great consternation ensued, which was soon appeased by the lady reappearing on the stage, evidently not much the worse for her shaking.

MISS MARIE LEYTON has imparted a certain air of novelty to her performance of the serpentine dance by decking her limbs with tiny electric lights of different colours; but the idea is by no means new. We remember the late Miss Harriet Laurie creating considerable effect a few years since by illuminating her dress in the same manner, and a glass of champagne that she held in her hand when she used to sing a convivial song literally sparkled with electricity. Miss Nellie Darrell, a lady better known in the provinces than in London, has also worked electric lights as additional embellishments to her costumes. The idea is a pretty one, and it is a wonder that it has not been very much more extensively adopted.

MDLLE VICTORINA made her first appearance at the Alhambra on Monday. She handled weights of 56lb., 65lb., 130lb., a dumb-bell of 180lb., and a total burden of about 865lb., also carrying a small black pony off the stage on her shoulders. Mdlle Victorina's performance was heartily applauded, and she is evidently a profitable acquisition to the Alhambra company.

WANTED, to Buy, a Set of Jack the Ripper Victims. Address, D'Arc's Waxworks, Cardiff. *3/12/1892*

MR EDITOR. – Sir, allow me to state that I introduced the electric light in a song and dance, my dress being adorned with coloured lights (upwards of forty), each light changing colour while dancing. I may state I first produced the novelty in the year 1888, having had the sole right to work the same. Since my husband, Mr Harry Cambridge, has been seriously indisposed, I was compelled to discontinue the idea, as I could not trust any one but him to work the electric battery. Miss Harriett Laurie was the first lady to introduce the idea of the electric dance, and myself, the undersigned, was number two.

Yours truly, NELLY DARRELL, the "Electric Spark" (title registered, No. 23,839), Cromwell's Varieties, Sheffield, Dec. 6th, 1892.
10/12/1892

AT the Goole Theatre Mr J.M. Robertson's *Western Life* company, playing *Drink*, opened on Monday night to a good audience, but on Tuesday, shortly before 7.30, the lessee (Mr C. Bromley) came before the curtain and announced that no performance would take place, since a quarrel was in progress between two of the male members of the company. He said it was presumably owing to financial matters, and he concluded by requesting the audience to keep order until he had made arrangements for the refunding of their money. This was done, and the audience quietly left the theatre, and remained outside in groups discussing the novel situation. On the stage a smart row was in progress between the manager of the company (Mr Hopper Clinch) and another member of the company. Mr Bromley sent for the police, and upon the arrival of Inspector Birkhead, P.S. Huntington, and a constable, he gave them instructions to remove the company from the theatre. After considerable noisy discussion, in which one member was summarily ejected, the remaining members left quietly, and the incident terminated.

AT the Goldfields Hotel, Johannesburg, on the 11th ult., a pleasing little ceremony took place, Mr Edwin Cleary, "Professor" Kennedy's manager, being presented with a shield of gold by a few admirers for having saved from drowning Mr Gomer May, of the Standard comedy company. A party of gentlemen, closely connected with the profession, were bathing at the waterfall near Mulder's Drift, when Mr May was sucked down by a small waterspout. Mr Cleary immediately went to the rescue, and, at imminent personal risk, rescued that gentleman from what appeared to be certain death. Mr Gomer May made Mr Cleary a special presentation of an alluvial nugget scarf-pin.

ONE of the Brothers Griffiths has been the victim of a rather serious accident during the week. The brothers represent the wolves in the pantomime at Drury Lane, and prepare to eat up Little Red Riding Hood by a little exercise in the bed-room scene, going through a very agile and amusing performance upon the horizontal bar at the back of grandmother's bedstead. On the occasion referred to the supports of this bar gave way, and the performer fell heavily on the stage, bringing the bar down with him on to his face, smashing his nose and injuring one of his eyes. Surgical aid was, of course, found necessary, but the injured artist has pluckily continued his part.
31/12/1892

4
1893
THE STUFFED BABY HAS WON THE DAY

MISS LOTTIE COLLINS has a rival at last. At Forepaugh's famous circus there is an individual who draws crowds to witness his performance of the immortal dance, which he executes with infinite spirit on a narrow platform, dressed the while in a red "accordion skirt," a large Gainsborough hat with a huge white feather, and other garments to correspond. And the latest exponent of Taraboomdeayism is a horse.
7/1/1893

A ROW AT THE WINGS.
Flora Moore, an American serio-comic vocalist, was summoned at the Southwark Police Court, on Wednesday, for assaulting John Constantine Rich, a comedian, at the South London Music Hall, London Road. Mr Armstrong, solicitor, prosecuted; and Mr J. Sydney defended.

Mr Armstrong, in opening the case, stated his client had expressed his willingness to settle the case without coming into court if the defendant would give an unqualified apology for her conduct. This the defendant had refused.

The Magistrate – Is it too late now for that course to be adopted? It seems a pity for two members of an honourable profession to have to come into court to settle their grievances.

Mr Sydney declined to give an unqualified apology, and the case was got on with.

Mr Armstrong stated that it was customary for artists on the music hall stage to perform in various characters, and, in order to be as prompt as possible in their changes, they frequently brought their costumes to the side of the stage. Miss Moore and the prosecutor adopted this course, and as the latter sang "The Sheeney Man" and other character songs, he required several changes. Mr Rich's basket, containing his costumes, were brought down and placed with those of Miss Moore (who was then performing) behind a screen. When Miss Moore had finished her song she came off stage in a "tiff," probably because she did not get a flattering reception, and, seeing the basket belonging to Mr Rich by the side of her clothes, she became very angry, and said "If this basket is not shifted I shall chuck it out!" It wasn't shifted, and she threw a pewter pot, containing water, over the screen. The water went all over the prosecutor, and the pot struck another man standing near. These American ladies, said Mr Armstrong, must be taught that they cannot come over here and conduct themselves in this way.

John Constantine Rich, comedian, was then called, and deposed that on the evening of the 7th he was fulfilling his engagement at the South London Palace. He had to go on stage immediately after the defendant, and had a basket containing his costumes brought up in readiness. This basket was placed behind a screen where Miss Moore's clothes were. When the defendant had finished her first turn, she came off and found the basket there. She said to her maid, "Whose -------- basket is this? Shift it." Witness, who was at the side of the stage at the time, told her not to shift the basket, as it was all right where it was. There was plenty of room for the defendant to dress, notwithstanding that the basket was

behind the screen. She then said, "If you don't shift it I shall fetch my husband to give you a hiding." Witness then asked who was her husband, and she replied, "Tom White." This gentleman was a personal friend of witness; and witness doubted very much whether he was the husband of the defendant. He told her so, and she then threw a pewter pot containing water at him. The water went all over witness, but the pewter pot struck a fireman. He immediately informed Mrs Poole, the manageress, of what had taken place, and hence this summons. Mr Sydney – Was there sufficient room behind the screen for Miss Moore to change her dress when this box was there? Witness – Of course. Mr Armstrong – My friend has not been behind a stage or he would not ask that question. Mr Sydney – No, I am not in the habit of frequenting music halls. Mr Armstrong – Then you lose a great deal. Mr Sydney (to witness) – When you were behind the screen didn't Miss Moore ask you to leave because she wanted to change her stockings? Witness – No. Wm. Howell, fireman at the South London Music Hall, gave evidence as to the throwing of the pewter pot. He did not hear prosecutor use bad language, but defendant called Mr Rich a filthy name because he would not shift his basket. The latter did not cause any obstruction. – Chas. Tarrant, music boy at South London, said he saw Miss Moore throw the water over the prosecutor, and Florence Sneezum, defendant's maid, deposed that her mistress did not use bad language towards the complainant. Mr Dickinson ordered the defendant to be bound over to keep the peace for six months, and to pay 2s. costs.
18/2/1893

ON Saturday evening about ten o'clock, while the last act of *The Fast Mail* was on at the Public Hall, Barnsley, Mr Frank A. Gordyn and Mr Gerald Spencer were in the box office counting up the cash, when a very black looking gentleman, evidently a collier, who was about three parts drunk, lurched up to the pigeon hole and, in a very husky voice, desired to know what time the next train went to Silkstone. He was informed that the last train on that line (*The Fast Mail*) had gone, when angrily he told his informers that theirs was "a rotten line" and that they could go to h---.
25/2/1893

WANTED, Young Lady Sopranos, to Yodel. German preferred. Comfortable Engagement. Photos, De Wing and Nice, 122, Fleet Street, E.C.
4/3/1893

ACTORS are the most superstitious of beings, and the old theory of the luck a black cat brings to a theatre is well known. At no place is a black puss more welcome than at the Comedy Theatre, where a celebrated feline dramatic critic resides. On a first night the cat invariably does one of two things. If he approves of the play he solemnly walks on to the stage, looks at the audience, and then goes off; but if, on the other hand, he has no great opinion of the piece in progress, he sleeps in Mr Charles Hawtrey's dressing-room. The cat – his name is "Godpapa" – has never yet committed an error of critical judgement. Each piece he has approved of has been a great success, and from those he has slept through the public have carefully kept away. A few such cats ought to be useful at dress rehearsals. They might save their owners no end of money.

MESSRS CATHCART, PETO AND RADFORD, of Hatton Garden, make a speciality of the small electric lights now so much in vogue in jewellery, stars, fancy costumes, &c. We were shown lately a variety of novelties made by this firm – scarf pins representing miniature carriage lamps, skulls with the electric light streaming through the coloured eyes, stars for the hair, set with brilliants that flash with hundreds of rays from the small lamps concealed beneath. We understand this firm has supplied most of the novel electrical effects seen at Covent Garden costume balls. The batteries supplying the current to these little lamps are made as small as possible, and weigh from fifteen to twenty-five ounces.
11/3/1893

THE multitudinous beauties of the pantomime *Little Bo-Peep* have served to maintain its deserved popularity to the very last nights of its career, but with the coming of these last nights and days – for the matinées are still well supported – Sir Augustus Harris has added to the number, and in the "Rainbow Dance" had introduced an effect that is as novel as it is pleasing. About twenty of the principal members of the corps de ballet arranged in white voluminous skirts, made additionally extensive by a contrivance carried by the wearers, go through the serpentine dance under quite new conditions, for as they dance they are occasionally almost lost to view in clouds of steam, upon which coloured lights are made to play with most curious and charming results. The dance has been hailed with shouts of approval and delight by all whose good fortune it has been to see it at Drury Lane.

TO THE EDITOR OF THE ERA.
Sir, – I send you the following narrative of what occurred to our company last week at Stalybridge. Our acting-manager was greatly astonished the other day at having a number of men present themselves for free admission on the strength of their being the bell-ringers of a church close by the theatre. Naturally he refused to pass them, when one of their number (the leader) declared that if they were not allowed free admission they would "break the contract." Upon it being explained by the resident manager that it was arranged they should have free access to the theatre providing they refrained from ringing their bells during the performance and upsetting everything with their din, our manager bowed his best, and gave orders for them to be admitted. This is the latest up-to-date artifice for getting a free pass. Faithfully yours, HERBERT SHELLEY. Walsall, March 13th.
In the next issue the manager, Mr Brough, stated that not only had he refused to admit the bell-ringers, he had threatened them with legal action if they rang their bells during the performance.

WANTED, Known, the Misses Dora and Edith Stanley, Miniature Lady Ventriloquists, Youngest existing. Ages Eleven and Twelve. Seven figures. Immense reception, Manchester District Concerts. Offers invited, Halls, Aquariums, Piers. Agent, A. Williams, Droylsden, Manchester.
18/3/1893

ON Thursday, at the Chester County Court, Mr Lionel Dainer, a member of Mr F.R. Benson's Shakespearian Company, and Mr Jalland, the manager, brought an action against Mr Poultney, of Chester, to recover £2 damages for ejectment from their lodgings. Apartments were taken for plaintiffs during the visit of the Benson company to Chester. They arrived on a Sunday, and in the evening had two other members of the company for guests. The evening was spent in playing poker over hot whiskies. Four piles of money were seen on the table by the landlady, who expressed her indignation at such proceedings on a Sunday, and called her husband and her daughter, and finally a policeman was summoned, and plaintiffs and their guests were ejected, one of them forcibly. It was then after midnight, and they proceeded to the Westminster Hotel. They brought the present action to recover damages. The judge gave judgement for the amount claimed, but the only costs he allowed were Court fees, as he thought they might, as gentlemen, have refrained from playing poker when they found the members of the family were opposed to it. It has been well remarked that this may be good Sabbatarianism, but it is hardly good law.
25/3/1893

MDLLE PAGANINI, aged eleven years, daughter of Paganini Redivivus, will shortly make her first appearance on any stage at Mr Morritt's afternoon entertainment at the Prince's Hall. She will be announced as "The youthful empress-queen of tragedy, comedy and song." Her initial effort will be Lady Macbeth's sleep-walking scene, which she will occasionally vary by giving it in German, French, and Italian, and also singing it in operatic form to music specially composed for her by Paganini Redivivus.
1/4/1893

AT the Star Music Hall, Liverpool, on Monday evening, Mr D.W. Watson, the one-armed cornet soloist, was carried across the high wire by Otto Menotti, the great wire cyclist, whilst playing a cornet solo. At the conclusion of the journey the feat was loudly applauded.
15/4/1893

AN accident, which caused considerable alarm among the audience, is reported to have occurred on Wednesday night at the Alhambra Theatre. While one of the scenes in the ballet of *Aladdin* was being set, several heavy pieces of the woodwork became detached, and fell upon a group of the ladies of the corps de ballet. Several of them were knocked down, while one young woman was precipitated into the orchestra. Consternation for the moment seized the audience, but the curtain was promptly lowered. Shortly afterwards the stage-manager, Mr T.C. Burleigh, was able to announce that in no case had very serious injury been sustained, and in due course the ballet was proceeded with. We are assured that the reports of the affair have dealt in a good deal of exaggeration.

FIVE POUNDS REWARD. – Left Home, a Young Lady, wishing to go on the Stage. Tall, pale, blue eyes, fair hair cut short and curled. Will probably apply to Theatrical Agencies. Five Pounds will be paid for information leading to her discovery.
Address, A.F., Scadding's Library, Belgrave Road.

ROBERTINA. – Return, and you can go on the Stage properly introduced.
22/4/1893

AT the Manchester Assizes, on Monday, before Mr Justice Charles and a jury, Miss Harriet Richardson, an operatic vocalist, sued Mr Anderson, senior partner in the firm of J. Anderson and Son, wine and spirit merchants in Newcastle-on-Tyne, to recover damages for breach of promise of marriage.

The plaintiff, a good-looking young lady, fashionably dressed, in the course of her evidence said her father was in the wine business, and died when she was very young. She was now twenty-eight. She became a governess, but did not care about that, and went on to the stage in comic opera. She was in the chorus, and had 35s. a week, and matinees brought it up to £2. In 1890 she went to Sheffield on tour with one of Mr D'Oyly Carte's operas. She was introduced to the defendant by Mr Edmund Tearle, a gentleman well known in the theatrical profession, who opened the Theatre Royal there. The next night she was introduced to the defendant again by Mr Hart, who, she supposed, did not know she had been introduced to him before. At that time she was living with Miss Belmont, another member of the company. The defendant called at their lodgings, and, presenting his card, said he was a widower in search of a wife. He took her and Miss Belmont out for drives, and acted towards her in a perfectly polite and courteous way. From Sheffield they went to Newcastle, whither the defendant followed her, and continued to pay her attentions. At the station, on going away from Newcastle, he kissed her and asked her to write to him, saying how she was getting on. She did not know at the time that he was a married man. Afterwards the defendant followed her to Bradford, Middlesbrough and other places.

At Middlesbrough, on Oct. 2nd 1890, he asked her to invite some of her friends to supper at her apartments in her honour. She consented, and several friends were invited. After supper he invited the company to stand up and drink the health of "the future Mrs Anderson, now Miss Norah Gordon, his affianced wife." Norah Gordon was her stage name. Everybody was perfectly sober. Claret was drunk during the evening, and it was with the first glass of champagne that the toast was pledged. She considered the toast-drinking a perfectly serious affair. He remained with her half an hour after the supper, and asked her if she thought him too old to become her husband. On the following day, and subsequently, he was most marked in his attentions, and introduced her to various people as his engaged wife. At Workington, whither he followed her, she informed him that her sister wished her to go to Italy as a companion to a young heiress. He said, "My darling, you had better remain and be my companion, and go to Italy with me for my wedding tour." She consented to stay in this country. She afterwards introduced the defendant to her relations in Manchester. Although she did not know at the time he was a married man, she was aware he had children. Before leaving Manchester he made her promise that she would not take another theatrical engagement after she had finished with the one she had. Afterwards, when they met at Bradford, the defendant said he would not marry her until after his daughter's wedding. At the close of her theatrical engagement she did not enter into another engagement for a year. Then she became pushed in her circumstances.

From February, 1891, until October, 1892, she never heard from the defendant, although during six months of that time she wrote to him often. In October, 1892, by which time she had taken another engagement, she met him at Newcastle accidentally. He seemed somewhat surprised to see her. He said he would walk with her to the theatre, and see her after the performance. At the close of the performance he wanted to accompany her to her apartments, but she objected, and he asked her to go to his office. She went to his office, and remained there half an hour. She tried to make him explain. He put her off by saying that he had been travelling very much abroad, and asked her to be a good girl and let that pass, and said he would soon make her love him as much as she had done before. He took her hand and asked her if she would let him measure her finger for a ring. He asked her what stones she would like, and she said diamonds. The following afternoon he came to her rooms, and brought the ring and a brooch. He put the ring on her finger, and asked her to allow him to kiss her, which she did. He made an appointment to meet her again, but did not keep it. She did not see him from that time, and she put the matter into her solicitor's hands.

Counsel for the plaintiff read various letters received by her from the defendant. In these letters he addressed her as "My dear Norah," "My darling," "My pet," and so forth, and generally described himself as "Yours most affectionately." To most of the letters he put his own name, but some of the were signed "J. Fairy." The plaintiff explained that that was what she called him.

Counsel, pointing to the defendant, a very portly gentleman, over fifty years of age – What, this gentleman here, you call a fairy? – Yes, I called him so.

Witness (continuing) – In one of the letters the defendant spoke of having met certain people, and said, "We had a little chaff, and the usual booze, my pet." With one letter he sent her a gold bracelet as a birthday present. In another there occurred the words, "Darling, I am longing to see your pretty little face again. – Always yours most affectionately, FAIRY."

In cross-examination, plaintiff strongly denied that she knew defendant's wife was living. He always represented that he was a widower.

Witnesses were called who bore out plaintiff's statement that defendant constantly spoke of her as his future wife.

Counsel for the defence, Mr Shee, said that the defendant had been guilty of foolish conduct, but there had been no wrong done to the plaintiff. In forming an opinion of the defendant's conduct, the jury should remember that people in the theatrical profession were not as straitlaced as people in other spheres of life, and they thought little of dinner parties, supper parties, drives, and so forth, which other people might consider very important. He denied that there had been any promise to marry.

The defendant, who is a short, stout, bald-headed gentleman, said that in 1891 his wife was alive, but an invalid. He was a wine and spirit merchant, and part of his business was to supply theatres with wines and spirits. He was always travelling, and was generally away from home from Monday morning to the Friday night. He travelled from Dundee to Birmingham, and was constantly meeting theatrical gentlemen. In his travels he often went to theatres, and he generally occupied a box.

Mr Shee – I think you kissed this young lady more than once? Defendant – Yes, in a friendly way.

It is difficult to kiss in an unfriendly way, but I dare say you kissed in a friendly way, and I dare say you kissed her on both cheeks? – Yes.

Defendant, continuing, said the supper referred to was given in the joint honour of the plaintiff and of Mat Robson, who was a very old friend of his. They had a very good spread. Before going to supper they all had liquor, and they had, of course, drink at the supper. He might have made a speech at the supper; he did not remember.

Witnesses were then called for the defence, who denied ever hearing Mr Anderson speak of the plaintiff as his intended wife.

The Judge, in summing up, commented severely on the conduct of the defendant.

The jury found for the plaintiff, and awarded her £150 damages.

6/5/1893

AT Saltaire an exciting scene was witnessed on Saturday night. Lowe and Castleton's company were performing the drama *Lord Anerley*. In the last act the villain shoots himself rather than be taken alive. Mr Wilford Selwyn, who was performing this part, accidentally shot himself, and the curtain was abruptly lowered. The actors rushed from behind the scenes calling out for a doctor. Mr Selwyn's left hand was found to be dreadfully shattered, and the third finger was amputated. Mr A.J. Lowe fainted, and was unconscious for an hour. Mr Selwyn was conveyed to the Sir Titus Salt's Hospital.

AT the West London Theatre, to quote the words of the song, "They have a little cat, and they're very fond of that;" but their affection has received a rude shock, and their feelings have been outraged by puss's conduct. She has eaten all the goldfish placed in the limpid and cool looking fountains and grottos that adorn various parts of the theatre.

ALL theatrical London was pained and shocked on Saturday last by the intelligence that Mr C.H. Fox, the well-known theatrical wig maker, of Russell Street and Wellington Street, Covent Garden, and lately residing at Castelnan, New Barnes, had on the previous evening in Hyde Park taken his own life, at the early age of thirty-four years. On Friday afternoon Mr Fox left his premises in Russell Street, having previously ordered his carriage to take him to a theatre in the evening. At half-past seven his body was discovered in Hyde Park, near Stanhope Gate. He had shot himself through the heart with a revolver. The particulars in connection with this tragic affair came out on Monday at the inquest held by Mr John Troutbeck, the coroner for Westminster, at St George's Hospital.

Mr George F. Fox, 154, Upper Kennington Lane, identified the body of the deceased as that of his brother, whom he last saw alive about twenty minutes to seven on the Friday evening. He then appeared in good spirits. Witness had never heard his brother threaten to take his own life. He had some slight business worries, as money was not coming in quite fast enough to allow him to discharge his present liabilities. Deceased was, however, perfectly solvent, for the book debts were £3,000 in excess of his liabilities. The deceased was married, and had one child.

Worie Hugo, a waiter, of 73 Featherstone Street, Hoxton, said on 7.30 on the Friday evening he was walking in Hyde Park, and when nearing Stanhope Gate he heard a pistol shot. On looking round to ascertain the cause, he saw the deceased fall off the chair on which he was sitting. He at once went for a policeman.

Police-constable J. Prince, 322 C, said he was called by the last witness to the spot where the deceased had shot himself. He found him lying on the ground, and saw that blood was oozing from his mouth. A six-chambered revolver, one chamber of which had recently been discharged, was found inside the deceased's shirt, which was unbuttoned. Witness at once conveyed him to St George's Hospital.

The Coroner then read the following unaddressed and unfinished letter, which was covered with blood, and which was found in one of the deceased's pockets: – "I am afraid I only told you a little of my troubles last night. I have been worse than foolish, and God knows how I shall get along. If I am sold up there will be enough to pay everyone. I am glad I did not borrow that £100 from you, for I owe you enough already. It is only just now that I see my true position. The prospects are very disheartening, and I am broken-hearted. All my speculations have been failures."

The Coroner added that the letter was dated May 11th.

Dr White, house-surgeon at St George's Hospital, said that when deceased was admitted life was extinct. The post-mortem examination revealed a bullet wound in the chest. The bullet had pressed the aorta and caused almost instantaneous death.

The jury returned a verdict of "Suicide whilst in a state of temporary insanity."

Mr Fox, who was only thirty-five years of age, started in business on his own account at the age of twenty. He was Mr Henry Irving's principal wigmaker, and, when the Lyceum company made their first voyage across the Atlantic, they took with them eleven hundred wigs of Mr Fox's manufacture. Examples of his skill have been seen on the heads of most of the leading members of the profession. For the production of *The Dead Heart* alone he made no less than four hundred and fifty wigs. Mr Fox was very popular in the profession, where his courtesy and deep interest in his work made him liked and respected. His latest venture was a provincial tour of the farcical comedy *The Noble Art*. The business will be carried on under the same name by Mrs Fox and Mr George Fox. Mrs Fox desires to thank very sincerely the numerous friends who have written her letters of condolence.
20/5/1893

HERE is a story which has the reputation of being true. A certain touring manager was arrested the other day on the charge of having opened a telegram addressed to an actor in his company. The manager admitted the charge, and gave his own version of the affair: – "M. – the actor – had been telling me for a fortnight how ill his wife was, and that he was liable to be called to her at any time – she was at Blankville. One night a telegram for M., from Blankville, was handed in at the box-office; and, as he was acting, I opened it, thinking that it might contain fatal news. But it didn't. It only said, "Meet me at once as Dashborough; good engagement for both of us. We open on Monday. – JENNIE." I refastened the envelope and gave it to M., who tore it open, and cried "My God! She is dying! I must leave tonight. Will you advance me the fare?" He did leave that night – indeed, he left that minute; but what I advanced to expedite his departure was not a fare. That is why he brings this action."

AT the Bow Street Police Court, on Saturday, Emilio Schierso, giving an address at 43, Brook Street, Westminster, and described on the charge sheet as a "globe-runner," was charged with disorderly conduct and an obstruction in the Strand. The accused, who was attired in a straw hat, a blue-and-black striped "blazer" and knickerbockers, was brought into court with a large round globe, on which, it appeared, he intended to travel from London to Manchester on his return journey. Police-sergeant James Harris stated that at a quarter-past twelve o'clock noon on Saturday he saw the defendant on the roadway in the Strand on the globe, with a flag in each hand, and a crowd of 300 or 400 people following behind. As owing to this crowd the traffic proceeding eastward was impeded, he asked the defendant to get off. He refused, and was taken in custody. Defendant denied that he stopped the traffic in any way. A witness, who described himself as a sketch artist on the music hall stage, who had attended the defendant on his journey from Manchester, and his manager were called for the defence, and whilst admitting that some people followed him, denied that the traffic was impeded. Mr Lushington, on the defendant undertaking not to repeat his attempt in a crowded thoroughfare like the Strand, discharged him. Defendant on leaving the court jumped on his ball and made a triumphant progress down the corridor and across the station yard.

WANTED, a Ventriloquist who can imitate Larks and work a Boy figure. Address, EDITOR, 58, Murray Street, London, N.
27/5/1893

A SINGULAR accident occurred the other night during the performance of the comic opera *Pepita*, at the Theatre Royal, West Hartlepool. Inigo, played by Mr Lytton Grey, was proceeding with his part in the last scene, and was in the act of flourishing his sword when the blade suddenly parted with the hilt and flew with great velocity over the orchestra, just missing the leader, and descending amongst the occupants of the stalls. A gentleman who was sitting in the second row was struck on the head by the weapon, which afterwards alighted on the head of an elderly lady, crushing her bonnet and causing her to utter a loud shriek. Happily no one was seriously hurt, though the gentleman who was hit on the head was stunned for a moment, and subsequently had to leave his seat and proceed home. Mr Lytton Grey was also somewhat unnerved by the accident, and proceeded with his part with some difficulty.

THE ELECTROPHONE.
THE theatrophone that has been established in Paris for some time, and has attained no small popularity, is to be introduced to London under the name of the electrophone, and a syndicate has been formed for its working in connection with the National Telephone Company. The said syndicate on Wednesday evening afforded a large number of guests an opportunity of testing the powers of the instrument at their offices in Whitcomb Street, Coventry Street, and a curious spectacle these guests presented, as with jaws in a metal framework they applied small knobs at the ends of rubber tubing to their ears and put on quite an ecstatic look as they took in the music of the theatre that at the moment happened to be switched on. We experimented with the Empire and the Shaftesbury, enjoying the orchestral performance at the former and the catchy music and frequent applause and laughter in connection with *Morocco Bound* at the latter. The object of the Electrophone Syndicate is to connect places of entertainment with hotels, clubs, restaurants, cafès, depôts, hospitals, bazaars, throughout the United Kingdom. They do not stop at theatres, for cathedrals, churches, chapels, and private houses are included in their ultimate scope. Even the Houses of Parliament may possibly, it is thought, be brought under the influence of the new wonder. The Syndicate has a box at the Earl's Court Exhibition, near the Welcome Club, and there the performances at four theatres can be heard to perfection. It is intended to make a great effort to reproduce at Chester the music and parts of plays at London theatres on the occasion of the banquet to be given to the Prince of Wales. In addition to the theatres named above, communication was held on Wednesday with the Trafalgar Square; and the Lyric, the Gaiety, Criterion, Alhambra, Prince of Wales's, Olympic, Comedy, Grand, Royal Aquarium, and Theatre Royal, Brighton, are to be added to the list.
17/6/1893

WANTED, to Sell, Mummy Egyptian High Priestess in superbly decorated Cartonage Case, 4,600 years. Unopened. Therefore contains Valuable Diamond Jewellery. Price £12. Wanted, Wax Cylinder, Edison Phonograph. ALBERT BLAKE, Publisher, Portsea.

MUSICIANS are Cautioned against accepting Engagements for JOHANNESBURG, SOUTH AFRICA at a Salary of less than £5 per week, as £2 in England is equivalent to £5 in Johannesburg. They are also notified that all Agreements signed at home have to be confirmed on arrival at Cape Town, and also in Johannesburg, and are even then null and void Thirty-five miles from Johannesburg.

SOUTH AFRICA. – The Johannesburg Orchestral Musicians have formed themselves into a Ring to try and keep up their exorbitant Salaries. The statement that £2 in England is as good as £5 in Johannesburg is absolutely false, as is the statement re Legality of Contracts made in London. LUSCOMBE SEARELLE.
8/7/1893

MR WILSON BARRETT was the recipient of a curious set of presents on the closing night of his stay in Montreal, when he played Hamlet. About five hundred students of McGill University hired the upper part of the house, and in the graveyard scene began sending boxes of cigars and wine from the gallery to the stage by means of a wire they had laid. The lordly Hamlet in vain attempted to ignore these malapropos tokens of good will. The students would have an acknowledgement, and the moody Dane had to step out from the scene, unhook the presents, and smilingly bow his acceptance.

MRS URWICK hereby begs to tender her Apologies to Mr Douglas Cox for having caused to be Represented his Play entitled "Freezing a Mother-in-Law" at St Peter's Garden Fete, Clapham, without first having obtained his permission to do so.
15/7/1893

ON Tuesday evening quite a sensation was caused at Spennymoor Railway Station by the arrival of a couple of Russians and a huge bear, to which all on the platform gave a wide berth, although the Russians, Messrs Petroff and Ivanoff, in broken English tried to persuade the passengers that the animal was quite quiet. The trio was met by Madame Zaleska, who conducted the new *Matrishka* artists to her residence, Eden Cottage, followed by some hundred representatives of Young England. Madame Zaleska leaves Spennymoor this morning with the Russian bear, new scenery, and a portion of her company to open at the Theatre Royal, Birkenhead, with the play named.

AT the North London Police Court, on Monday, Mr Lane had before him an amusing case involving the ownership of a dove. The complainant was Mr George W. Hunt, the composer of the once-celebrated song "We don't want to fight, but, by Jingo, if we do!" and the defendant Mr John Lundy, a City merchant. The parties are near neighbours in Graham Road, Dalston, and Mr Hunt said that a fortnight ago he lost a pet dove which he had kept in a cage in his garden for four years. He subsequently saw an ancient dove in a cage in the defendant's garden, but that dove was not his. A day or two after a painter employed on the houses brought witness an old dove, which he recognised as the one he saw in the defendant's garden. Then he heard his own dove cooing in the defendant's garden, and on going to see the bird he at once recognised it as his. The defendant, however, refused to give it up. The complainant valued his dove at £1 1s.

Cross-examined – He was unable to say if his dove was a cock or a hen. Although he had had it four years he had never inquired as to its sex.

Mrs Goodchief, residing in the same house as the complainant, said she recognised the dove in the defendant's garden as Mr Hunt's.

Mr Lane – But all doves are very much alike. Witness – Yes, but this dove laughs at me.

The defendant said it was impossible for the witness to see the dove three or four gardens off. Witness, however, said that she distinctly saw the bird laugh at her.

The defendant said that the dove the complainant claimed had been in his cage for four months. He also bought the one the painter took to Mr Hunt for sixpence. Mr Lane said it was obvious that a mistake had been made, and he dismissed the summons. The defendant asked for costs, saying that through a sixpenny dove he had been kept from his work on 'Change. Mr Lane allowed 5s. costs.
29/7/1893

AN amusing incident occurred at Torquay on the opening night of the South company of *A Woman of No Importance*. Having the same set for the second and third act there was not a very long wait, so some of the occupants of the gallery had not returned to their seats before the curtain was raised. They kept straggling in, so Mr Mouillot went to the gallery door to ask the "boys" to make as little noise as possible. The inevitable Irishman turned up, and on being asked to make as little noise as he could, he replied, "Oh, begorra, I will that, sir. I'll tell you what I'll do for you and Mr Oscar, as I knew him well,

I'll take off my boots," and he did, boldly entering the gallery boots in hand. Another straggler, coming in later, was not so polite, and was making a noise when descending the gallery. The Irishman's voice came out loud and strong – "Take off yer boots, ye blackguard, and show yer respect to art."
2/9/1893

MR W. MORTON, of Greenwich, is nightly distributing at his "model theatre" dozens of cards designed to advertise his tour with *Ups and Downs of Life*. On each card is a picture of a lady and gentleman approaching the entrance to a theatre, under the arch of which is a board with the directions "*To the Ups and Downs of Life*." In the centre of the card a flap can be raised at right angles to the rest of the "throwaway." By pulling up this flap and holding the card so that the flap casts no shadow; and then resting the tip of the nose on the top edge of the flap and watching the figures for a moment, the lady and gentleman appear to walk into the theatre. These cards are given away by the attendants in the intervals of the performance at Morton's Theatre each evening, and the spectacle of the whole audience with the nose of each individual on the edge of the flap above-mentioned is very amusing.
9/9/1893

A WEEKLY society paper keeps a female physiognomist, who, on the receipt of a photograph of any purchaser of the paper, writes out a description of the character of the sender, which is published the following week. In answer to a male correspondent, the physiognomist says: "No wonder that from your earliest youth you have wished to go on the stage, for your face shows all the qualities which tend to make a great actor. The forehead gives intuitive perception of character; the eyebrows power of affecting jealousy and sensitiveness; the eyes imagination; the nose courage; the lips wit, fluent speech, and delicacy of intonation; and the chin sympathy and refinement. Why not go on the stage at once? You have every indication of success in such a career." Can it be wondered at that the stage is over-crowded, when such decided and unhesitating advice as this is given, without the advisor having even met, personally, the individual she counsels?

MR BRANDON THOMAS a day or two ago received by post from the Cape a mysterious parcel. It proved to be a large slice of cake – not wedding cake, but good, honest, substantial plum cake. Fearing that it had come to him by mistake, Mr Thomas ate it hurriedly, before the postman could reclaim it. He could not imagine the meaning of the incident, although the attack of indigestion which followed secured him plenty of time to devote to the elucidation of the problem, which was a sort of current topic among his circle. A later post brought a Johannesburg paper, in which the explanation was found in the following paragraph: – "*Charley's Aunt* has broken the record of the consecutive run of any play or opera in South Africa, and in recognition of the achievement I have decided that this week the members of the Hawtrey comedy company take the cake on the understanding that a large slice of it be sent to the author, Brandon Thomas."

"DADDY WOULDN'T BUY ME A BOW-WOW" is not appreciated in Denmark, a fact which we would emphasise for any of our readers who are contemplating spending their holidays in that country. On Thursday, 7th inst., a Birmingham solicitor, who is well known to members of companies visiting the Midland metropolis, invited the staff at the hotel at which he was staying in Copenhagen to supper at one of the late cafes. All being Danes, they were ignorant of the bewitching attractions of Mr Arthur Roberts's latest success, so, on the way to the cafe, the host sought to entertain his guests with the story of daddy and the much-wished-for bow-wow. He was arrested, taken to the police-station, and would have remained the night but for the persistency of his guests, who succeeded in bailing him out by depositing ten kroner as a guarantee for his reappearance when required.
16/9/1893

AN amusing incident occurred last week during Miss Vesta Tilley's engagement at the Gaiety Theatre, Oldham. About 7.30 on Saturday night a wagonette drew up at the front entrance, containing a dozen or so of very old women, who had subscribed to hire the vehicle, and had driven from Lees, near Oldham, to hear Miss Vesta Tilley sing. They helped each other down carefully, brought out their umbrellas and wraps, and small bags, from which peeped the small necks of small bottles, and, in fact, everything necessary to make their night drive comfortable. In a body they made for the pay box and paid their money. To their surprise, the money-taker returned their cash, informing them that not a seat was to be had. It took some time before the old ladies could be made to understand that they could not go in, but when they at last grasped the situation, they gave the poor money-taker a piece of their mind. After much persuasion, they were all safely packed back in the wagonette, one old lady being heard to remark as they drove away, "I'll be bound my mon has told yon money-taker not to let me in."
23/9/1893

WANTED, to Sell, Extraordinary Living Curiosity, Healthy Duck, having Three Legs, namely, Two Duck's and One Hen's Legs. Wonderful freak. Price 10s. Living for small Showman. 17, Spiceal Street, Birmingham.
7/10/1893

A MEMBER of the Hardie-Von Leer company on tour is S. Ojijittekha Sero, a chief of the Mohawks, and an extraordinary example of Indian culture and intelligence. He can discuss Herbert Spencer, has lectured in order to show that the Indian is not as he is represented in the past or the present, and is the only Indian member of the Actors' Association.

MISS EVA LESTER, music hall artiste, was summoned to the Lambeth Police Court, on the 13th inst., by a cabman named Parsons, for 25s., which he alleged to be due to him. The complainant stated that he "picked" the defendant up at the Horns, Kennington, about three o'clock in the afternoon, and drove her about until about one o'clock the next morning. The last call was at the Horns, which they left at closing time. The defendant had not paid him a penny.

The defendant said she engaged the complainant between three and four o'clock in the afternoon. He put her down at her house between six and seven. She then asked him what his fare was, and he replied, "Well, 7s. won't hurt you, will it, Miss Lester?" She paid him 7s., and gave him a brandy and soda. He said he felt hungry, and she told him to go into the kitchen and have a mutton chop. About half-past seven she was going out with her dressmaker. The defendant told her not to walk, and he would drive her about as long as she liked, as she had been very kind to him. He drove her from place to place, and set her down at her house in Hilda Road, Brixton, about one o'clock. He did not ask for any money, but said he would call in the morning to see how she was.

The defendant's dressmaker gave corroborative evidence, but the complainant, recalled, positively denied that he received 7s.

Mr Biron said he considered the 7s. settled the account up to six o'clock, and that the mutton chop and brandy and soda squared it up to eight, but the defendant must pay for the remainder of the evening. He made an order for the payment of 12s. 6d. and 5s. costs.

In the course of an interview, pantomime star George Lupino spoke about his early career as a ballet dancer:
Time was when the male dancer fairly divided honours with the premiere danseuse, but it is not so now. Perhaps the public thinks grace effeminate in a man; at any rate, does not appreciate it. "I found," says George Lupino, "that, in a manner of speaking, I got more applause for sitting on stuffed babies – more money also – than I got for operatic dancing. Besides, you can sit on stuffed babies till extreme old age

overtakes you; but the day of the dancer as a public favourite is short. So the stuffed baby has won the day."

NOTICE TO ARTISTS. – Re. Four-Legged Freak Dance, as Performed by Miss De Laine at the Royal Aquarium for the past Six Months. It is useless writing for permission to use same in Pantomime, as the above is Patented, and if permission is given, you cannot obtain the Mechanical Legs only through TOM PRITCHARD, 167, Stamford Street, who is prepared to Sell One Set in each Town.
21/10/1893

AT a recent performance of *Faust* by Mr J.W. Turner's company in a certain north-country theatre, Mephistopheles had just disappeared down the trap with Faust, when the old woman who had called for the company's washing, and who was standing at the wings, was heard to exclaim in excited tones, "Oh, where have they gone to?" "Gone to? Why, to the devil. Go and see," replied one of the supers. Whereupon the inquisitive old dame trotted nimbly on to the stage, and when the curtain again went up her portly form was disclosed leaning over the trap, and illuminated by the glare of the red fire which ascended from the depths beneath. "Come off," roared the manager; but the old lady, apparently oblivious of what was going on around her, continued to gaze down the trap until the curtain was finally lowered.
28/10/1893

SIR ARTHUR SULLIVAN was, we hear, so much annoyed by the substitution of a female for a male Nanki-Poo in the revival of *The Mikado* at the Unter den Linden Theatre, Berlin, that he tried to stop the performances, and took legal advice as to his power to do so. However, the opera is still being given, with Frau Ilka Von Palmay in the part originally sustained by Mr Durward Lely.

WHAT becomes of heavy-weight pugilists when they become too heavy-weight? This is a riddle whose answer changes with the years; for whereas of old their invariable practice was to take a public-house, they now, with a like monotony, drift towards the stage. Mr John L. Sullivan led the way as a full-blown star. Mr Peter Jackson, champion heavy-weight pugilist of Australia and England, is at least a "central attraction" – a delicate distinction which none but an acting-manager can properly appreciate. Peter is now playing Uncle Tom in a grand spectacular production of that gentleman's *"Cabin,"* to which he gives additional interest by a sparring match with one Joseph Choynski – also not unknown in the ring – between the second and third acts. If this be not the realistic and advanced drama, we humbly ask what *is*?
9/12/1893

WANTED, for Small Child, Decapitation Trick. Particulars and price to A., 221, Vauxhall Bridge Road, S.W.

PROFESSOR ENOCH, a hardy Yorkshireman, whose performances in the Aquarium tank are so well known to London sightseers, is now in New York at the Park Theatre, where he is performing his celebrated feat of playing the trombone under water. American critics are uncharitable enough to suggest that certain vocalists who sing out of tune might try warbling an aria in a similar sub-aqueous position to that adopted by the Professor.
23/12/1893

5
1894
THE BEAUTIES OF HER INCOMPARABLE BUST

ALLEGED THEATRICAL FRAUDS.
AT the Westminster Police Court, on Monday, Henry Gartley, described as a theatrical agent, late of Claverton Street, Pimlico, and Victoria Street, Westminster, was brought up, on remand, charged with obtaining money by false pretences from young women desirous of getting on the stage. Mr Sims prosecuted for the Treasury. The accused was a super., paid at the rate of 15s. a week, at the Adelphi Theatre. It had already been given in evidence that that he advertised for young people desirous of getting on the stage, and that his correspondence with histrionic aspirants was of a most extensive character, hundreds of letters having being seized by the police.

The American young lady, Hazel Thornton, otherwise Coleman, recalled, and cross-examined by Mr Dutton, said that when she took her lessons at Claverton Street, she did so in the office. There was a stage fitted in the office. She had two lessons – each lasting half an hour. The arrangement with the prisoner was not that she should pay four guineas to be trained for the stage. She was to pay two guineas for elocution, and two for being introduced to the Comedy company. Prisoner said nothing to her about bringing out a play in the provinces, which she was to enter if she got on well. She told the prisoner at the outset that she had been engaged in the ballet at a New York theatre – the Casino. She had three months experience as a ballet dancer.

Mr Dutton (for the defence) – Surely, my girl, with your New York experience, you never expected to be trained as an actress for the London stage for two guineas? Witness – I really did. That is all the man asked me. I was to be "educated in the dramatic art."

In answer to further questions, Miss Coleman said that the number of lessons she was to receive was not stipulated.

Mr Dutton – I suppose you were satisfied with the two lessons you had – prisoner did his best to train you? – Well, I learnt the part myself, but he showed me "the expression."

But you have improved slightly? – Well, a little.

May I take it that if you had gone on with the prisoner's tuition you would have become efficient? I would *what*?

"Efficient" – you know what that is? – Yes, I think so.

You did not give the defendant the opportunity of finishing you off as an actress? – Well, that was his fault. Why did he run off and hide in a doorway?

But you knew he was taking a more suitable office in Victoria Street? – No. He never told me. The first idea I had that I was "being done" was seeing everything packed up for removal. I guessed he was waiting "for the truck."

Miss Kate Fidler, a tall, stylishly-dress young lady, said she resided at a hotel, the Ring of Bells, Winslow, Cheshire. Her father kept the house, and she resided with him. In November last she saw an advertisement for lady and gentleman amateurs for "long tour of an established success." She wrote an answer to the advertisement, and got into communication with the prisoner at Claverton Street, Pimlico.

Mr Sims at this juncture put in the whole of a long correspondence between the prisoner and witness. Miss Fidler wrote that she should very much like to join his company. She said that she had not been on the stage before, but would very soon pick it up. She added that she had two sisters on the stage with Henry Dixey's company in America, that her age was eighteen, her height 5ft. 8in., and that she was slender. Prisoner in answer to this wrote that no doubt she would suit to take light comedy in his company, which was formed. She would be required to come to London about four days before the departure of the company for rehearsals. Her salary would be two guineas a week and all travelling expenses. In a further letter of Nov. 30th prisoner said the tour was postponed, and told the young lady that as she had not been on the stage before he should require a small premium of £4. Assenting to this Miss Fidler sent the prisoner £1 on account, and received a part purporting to be that of Nora, and a memorandum of agreement relating to an engagement in *A Woman's Vengeance* company starting on tour Jan. 9th.

Mr Dutton, in cross-examination, asked the young lady if she did not part with her money for tuition.

Mr Sims objected. The girl never saw the prisoner, and the whole negotiation was in writing. The agreement spoke for itself, and there was not a word about tuition from start to finish.

Miss Rose Varens, a young lady described as an actress, now of the Tyne Theatre, Newcastle-on-Tyne, deposed that in June last she was living in Liverpool Road, Islington. She was desirous of going on the stage, and, seeing an advertisement in a theatrical newspaper, she answered it. In the result she went and saw the prisoner at a house in Winchester Street, Pimlico. She asked him if he could get her a part on the stage. He said yes. He had a company going out the first week in August, and could train her for a part if she paid him ten guineas.

Mr Sims – Did he say what the company was? – Yes. A burlesque company, *Dick Whittington Up to Date*. He asked me what part I would like – a girl's or a boy's. I said I should like to be a boy, and he said he would give me second boy.

What did he say about his own connection with the piece? – He said that he was to be the manager, and perhaps he would take a part himself. I was promised between £2 and £3 a week salary, and that the burlesque would be turned into a pantomime at Christmas. I agreed to the prisoner's terms, and paid ten guineas in two instalments. I was to commence rehearsals when I liked, and I elected to begin on the following Monday. I went to the same place.

And what did the prisoner do for you? – He showed me a few steps in dancing. On another occasion, a week later, he taught me a song, "Far Away in Dreams," which I was to learn for my part. There was also another song, "Ding, Ding, Dong."

Mr Sims (producing it) – Written on the back of one of the prisoner's memo. forms, where he describes himself as "Musical Director of the Grosvenor Academy."

Witness, resuming her evidence, said that she could never get her part. Prisoner always told her that she should get it later on. He said at last that she should play Dick, the principal boy. He gave her a list of provincial theatres where he said the company was booked. She knew that one of the theatres was the Royal Opera House, Chatham, and another the Theatre Royal, Stratford. In September prisoner told her that they would open at Stratford within a week. After this she made inquiries at Stratford, and found that nothing was known of the prisoner or his projected company.

Mr Sims said that after this witness could not see the prisoner, who was out when she called. Some letters passed between the parties, Miss Varens writing that she had been treated very badly, and that she would be humbugged no longer. She asked for the return of the ten guineas, and threatened to make the matter public.

The next letter from the prisoner was dated Oct. 6th, and was addressed from Claverton Street. Gartley wrote: – "When you are proficient I will get you an engagement, but you know as well as possible you are not. As to returning you the money, what do you think? You have had half of your tuition in dancing, songs, elocution, &c. I think you must be 'off.' I should advise you to be careful. I have seen my solicitor, and he has advised me properly." Miss Varens identified her reply, the reading of which occasioned a good deal of laughter. She considered that the prisoner should at least write like a gentleman, and not ask her if she was "off." The letter went on: – "No, indeed I am not; I think it is no more than right that at least you should refund me half the money I paid you. I have learned precious little elocution, and certainly I don't know what '&c.' stands for. The dances you showed me nearly every street urchin knows."

Mr Sims – I believe the prisoner told you that you would require some stage accessories? – Witness – Yes. He said that I should have to buy my own tights and shoes, and that he could get them for me. He charged me 35s. for the tights.

Mr Sims – When you were carrying on this negotiation with the prisoner how old were you? – I was seventeen. I had no business experience or knowledge of the world. I had been living with my parents. I had only played in amateur theatricals and at private parties.

Mr De Rutzen complimented all the young women on the intelligent and ready manner in which they had given evidence.

Cross-examined – Miss Varens said her lessons commenced in June and continued till September. She might have had twenty lessons altogether. In September she was taken ill, and was indisposed for a few weeks. In October she got on the stage, but not through the prisoner. She went with a touring company till she got her present engagement in pantomime at Newcastle.

Mr De Rutzen further remanded the prisoner, Mr Sims stating that the Treasury had other witnesses to call.

The accused, who also called himself Lord Henry Gartley, was later sentenced to ten months' hard labour.

WANTED, Proprietors not to Worry. John R. Preston, Advertising Manager, &c., is not Dead. Thanks for Wreaths and touching condolences. Now Engaged.
13/1/1894

THE following letter, with many others of the same tenor, has been received by a prominent provincial manager: – "Dear Sir, I wright to you to see if you could take me on the stage you do take girls to learn at the back I will try to learn quick I am very good at lerning I can jump about like fun do have me on for I do love it, it is so nice. I am 17 age and an Irish girl shall you saend for me to see what I am like I am a jolly girl I shall be very glad indeed if you will have me let me know as soon as you can please, Yours truly, -----."
20/1/1894

MR EDWARD MARTIN, the manager of the People's Palace, Sunderland, where the Amazon troupe of Dahomey Warriors had been performing, was charged, on the 26th ult., at the instance of the Corporation, with permitting overcrowding. The town clerk stated that forty-six of the Africans lived in one house. After evidence had been given, Herr Guiner, manager of the troupe, stated that they had been allowed to live in Oxford Street, London, and also in Newcastle without interference in a house containing one room less than this one. The Bench ordered the nuisance to be abated within twenty-four hours, and ordered Mr Martin to pay the costs.
3/2/1894

MR F.R. BENSON had a curious gift made to him last Saturday by the students of Queen's Hospital, Belfast. The quay from which was to start the steamer that was to carry away Mr Benson and his company was lined, twelve deep, with hundreds of people; and the actor was presented, in the saloon of the vessel, with a human skull, trepanned on the back with a silver plate, with "Alas! Poor Yorick!" engraved on it. The skull was christened in champagne, and then the vessel started, amidst cheers and the singing of choruses.
10/2/1894

MR PETER JACKSON, the pugilist, whose skin is ebon-hued, has, it is said, the ambition to play Othello. Some inveterate joker will be saying "Moor's the pity." But why should not an intelligent fellow – which Jackson certainly is – whose complexion is the burnished livery of the summer sun, follow the example set him by Ira Aldridge, who starred in Shakespeare many years since at the City of London Theatre.
24/2/1894

THE late Mr Aynsley Cook had an amusing adventure in Liverpool a few years ago during the opera season at the Royal Court Theatre. Mr Cook, who was a man of tremendous bulk, hired a "four-wheeler" one night near the theatre, but the vehicle had not gone far before the bottom fell out. The artist shouted to the driver in the deepest bass he could command, but a strong wind was blowing, and the cab proceeded for a long way with Mr Cook running inside it before the jehu pulled up.

AT the Royal Court Theatre, Liverpool, on Wednesday, in the course of the first complete rehearsal of Wagner's *Rienzi*, an odd incident happened. In the destruction of Rienzi's palace several large stage batteries are discharged, and the explosion was so tremendous that it was heard a long way off. A great crowd of passers-by rushed to see what had happened, it being imagined that another Anarchist outrage had been committed.

ELEANOR LAWRENCE, a housemaid, was charged at the Marylebone Police Court, on Thursday, on remand, with attempting to poison Mrs Salmond, her mistress, and others. The prosecutrix is the wife of Mr Norman Salmond, who was with the late Madame Patey on a professional engagement at Sheffield. The prisoner had been in Mrs Salmond's service since November. On the 23rd ult. everything in which the water from the cistern in the house was used tasted of carbolic acid, and the prisoner subsequently confessed to a police constable that she had thrown carbolic acid into the water in the cistern in revenge for being dismissed without a character. She was committed for trial.
3/3/1894

ON Wednesday morning a suspicious-looking tin canister was received at Frank Hiam's conjuring depôt. It looked very much like an infernal machine, and not one of the firm would open it. At last it was taken to Old Street Police Station by Mr Frank Hiam's sons, Arthur and Fred. There it caused some consternation, and at last was put into a bucket of water. On the tin being opened everyone was surprised to see inside a small red orb, which looked very much like a bomb, but on examination was found to be a billiard ball.
10/3/1894

SENSATIONAL melodrama has its perils and its sacrifices. Mr Frank Oswald, who was appearing in Mr John Lawson's *Humanity* company at the Theatre Royal, Blyth, on Monday, had a painful accident. In the "death struggle," when mirrors, window panes, and globes were being shattered in every direction, a piece of broken glass almost severed his nose from his face. The scene was abruptly terminated, and the nose was stitched into its natural position. Only some two or three months since Mr Oswald fractured his arm while taking part in the same scene.

A PARCEL containing some theatrical lightning recently forwarded from a Holloway manufactory to a Stockport theatre caused considerable excitement in the neighbourhood of the Angel, Islington, by exploding in the carrier's office. The senders were fined £10.
17/3/1894

AT the dress rehearsal, which was almost equivalent to a first performance, of Massenet's new opera *Thaïs*, at the Paris Opera House, on the 16th inst., when Mdlle Sanderson, as the mocking courtesan, had to open her mantle and display to the monk Athanäel the beauties of her incomparable bust, something gave way, and the exposure of Mdlle Sanderson's handsome person was so complete that a murmur of startled surprise ran through the audience. This was an accident, of course; but it is curious to remember that an exactly similar mishap happened to Mrs Brown Potter when she appeared for the first time as Cleopatra in New York, and had to undo her bodice to apply the asp to her breast. Surely some method could be devised by which these little accidents might be avoided?

THE MYSTERY of Ibsen's mane is a mystery no more. Most people to whom the Norwegian dramatist's portrait is familiar must have wondered how he managed to keep his hair in such a persistently "flamboyant" state. From American sources we learn that he always carries a comb and a looking glass, the latter being concealed in his hat. By means of these he is able to frequently and stealthily adjust his locks.

WANTED, it Known, that Townley, the Ancient Juvenile Lancashire Singer, is keeping the Audience in complete Torture, Nightly, this Week, at People's, Oldham. Remains another week. Write above.
24/3/1894

THE recent disgraceful disturbances at the Opéra-Comique Theatre, Paris, on the occasion of the appearance there of Mdlle Jane Harding, have been dealt with by the Correctional Tribunal. It was shown that after hooting, hissing, and catcalls had been heard, Mdlle Harding was struck by a dead rabbit, a codfish, and other items thrown from the upper circle by a Mdlle Victorine Beaucarne, who tried to dismay Mdlle Harding by writing "I have your certificate of birth, and we will have a good laugh in court about your tender youth, for you know you are not exactly twenty-five years old." The judge fined Mdlle Beaucarne ten francs, and said he was sorry he could not send her to prison.

THE amusements provided at Canterbury during the visit of our civic forces included a novel entertainment. The ancient cathedral city had just been connected by telephone, and the National Telephone Company took the opportunity of experimenting with the wires by connecting the London music halls with the premises of Councillor Lukey, the Mayor. Some of the leading townspeople, besides a large number of Volunteers, took advantage of the opportunity of listening to the variety stars, and the results were completely successful, the songs being perfectly audible, although the distance was about sixty-five miles.
31/3/1894

WANTED, to Buy, Two Performing Chairs; must be strong and in good condition. ATHERTON, St Helena Tavern, Rotherhithe, London, S.E.
21/4/1894

MISS ELLALINE TERRISS, on her first appearance in *Cinderella* at Abbey's Theatre, New York, took the house entirely by storm. She had an "ovation" lasting nearly two minutes; and at the end of this a shoe 3½ft. long and 3ft. high, made of pinks, roses, and pansies, was handed over the footlights.

TO THE EDITOR OF THE ERA.

Sir, – The following verbatim copy of a letter received by me a week ago whilst playing in a large provincial town may be worth quoting, as showing that a glamour evidently yet hangs about the stage – for some people – even in this *fin de siècle* age:

Oldham, April 19th, 1894.
Dear Miss Terriss, I have seen you many times, and possibly you have never noticed me! The more I see you, the more I like you. Rather an abrupt way of introducing one's subject, but I am an abrupt customer. Now to the point: are you tired of professional life, and if so, and not engaged, would you care to become the wife of a tradesman? I am in the refreshment line at Oldham, formerly a cavalry non-commissioned officer (aged thirty-four). You are just the lively little soul I have been looking for! And if I have not offended you too much by this awkward way of introducing myself, please drop me a line by return and oblige. Yours very truly, -------

I suppress the name for obvious reasons.
Yours truly, FLORENCE TERRISS.
Victoria Theatre, Newport, May 1st.
5/5/1894

WANTED, a Coloured Boy, about Thirteen, as Page to Madame Sartis Lindsay, the only Lady Dentist in England. Thanks to those who answered my advt. Am suited. Yours truly, LITTLE AGGIE. Address, 20, King's Road, Peckham.
26/5/1894

MR LEWIS GILBERT, acting-manager of the Gaiety Theatre, West Hartlepool, appeared at the police court in that town, on Tuesday, to prosecute a young man named Geldart, who whilst employed in the establishment stole a revolver from the property-room, after having read a cheap novel called "Deadwood Dick." Mr Gilbert said he never knew a property man to be influenced by romance in this way before. Geldart was fined 10s. and costs.
9/6/1894

A BRIGHT spot in the otherwise wearisome amateur performance at St George's Hall on Thursday last of a burlesque called *Beauty and the Beast* was the appearance of the two daughters of the Earl of Ellesmere, who, by the mother's side, are related to the great house of Cawdor. Lady Beatrice Egerton as Tapioca sang with a good deal of *chic* a ditty in which she described herself as a "risky, frisky, *fin-de-siècle* girl," and justified the description by a saucy little kick-up dance. Lady Mabel appeared as Cocoatina (otherwise Beauty), and thoroughly professional was the manner in which she did a pirouette at the end of a dance.
16/6/1894

THERE were three unlucky incidents in the production of *The Texan* at the Princess's Theatre, on Thursday. The first was the exclamation "Bad, bad!" uttered by the doctor, really in reference to his patient the Major, but taken by the audience to refer to some brandy which he was fetching from a cabinet; the second was what sounded like the falling of a big stone on a wooden floor, but was explained, by a remark of one of the characters, to be the front door closing; and the third was the exclamation of William Plainleigh, "I should know that scream!" suggesting that he was unpleasantly familiar with the peculiar shriek of his passionate and faithless spouse, now Mrs Major Tyrell. And why did the old dame in the last act walk off apparently straight through the wall of her house, when there was a remarkably practical door "quite convanient"?
23/6/1894

LYCEUM "CINDERELLA" CO. AT SEA.
(BY ONE OF THE COMPANY.)

THE Lyceum *Cinderella* company, which arrived in England on Wednesday last, had a startling accident soon after leaving New York, on the morning of June 20th. Everything went well till about midnight. Mr Fred Dangerfield, the Anglo-American scenic artist, now of the Chicago Opera House, and myself were standing on the lower deck on the port side, when, about twenty minutes past twelve, Mr Dangerfield cried, "Good heavens! Look at that vessel coming right into us!" It seemed to loom up out of the mist. I could hardly believe my eyes. It was about 100 yards away when we first saw it, and was coming right straight into us on the port side just above the bridge. "Run, run, old man!" said Mr Dangerfield. I started towards the stern, but before I had got 20ft. the vessel crashed into us. The noise was like the cracking of millions of walnuts. In an instant we were enveloped in steam. Mr Dangerfield's trousers were torn by the iron wreckage and his leg cut, and when the hot water pipes were cut through he was covered with dirt and steam.

The force of the collision threw me on my back, and as I lay there I saw the other vessel scrape along the side of the *New York*, going towards the stern. We had caught her anchors, and the chains were dragging from their boat to ours. It was all done so quickly that I could hardly realise for a few seconds what had happened. When I did, I ran down the first opening aft way to tell the ladies to get up. At the second-class cabins I met crowds of people all coming up the gangway, most of the men having only their pants and night shirts on, and the ladies all in their night-dresses, with what few things in their arms they could manage to collect. Several of the boats were lowered, and preparations were made for getting the ladies into them. I tried to assure them that it was all right, and asked them to go below again.

I then went back to the first-class cabins, where everybody was perfectly orderly, especially the ladies. Most of them had put on life-belts, and everybody was prepared for the worst. They tested the depth of water in the hold, and found that we were not making any at all. This reassured everybody, as we had evidently only been struck above the water-line; but the accident was quite sufficient to keep a good many people from turning in for the rest of the night.

We stood by the other vessel for some time, till she signalled that she was all right, and we signalled the same. I only hope she was, as she must have been in a dreadfully damaged state, considering the amount of timber and iron she left behind with us. I sat up for the rest of the night, in case of accidents. Next morning I had a stiff leg. The surgeon sent me bandages and a lotion, and I had to remain below. Considering we were only 20ft. away at the time of the collision, it is a marvel that Mr Dangerfield and myself escaped with our lives.

30/6/1894

THE production of the new drama *The Terror of Paris* at the Victoria Theatre, Burnley, by Messrs Dottridge and Longden's company, was so successful that those gentlemen have resolved to send it on tour at Christmas. The piece contains two sensational scenes: one in which an Anarchist leader making his escape crosses a street on the telegraph wires, and the other in which, in a pretended glass-blowing factory, he threatens to "blast the eyesight" of a traitor with a mass of molten glass.

7/7/1894

WANTED, to Sell, Performing Dog, Performing Goose, Five-Legged Dog, and Large Horse-hair Mattress. CHARD, Belford Hotel, Harrogate.

28/7/1894

THE Rev Geo. Wallace, the pastor of the Congregational Church in Portland, Oregon, preached an extraordinary sermon on Sunday night, directed at Mr Kyrle Bellew and Mrs Potter, who are acting at the Marquam Grand Theatre, and who were in church during the discourse. Mr Wallace commenced by saying that he desired to emphasise the fact that a mass of impurity had been poured upon the city during the week by the performances at the Marquam Grand Theatre. So vile were they in their character

that that they ought never to be tolerated in any community. There was perhaps some talent in their performances – at least he gave them credit for that – but they had taken that talent and linked it with all that was vile and abominable in the production of a class of French plays that were an insult to the American stage and people. During the delivery of these remarks Mr Bellew and Mrs Potter were evidently ill at ease. They occupied a prominent place in the church, and all eyes were riveted upon them. At length both of them, after whispering together, left their seats, and walked down the centre aisle, and left the church. When they were almost half-way down the church the preacher called out, "These are the parties of whom I have been speaking."
4/8/1894

THERE is a well-known station on a certain railway where tickets are carefully examined, and woe betide the artless young lady who travels with her pet pug or guardian collie. The officials are always on the look out, and it is not the slightest use saying that "such-and-such a company always lets the dear darling go through without paying for it." Thus found Miss Lingard the other Sunday when travelling with the *Woman of No Importance* company from the Midlands to the North. Lancet, her favourite Skye terrier, just awoke as "all tickets" was being called, and would assert himself when the collector came to the door. "Want a ticket for the dog, mum." "Oh, we never pay for him," she answered in her most pleasant and convincing manner. "Well, you must pay here," replied the man with the punching machine; and pay she had to. The scene was changed. A week had elapsed, and poor Lancet had met with an untimely end in Edinburgh. Miss Lingard had only time to get her favourite pet nicely stuffed by a local taxidermist and sent down to the train on Sunday morning. The journey back was by the same line, and they went through – well, the same particularly particular station. Once more came the cry, "All tickets ready!" and the lynx-eyed collector, looking out for canine fares, came along. "Must have a dog ticket, mum." "But, please, collector, I haven't got a live dog." "What do you call that on the seat, then? Why, it's the same one you had last Sunday going through." "Yes," replied the fair Mrs Arbuthnot, wearily; "but I decline to pay for him till you put him in the guard's van and tie him up." "All right, mum, that's easily done," and the energetic young man made a reach for the dog. There was no responsive bark and no aggressive bite; and as he held the poor stuffed animal up even the heart of the dog detector was touched. "Beg pardon, mum, I'm sorry he's dead. I had a good fox-terrier of my own that died last night. Right here, Jim," and with a suspicious flick of the coat sleeve across his eye he signalled the guard to clear the ticket platform.

AN alarming accident befell Miss Maud Dowd, one of the ballet dancers engaged at the Winter Gardens, Blackpool, last Saturday evening. Whilst changing her costume for the Scotch ballet, she incautiously stepped on to the glass roof over the "Ally Sloper" gallery, and fell with a sickening crash amongst the promenaders, breaking her right wrist and and cutting herself badly on the face. She was in a semi-nude condition at the time, but a gentleman gallantly placed his coat around the unfortunate lady, and carried her into a private apartment, where Dr Richardson dressed the wounds.
11/8/1894

WANTED, Known, Captain Paul Boyton's Celebrated Performing Seals will be at Liberty to accept Engagements from October onwards. Can Perform on any Stage. No Water required. The Best Act of the Kind in the Universe. These Highly Trained Animals Play all sorts of Musical Instruments – Banjos, Drums, Tambourines, Zithers, &c, – Fire off Guns, Sing, Clown, Play at See-Saw, and numerous other Tricks. An Excellent Fifteen to Twenty Minutes' Turn. For terms and Dates, address, Captain PAUL BOYTON, Earl's Court, S.W.
18/8/1894

MR COMYNS CARR'S company had an adventurous journey back from Brighton after the special matinee of *The New Woman* on Thursday. In consequence of two engines having run off the line at Victoria, the Pullman train in which Mr Carr's company was travelling, and which is due at Victoria at 7.0 p.m., was brought to a dead stop midway between Clapham Junction and Battersea Park, where it remained until about ten minutes to eight o'clock, and then crawled slowly forward to the platform at Battersea Park and again pulled up. As it was then five minutes to eight, and no information could be obtained as to when the train would reach Victoria, the company decided on the desperate expedient of leaving the train at Battersea Park, although there were no cabs or means of conveyance for the baggage and wardrobe at hand. Several ladies and gentlemen started in a tramcar for Vauxhall, and took cab from there to the Comedy. Three or four other ladies stopped the driver of a covered van, and bribed him to gallop to the theatre, and finally the luggage was got away on two four-wheeled cabs. The first member of the company reached the Comedy at 8.20, five minutes after the curtain should have risen. The rest arrived within a few minutes, and in less than a quarter of an hour the curtain had gone up on the first act of *The New Woman*.

IT is not often that people at a play protest as openly against its impropriety as was done at the Prince's Theatre, Kew, on Wednesday evening, in the course of the production of a new piece called *A Black Dove*. At first the eccentric nature of the dialogue seemed to conceal the motive of the plot from the unsuspecting public; but when it was realised that Sir Harry Marsden had unwittingly been living in unholy wedlock with his own daughter a large party in the centre of the room rose simultaneously and marched out of the building, in spite of the protests of the remaining portion of the audience.

AT Koster and Bial's Thirty-Fourth Street Music Hall, New York City, a short time since, an incident not down on the programme was the entertainment of an innocent, but nevertheless very lively, little bat, who divided his time during the entire evening between the audience and the stage. During the early part of the performance the animal began by flying along the mezzanine box tiers and paying his respects to the lady occupants' headgear. When the house was darkened and the curtain drawn to show the living pictures, attracted by the bright glare of lights behind the frame, "Mr Bat" first gave his attention to Tannhäuser and Venus by lighting upon the shoulder of the young lady who poses as Venus. The consequence was a quick convulsive movement, a scream, and complete demoralisation of the picture. Afterwards, with a swoop down the auditorium, he flew direct towards the frame containing a burlesque of the Three Muses, and fastened his claws firmly in the wool which adorned the head of a little Negro boy, who was the central figure. The result was a yell, and the little chap bounced out of the frame, and rolled on to the stage. With the last picture, "Diana's Chase," in which fourteen figures are shown, his "Batship" played sad havoc, and the curtain was rung down, the stage being in dire confusion. Up to the present time "Mr Bat" is still at large.
15/9/1894

AN extraordinary outrage was perpetrated at Blackburn Theatre Royal, on Tuesday night. During the performance of *A Gaiety Girl* a well-dressed woman swung open the doors of the promenade round the dress-circle and made a dash past the doorkeeper. He caught hold of her, but she upset him, and, running to the dress-circle, hurled a brick which she had concealed under her cloak right into the crowded seats, striking a gentleman heavily on the back. A scene of great excitement followed. The woman has since been certified to be insane.

STAGE-STRUCK INDEED.

Mr Herbert Barr sends us the following letter which he has received from a correspondent who wants to go on the stage: –

Dear Sir, – Observing your advt. in The Era *for a smart young comedian, I beg to offer myself as a candidate for the vacancy. My age is eighteen, therefore I am but in my years of youthfulness, but as an actor I am truly great. I am the writer of fully nine books on burlesque, involving songs, stage motions, hideous hubbubs, caricatures, and many more creations pertaining to the acting art. I have served over three and a half years in the commercial creation to my heart's dissatisfaction, for like the majority of talented aspirants I find commerce sad and sickening. The reason why? I have that soul, the devotional instinct of a great actor. When on the boards (or elsewhere) I am a supremely energetic actor, and I always strain to create a consternation that would repel the idea that there is a limit to eccentricity. My height is 5ft. 6in. Sorry to state, no photos. My plight just now is truly a piteous one, for I am idle and almost penniless (an element of danger).*

Nowadays, 'tis a vain endeavour to persuade desperate men the honest measure of my abilities, as I am unknown and regarded as one of the stage-struck brigade. To substantiate this as a wrong, gross, insultive theory so foolishly propounded, I offer this defence.

From my earliest moment I was conscious of a propensity for the dramatic world, and to enhance this consider I could write a finely styled burlesque when just about twelve years of age, as my books can vouch for. The secret of acting is earnestness; earnestness is everything in an actor, for if you are apathetic you are lost. I close, and fervently pray you will extend the palm of generosity towards me, and so earn my life-long gratitude. I entreat expedient action. Very truly yours, ---------.

P.S. – Terms depend on your own wise counsel.

AT Marylebone Police Court, on Tuesday, Nathan Barman, a smart-looking young man, a native of the United States of America, who refused his address but described himself as an actor, was charged, before Mr Plowden, with being found in a dusthole and having no visible means of subsistence.

Police-constable Smith, 484 X, deposed that shortly before three o'clock that morning, while passing along Elgin Avenue, Maida Vale, he heard a noise as of someone snoring proceeding from No. 17, and upon descending into the area of the house he found the prisoner fast asleep in the dusthole. He aroused him and asked his business there, and received the reply that he lived there. The inmates were consequently awakened, but they denied that he lived there, adding that he had done so some time previously. Failing to give a satisfactory account of himself he was taken into custody.

The prisoner, speaking with a decidedly American accent, said he gave as full an account of himself as he thought necessary. He gave addresses at hotels, but because he would not say where he then lived he was locked up. At one time he lived at 17, Elgin Avenue, but left because he had no funds wherewith to pay his debts – his money not having arrived from "the other side" (America). The family were very respectable, and they kept him five weeks, but his conscience would not permit him to impose upon them any longer, so, contrary to their wishes, he left. He had a draft on a Chicago bank for £10. Last evening he went to the house and knocked on the door, but before anyone answered he fell asleep – being very tired – and did not wake until the constable shouted into his ear, "What are yer up to here?" At the station he was asked where he lived, and he said that he had stopped at the Metropole and Avenue Hotels, but that did not satisfy them.

Police-sergeant 22 X, interposing, said the American Legation had been communicated with in reference to the prisoner, and they had promised that when the Ambassador arrived he would attend to the matter.

Mr Plowden – We don't want to trouble the Ambassador because an American citizen is found here sleeping in a dusthole. (To the prisoner) – I don't think you were there for a mischievous purpose. Your attachment for the house is somewhat remarkable. You may go away.

22/9/1894

IN the second act of *Claude Duval* at the Prince of Wales's Theatre, on Tuesday last, a number of chorus ladies appeared as parlour-maids, with pretty aprons and French caps, carrying feather brushes in their hands. Somewhat inconsistent with their supposed menial condition was the fact that the hands of nearly all of them blazed and sparkled with dazzling gems. In these days of realistic detail, surely the stage-manager should see that such valuable and luxurious adornments are removed by ladies when impersonating servants, rustic beauties, and others in a humble way of life.
29/9/1894

A QUAINT incident occurred at Toole's Theatre on Thursday evening. During Mr Geo. Egbert's whistling solo he concocts a cocktail at one side of the stage. The property master having put a fresh-cut lemon on the chiffonier on Thursday, the fruit had the effect of making Mr Egbert's mouth water, so much so that he could not whistle, and was considerably embarrassed.
13/10/1894

ON Monday last, in the course of the visit to the Theatre Royal, Wolverhampton, of the *Woman of No Importance* company, under the direction of Messrs H.H. Morrell and Fred Mouillot, Princess Louise, the Marquess of Lorne, and the Earl and Countess of Dartmouth drove from Patshull to the Wolverhampton High Level Station, passing through the heart of the town, the streets of which were crowded. Among the private carriages at the rear of the procession was one drawn by a pair of greys, and having in the windows the announcement, in large letters, "This carriage is reserved for a Woman of No Importance."
20/10/1894

ON Monday, at the Wrexham Police Court, on an application being made for the renewal of the theatrical license for the Public Hall, the chairman of the Bench, a strong teetotaller, asked the borough surveyor if he had noticed certain placards on the walls of the town representing women in tights, and showing the naked figure, and whether they were in connection with any performance at the Public Hall. One of the secretaries to the Public Hall Company thereupon informed the Chairman, much to the amusement of those present, that the bills were advertisements of a temperance drink.

THE following letter has been sent to Mr Gus Elen from a young lady in Germany, and, after a perusal of it, our readers will come to the conclusion that the writer's future career is not likely to be retarded through an excess of modesty: –

Aug. 26th. Dear Mr Elen, – Please excuse my writing to you when I don't know you, but I saw a photo. of you last year in England, and you had such a kind face and jolly eyes, I thought perhaps you would help me now. I'm learning German here, and I have got into such a muddle with my allowance. I was awfully stupid a little while ago, and bought a lot of things I could have done without, and now I don't know what to do. I simply daren't write home for more money, and I don't know anybody I could ask. Won't you please send me a pound or two? I know it is most awfully cool of me to ask you, but you don't know what a bother I'm in, and the papers and everybody always praise you so tremendously that you must be making just heaps of money, so it wouldn't really make any difference to you, would it? Do, please. I have put in an addressed envelope if you will send me a bank-note; but I have not been able to stamp it, because, you see, unused English stamps are not to be had here. Oh, do please. Yours truly, ------. Please do, and don't be angry with me for asking you.

WANTED, Known, my Drama, "Jew Jacobs, the Curse of Nations," is still negotiable. Fortune for Lady capable of Duality. Call and read. G.H. BAKER, L.A.M., 35, Wharton Street, W.C. Jews, don't apply.
3/11/1894

FAIRIES IN CABS

TO THE EDITOR OF THE ERA.

Sir, – I belong to a comic opera company of between thirty and forty people. On arriving at a certain New Theatre Royal in the provinces I found it to be simply a large wooden shed, with a stage at one end. At back of stage were two dressing-rooms, 16ft. by 10ft. each. The dressing tables were narrow planks 6in. to 9in. in width and about breast high. The lavatory accomodation was a basin of water on the floor; no washstands. Buckets on the floor took the place of basins in the extra dressing-rooms we had to dodge up. This was done by placing wings at the side of the stage. So far, so good; lots of people have to do this sort of thing. My complaint is based upon the following: – On my arrival at the "theatre" I found the two dressing-rooms a mass of water, rain pouring in at the roof. Extra carpets were got by the local manager and laid on the wet floor, and the members of the company in the improvised wing dressing-rooms were provided with candles.

On the morning of the third day there was a rehearsal. On reaching the "theatre," during a downpour of rain, I found the rooms flooded, and in the auditorium the water was coming down in all directions. Some of our ladies wishing to enter the dressing-rooms had to raise their umbrellas, the boards of the roof covering these rooms being in many cases a quarter of an inch apart. In the boards at the sides were many holes, which enabled inquisitive gentlemen outside to look into the rooms.

The local manager told us that the felt had been blown off the roof, and that he had been trying to borrow tarpaulins from the railway companies, but could not get them. Tar was dropping from the stage roof at night, and seriously injured some of our properties. This place is known as a New Theatre Royal. Can nothing be done? Yours truly, GEORGE ASCOT.

P.S. – One thing I have omitted. Our musical director wanted to take the top off the piano, and was in the act of doing so when a voice said, "Don't take that off; the water is coming in, and the piano will be spoilt."

AT a recent performance in the Bilston Theatre, whilst the villain of the drama was pursuing the innocent heroine, the manager's black cat at the same moment took upon itself to pursue an innocent little mouse upon a ceiling made of sheets of tin fastened underneath the boxes. This caused great consternation owing to the inevitable clatter upon such resounding material. The startled audience thought the balcony was about to fall into the pit, and the players upon the stage paused in alarm. Puss having eventually captured her prey, quiet was again restored, and the drama was proceeded with.
24/11/1894

WANTED, a Wife who can Afford to Keep her Husband. Apply, McASKELL, Alhambra, Belfast, and please not to get Excited.
22/12/1894

A VERY sad event occurred during the performance of the pantomime *Dick Whittington and His Cat* at the Elephant and Castle Theatre on Boxing Night. Miss Kitty Tyrrell (Mrs Harry Ewins), who was taking the part of the Rat, after having appeared in the second scene, Fitzwarren's Kitchen, retired to the wings to await her re-entrance. She then complained of feeling faint, but a few minutes afterwards again went on the stage, took part in a dialogue in which she had to say "In due course his road to fortune he'll pave o'er my corse," and then made another exit to the wings. Here she was seen to stagger and reel, and was carried by her husband Mr Harry Ewins, who was taking part in the pantomime, and was also the clown in the harlequinade, to her dressing room. Restoratives were procured, but death appears to have been almost instantaneous. The audience were not made aware of what had taken place, and a substitute was found for the deceased lady. At the inquest, which was held at the Newington Coroner's Court on Friday afternoon, a verdict of Death from Syncope was returned.
Miss Tyrrell was only thirty-five.
29/12/1894

6
1895
THE PEA-SHELLING PRIMA-DONNA

THE young Earl of Yarmouth, the heir to the Marquisate of Hereford, is making a tour of the Australian Colonies, and towards the end of November was the guest of his Excellency the Governor of Tasmania. The Earl has a strong predilection for the stage, and while staying at Government House aroused great excitement in Hobart by allowing it to become known that he would take a prominent part in a theatrical performance to be given at the Theatre Royal, in aid of a local charity. On the evening in question, Nov. 19th, the theatre was crowded with the elite of Hobart, Lord and Lady Gormanston and many of the officers of Her Majesty's ships *Katoomba* and *Goldfinch* being present. It having been whispered about that the earl, as "Mdlle Roze," would give an exhibition of the famous serpentine dance *á la* Miss Loie Fuller, public curiosity was intense. The earl, having appeared in a farce entitled *A Pair of Lunatics*, in the farce *Domestic Economy*, in which he impersonated an ill-used mother, and having taken part, in much-abbreviated skirts, in a dance in which he is described as having "kicked as high as the most exacting ballet mistress could desire," achieved his crowning triumph in the serpentine dance.

The following account of this remarkable performance is given: – "The stage was darkened, and then suddenly in the centre the Earl of Yarmouth appeared in a circle of limelight clothed in an exact facsimile of the flowing drapery which Miss Mary Weir used to appear in when giving the same dance at the Princess's Theatre. He also had golden curls falling down his back, and in his whole make-up equalled the best efforts of the most experienced female impersonator ever seen on any music hall stage. The limelight man was fully equal to the unprecedented occasion, and his lordship, whirling with his drapery in each hand in the most approved fashion, gyrated before the astonished throng in one wild blaze of kaleidoscopic colours, and danced with unabated vigour in aid of the funds of the Girls' Industrial School and the Dorcas Society. Then the limelight man began to project pictures upon the whirling skirts of the noble earl, who displayed first of all Sir John Millais' well-known work entitled "Bubbles"; and, after the portraits of the Prince and Princess of Wales and the Duke and Duchess of York and Lord Gormanston and Lady Gormonston had been shown, still the Earl of Yarmouth whirled his white silk skirts with the dexterity of Miss Bella Bashall combined with the gracefulness of Miss Mary Weir. Thunders of applause greeted him, and several large bouquets were thrown to the almost exhausted nobleman, who concluded with a quick pirouette and final bow of salutation."

THE blackmailing system has broken out in South London. Already three or four of the most prominent artists engaged at one house have been molested after leaving the theatre at night, and threatened with what in professional parlance is known as "the bird" – that is, hissing and expressions of disapprobation from the audience – unless their tormentors are well paid to remain quiet. A little after twelve o'clock on Tuesday morning a young lady employed at one of the South London houses was threatened with personal violence unless she complied with this impudent extortion, and being alone and seriously alarmed she handed over the whole of the contents of her purse. Mrs Poole, the popular manageress of

the South London, had heard of one case which occurred last week, in which one of a pair of Nigger artists was assaulted by a rough on pay night while his colleague was gone to the stage-door entrance to draw their salary.
5/1/1895

ON Monday, when Mr John Humphries' *Dark Continent* company was playing at the Prince's Theatre, Accrington, one of the pedestals in the hotel scene, being badly connected, allowed a large volume of gas to escape, which, rising to the lighted burners, immediately ignited with a loud report. The noise and the shouts of the audience caught the attention of Mr Charles Herberte, who was on the stage, and he promptly and quietly wrapped the tails of his frock-coat round the pedestal and extinguished the flame, earning a hearty round of applause from the audience.
12/1/1895

MISS EDITH COLE, who is appearing as Josephine in *A Royal Divorce*, in the provinces, told a north-country interviewer the other day, in reference to a pretty basket of flowers handed to her on her first appearance at Darlington, that she wished that some great actress would set the fashion of having gloves or even stockings thrown on to the stage. They would, she thought, be more permanent tokens of respect, for a pair of gloves could be worn for a fortnight at least, whereas, she added, the poor flowers thrown on to the stage frequently drooped and died before they were got out of the theatre.
19/1/1895

THE SIX COLOURED MEN who represented the "Brave Matabele Warriors" in the Tableaux Vivants at the Empire Theatre wish to heartily thank Geo. Edwardes, Esq., C.D. Slater, Esq., and J. Cabel, Esq., for all their kindnesses. We also wish to thank the whole of the Permanent Staff of the Empire for their Kind behaviour towards us. THE SIX COLOURED MEN.
26/1/1895

IN the presence of a crowded audience the Grand pantomime was played for the last time on Saturday, and the occasion was made a pretext for some unexpected and unrehearsed effects. A number of young men, supposed to be medical students, secured nearly all the seats in the stalls, and proceeded to make things lively by taking up the choruses and delivering volleys of flower "button-holes" to their favourite performers. While the scene in which the shipwrecked comedians sit down to eat the "property" kipper was being played, they sent on the stage a perfect storm of red herrings. Later, when Mr Harry Randall was singing his amusing parody of "Baby," a shower of dolls – baby dolls – came from these hilarious gentlemen, and further on bouquets of vegetables for the comedians, and pretty flowers for the ladies. When, however, a disposition to supply oranges and lemons set in, the management stepped in with a warning, and for the rest of the evening these choice spirits contented themselves with roaring choruses and demonstratively applauding.

PONTO is no more. Ponto was a black retriever, the faithful companion of Mr Gus Elen, and the devoted guard of Mrs Elen. Poor Ponto was a victim to the recent inclement weather. Her loss is very much felt by her late master and mistress. A companionship of eight years cannot be altogether forgotten, and Ponto's head will be stuffed and mounted and placed in a position of honour in her master's studio.

ON Monday Miss Annie Oakley will give exhibitions of her marvellous shooting powers at the Alhambra, the management having engaged her for a few weeks prior to her return to America.

WANTED, the Address of Madame Alma, Female Horse Lifter (was at Whitechapel), or another same Business. WALTER TAYLOR, 43, Stanhope Street, W.C.
2/3/1895

MR W.M. THOMPSON, the George Forrester of *The Fatal Card* company, now appearing at Palmer's Theatre, New York, wears the key to the door in the office scene of the third act of the piece on a chain fastened to his clothes. The reason of this precaution is that, owing to the loss of the key the other night, Mr Thompson and his fellow villain, Mr W.J. Ferguson, were obliged to perform some extraordinary feats in passing through apparently solid walls in order to do their share in the murder scene. The tragedy was changed for the moment into a farce, and Mr Thompson is very properly determined such an accident shall not occur again.
9/3/1895

ON Saturday, at the South-West London Police Court, Mr Julian Cross, an actor, engaged at the Adelphi Theatre, Strand, applied for assistance in tracing the whereabouts of his daughter, Henrietta Cross, aged nineteen. Miss Cross was also engaged in the theatrical business, and had a part in the play *Tom, Dick, and Harry*, now on tour. Last Thursday evening she left her father's house, 13, Eglantine Road, Wandsworth, with the intention – as she declared – of going to Putney. Since that evening nothing had been seen or heard of her by her father. The latter, who seemed greatly distressed, could give no reason for her disappearance, as she was quite happy at home, and had always been a good girl. The only intimation she gave of her conduct was conveyed in a brief note addressed to "Mother," in which she asked forgiveness for bringing misery on them. The following was the description supplied by her father to the Press: – Five feet nine inches, dark hair, hazel eyes; handsome, and of stately bearing. She was wearing a brown skirt, a red Scotch plaid bodice, and black jacket trimmed with beaver, low shoes, and sealskin toque on the head.

THERE is no quite obvious connection between sanitation and Mr Oscar Wilde; but the Medical Officer of Health for the Borough of Cambridge has discovered sufficient to induce him to preface his "Report on the Sanitary Condition of the Borough of Cambridge" by a twenty-line quotation from *A Woman of No Importance*. It is true this excerpt is followed by half-a-dozen lines from a famous French novelist; but the association in the officer's mind of Zola with drains is easily understood.

MR JULIAN CROSS tells us that he has had no news of his daughter, Henrietta Cross, who disappeared from her home mysteriously on the evening of the 14th. He is reluctantly compelled to believe that the poor girl has lost her senses. In 1881 she was treated by an ear specialist, Dr Wright Wilson, of The Crescent, Birmingham, and he pronounced her cured, but he said a tumour might eventually form on the brain, though at that time there was no sign of such a formation. She was recently in the country on a two months' tour with the *Tom, Dick, and Harry* company, and frequently complained of pains in her head.
Henrietta Cross was never seen again.
23/3/1895

MR KYRLE BELLEW tells of a strange incident which happened on Mrs Brown Potter's eighteen months' tour round the world. During Mrs Potter's performance of Lady Macbeth in an Indian city the house was in almost complete darkness, the only light coming from the candle which she carried in her hand. A hideous vampire bat flew in at the window of the darkened theatre, and, attracted by the candle light, fastened on Mrs Potter's bare arm in the sleep walking scene and sucked her blood until the audience was almost hysterical with excitement. Mrs Potter's eyes were closed, and she was completely absorbed in her part. She went through her speech superbly, and as she retired from the stage the bat flew away. Mrs Potter was quite exhausted, and presently fainted. In her intense preoccupation she had not even felt the bite.

SAID a budding actor to a manager the other day, "What a wonderful thing is the human head. In the first place, it is there that intellect finds its seat –" "Seat!" interrupted the manager, "In *some* heads it doesn't even find standing room!"
6/4/1895

IN these end-of-century days a remarkable degree of perfection has been attained in the training of cats, and the latest examples to arrest our curiosity and to evoke our admiration are the sleek and gentle creatures that obey the command of M. Techow at the Alhambra. We say "command," but we should explain that the *dompleur des chats* makes his pets understand his orders without speaking a word – by gestures only. The cats number fourteen. Feline funambulism is not new to the London stage, but M. Techow's two cats make it funny. Approaching from opposite ends of the rope the two meet in the middle of the narrow causeway, and argue the difficulty out in cat language, until the one, finding the other will not give way, gets impatient, and jumps over. In another essay on rope walking the aggressive performer makes the other go backward. Whether the clown cat makes the other cats laugh we are not prepared to say, but his artfulness in shaking his tail to express a decided negative when invited to do some walking over bottles and other tricks is exceedingly funny. One cat is a splendid leaper, and the clarity of his movements in and out specially made frames is certainly remarkable. The animals go through their performance with both alacrity and cheerfulness. M. Techow's cats are a decided novelty, and they have come to stay.
13/4/1895

TO THE EDITOR OF THE ERA.
Sir, - Will you allow me to contradict an astonishing statement to which you called attention in the last issue of *The Era*, to the effect that one of the conditions attached by me to the performance of my play *Candida* was that Miss Janet Achurch should receive a salary of £50 a month. If I really had the power to fix what a manager would give, why should I be so unfriendly to Miss Achurch as to say £50, when I might just as easily have said £100 or £250? And, if I really had the power to fix what Miss Achurch would take, why should I rate her services at from eight to ten times the value of my own weekly services as a critic?

I should as soon think of interfering in the settlement of Miss Achurch's salary as she would, I presume, in the settlement of my royalties.

If ever I do interfere in the matter of salaries behind the curtain, I shall not begin with the £50 ones. It is the salaries of 50s. and less that require attention.
Yours truly, G. BERNARD SHAW.
London, April 18th, 1895.
20/4/1895

SOME of our readers may have considered the story which we repeated the other day about the vampire bat which sucked Mrs Brown Potter's blood during her performance of Lady Macbeth in Calcutta almost improbable, but a "rider" has been sent us, on the usual "unimpeachable authority," which is still more surprising. It seems that a naturalist who was observing the habits of the vampire in the vicinity of the Indian capital, noticed a large bat in a tree, surrounded by a semi-circle of his companions, going through a series of strange movements, and making what appeared to be intended for expressive gestures. It was evidently the creature who had imbibed, with Mrs Potter's blood, some of the dramatic genius of the tragedienne, and was endeavouring, in its dumb, animal way, to emulate her achievements.

AFTER McAnney's tricycle performance at the costume carnival in the Lambeth Skating Rink on Thursday night a fire broke out and completely gutted the building. Amongst other properties he lost two new bicycles and his Tower machine. This was especially unfortunate, as they had just cost him £75, his other machines being smashed in a railway accident in Germany at Christmas.   *27/4/1895*

THERE have been on exhibition at Reynold's Waxworks, Liverpool, two giant children. On Saturday night Mr Reynolds procured a four-wheeled cab to convey his protégés home to their residence in Ashton Street. All went well until the vehicle reached Wellington Rooms, Mount Pleasant. Here the weight of the children proved too much for the cab; one of the springs broke, the bottom fell from the vehicle, and the two giants found themselves standing on the roadway. It was with difficulty that they were extricated from the wrecked cab, and they fortunately escaped with a shaking and a few slight bruises. Another vehicle of sufficient strength was procured, and the youthful giants, who together weigh 592lb., were ultimately landed safe at their lodgings.
4/5/1895

THE other day, in a provincial town where actors' "diggings" are scarce and not over-comfortable, a member of Mr Van Biene's company had just quietly settled down in his apartments when in rushed unannounced a portly looking individual with his hands on his stomach and a demoniacal grin on his face. After glaring at the actor for a second or two, he proceeded in the broadest of Yorkshire dialects, "Eh, mister; eh, mister. I've gettin' a awful kind a-rumbling like here," passing his hands over his waistcoat. "Can ye give me somat for it?" "My good man, what's the matter? I don't know you," exclaimed the astonished actor. "Why, be'nt thou the quack doctor i't market-place?" asked the man. "No, sir; what do you mean?" indignantly responded the actor. "Get out." As the fellow retired the landlady explained, with many profuse apologies, that a "medical gentleman," who "stood" in the market-place, had only that morning vacated the rooms, and that the intruder was one of his unfortunate patients.
18/5/1895

WHEN recently the American *Wep-ton-no-Mah* company were playing at West Hartlepool one of its members, an American Indian, known as Chief Ga-ne-Gua, was attracted by the appearance in the audience of a young lady, Miss Emma Ireland. A day or two afterwards he made the acquaintance of the lady, and the result was the recent union of the couple at Leeds. The bridegroom belongs to the Onandoga tribe of the "Six Nations," their reservation being seven miles from the city of Syracuse, New York state, U.S.A. He was prominent in many sanguinary rebellions against the Federal Government, and has been wounded several times in these fights. The bride attended on the stage of the Theatre Royal, Leeds, with her husband, on the evening of the wedding and received the hearty congratulations of many friends who had come from other towns to attend the novel wedding ceremony.

MISS SISSIERETTA JONES does not like to be known as the Black Patti. The name was playfully used by a New York reporter, and has clung to her; but Miss Jones is a great deal more modest about her abilities than her description would suggest. Once, she tells you, she heard Patti sing, and wept – with admiration or desire, or both. Sissieretta Jones is a daughter of the south, but her people moved northwards when she was but a child. Her early years were spent at Providence, where they are much more tolerant of coloured folk than in the south. She was a popular singer at local concerts; and her growing fame suggested the more careful culture of her voice.

Sissieretta married while she was still a girl, and shortly went to the West Indies and South America, where for several years she was a great favourite. She had a valuable collection of medals and other mementoes of her visit to this part of the world. It was, however, on her return to New York that Miss Jones's greater fame began. Among her other exploits was a tour through the south, whereof she treasures the memory for two reasons – the white folks came to hear her, more graciously, she supposes, than they had ever come to hear a coloured artist before, while her own people were frantic with delight at her success. Coloured people are passionately fond of music, and have produced some sweet singers.

In the South the coloured people are rigorously divided from the white folk in places of entertainment; but Miss Jones is overjoyed to think that her tour may have done something to soften racial prejudice.

Till she came to Europe she had never sung in a variety theatre, and the smoke proved very disagreeable to her. Her appearance at the Palace was preceded by two engagements on the Continent. She has been gratified by her reception in London, and charmed by the novelty of her surroundings. Miss Jones avows a passion for music, and says it is her ardent desire to have more opportunities for study under the direction of some really able and distinguished teacher.

25/5/1895

MRS BROWN POTTER and MR KYRLE BELLEW'S opening performance this season at the American Theatre, New York the other day was marked by a painful accident. In the bathtub scene, in which Charlotte stabs Marat, Mrs Potter entered so faithfully into the spirit of her part that she accidentally inflicted a slight wound on Mr Bellew. Her alarm was great and obvious at the sight of the blood on Marat's fleshings, but the act was finished without serious interruption. When the curtain fell Mr Bellew went to his dressing-room, where a doctor stopped the flow of blood. He had been stabbed in the side with considerable force, but luckily the dagger struck a rib, and so saved him from serious injury; and he really lost less blood than did Mrs Potter when the bat fastened on her arm whilst she was playing Lady Macbeth in Calcutta.

A SUMMONS taken out by Mr James Leslie, manager for Mr Hermann Vezin, to have Mr Llewellyn Howells, a commercial traveller, of Swansea, bound over to keep the peace, was heard at the Swansea Police Court on Monday. Mr Leslie, manager of Mr Hermann Vezin's company, said he had to eject defendant from the theatre on the Saturday evening. On the Monday evening Howells said he would bring fifteen men to burn and wreck the theatre and kill witness, who also received a letter from defendant addressed "Leslie, blackguard manager, New Theatre, Swansea," containing the words "A thorough blackguard like you generally meets with his deserts. You will have yours." The Court bound over Mr Howells in recognisances in the sum of £50 to keep the peace for six months, and ordered him to find a surety in £25 to the like effect. He was further ordered to pay costs, including solicitors' fees. He was taken to gaol in a hansom, having failed to find the surety required.

TOM COSTELLO had a funny experience the other evening at Newcastle-on-Tyne. He was singing his new song, "The One-Legged Family," when a gentleman in the audience, afflicted with the loss of one of his nether limbs, arose in wrath, and in language unfit for publication declared that Tom was "getting at him" – "taking him off," in fact, and to add weight to his assertion threw his stick at the artist. Tom cleverly dodged this, and, singular to state, this "miss" was the "hit" of the evening.

AT the North London Police Court, on Wednesday, Nelly Seymour, a smartly-dressed young woman of nineteen, was charged, before Mr Paul Taylor, with annoying Mr Algernon Syms, an actor at the Britannia Theatre. The prosecutor stated that shortly before one on that morning he was proceeding from the theatre to his home in Springdale Road, Stoke Newington, when he was followed by the prisoner and another young woman. The prisoner made certain suggestions to him, which he resented, and he asked her not to annoy him again. The girl then made use of the most unpleasant language, and he had to call a constable and give her into custody.

The prisoner tried to conceal her tears, and denied the accuracy of the prosecutor's story. She said she did not know Mr Syms, nor did she want anything to do with him.

Mr Taylor – Do you know this woman? The Prosecutor – I do not know her, but there is another young woman in court who has "shadowed" me for months, and the prisoner, of late, has been her constant companion. They know me through seeing me on the stage. I had an accident at the theatre, and was laid up for three months with a shattered arm. The second woman to whom I have referred took apartments opposite my house, to my very great annoyance. That person made the bullets which this young woman fired. For about a week past these two young women have occupied a private box at the theatre, endeavoured to force their attentions upon me, and they have followed me home.

Mr Taylor – Are you a married man? The prosecutor – Yes, and I have a family.

Mr Taylor told the prisoner that there was no question in his mind that she had persisted in following the prosecutor, and that she had made improper proposals to him. Such attentions could not but be most annoying to a respectable married man. He fined the prisoner 20s., or in default fourteen days.

WANTED, to Buy, a Bear. Must be quiet. Address, G. HITCHCOCK, Post-office (till called for), Workington, Cumberland.
1/6/1895

"PALLETTARIA" BY AMATEURS.
It is a long time since so uneven and imperfect an entertainment has been presented to us by amateurs at St George's Hall as that furnished with no inconsiderable amount of accessory pretentiousness by the Royal Academy Students' Dramatic Club on Tuesday last. *Pallettaria,* for what it is evidently intended to be – a skit upon or *revue* of contemporary art – is by no means badly put together, and, from what the speakers and singers allowed us to hear of the words and lyrics, we imagined that the authors, the "Brothers Brush," deserved a share in the commiseration so well earned by the audience. Quite half of those appearing in this original musical anachronism were "rank duffers" of the rawest type, who knew neither how to walk, how to pronounce English, nor how to sing in correct time or tune. The entertainment as a whole was, indeed, many degrees below the standard of clubs like the Whittington and the Vaudeville, which are recruited chiefly, so we have been informed, from the prosperous commercial class in the City and elsewhere; and the agony caused to the sensitive ear by the sounds from many of the speakers and singers was increased by the efforts of an execrable orchestra. (…)

If we deal with the principal members of the cast in detail it is only in order that our censure may, if necessarily severe, be discriminating also; for the entertainment, as a whole, certainly did not deserve exhaustive notice. Mr Harold Speed sang nicely and looked well, but his acting was feeble. Miss Isabel Pyke-Nott's method of suggesting queenly grace chiefly consisted in elevating her nose in the air. Miss Isabel Coates and Miss Colyer as the King's sisters vied with each other in weakness and amateurishness; we hesitate to which lady the palm should be awarded. Mr E.H. Read as Prince Amor exhibited by turns nervous and jerky effrontery and moist and uneasy bashfulness, and constantly clipped his words and phrases. Mr Lewis Baumer was, at least, distinct and cool as Antenor; but such a mooning, shambling, slouching performance as Mr C.Q. Orchardson's as Frusino is seldom seen in a modern amateur entertainment. Mr G.F. Metcalfe's enunciation was fairly good, but the inexperience of the raw amateur peeped through his capital make-up as Nicobulus. Mr W.H. Byles danced nimbly but without finish as Beachaume. Miss Anna Kinnison evidently appreciated the point of the humorous verses she intoned, and it was rather unkind of her by her indistinct delivery to prevent the audience from enjoying the joke, thus keeping the fun quite to herself. Her skirt dancing was of the "back drawing-room after ten lessons" order. Mr Charles Capper whistled well, if not phenomenally, as Siefel; and Mr Walter Churcher showed genuine low comedy gifts as Arthur Smythe-Jones, working very hard, being always alert and active, and speaking his lines with very acceptable distinctness. Miss N. Du Maurier as May displayed vivacity without self-control in her acting, and in her dancing lightness without training. The stage-management was imperfect, and at one time the performance nearly came to a stop altogether. If the piece had been rehearsed, it was evident that the rehearsals had not been properly conducted. It is a pity that so many pretty dresses by Messrs Harrison, and so much "kind assistance" from R.A.s and others, was wasted on an entertainment which, taken in its entirety, would have brought the blush of shame to the cheeks of the committee of any of our established amateur associations. Most of the young ladies and gentlemen appearing at the St George's Hall on Wednesday should, for the future, have the doors shut upon them by their friends, that they may play the fool nowhere but in their own studios.

ON Saturday, at the Thames Police Court, Henry Rabbinowicz, an actor in a Yiddish dramatic company, was charged on remand with stabbing Simon Silberstein and Harris Levy. Mr Bedford defended. The evidence showed that while the prosecutor was taking part in a performance at the Phoenix Hall, Commercial Road, he was called outside. Some fifteen men, all of them Hebrews, then came up to him and asked him to stand them some drink. He declined, and they attacked him. In the struggle the two men were slightly stabbed with a small penknife. Mr Bedford said that, in addition to the blackmail demanded from the prisoner, there was some jealousy against him on account of a woman named Matilda. All he did was done in self-defence. The prisoner was discharged.

WANTED, to Sell, to Waxwork Showmen, Head of Jabez Balfour*, also Oscar Wilde, 20s. each, to clear; some Hands, 4s. pair; also some Cheap Figures, Complete, and Dressed Ready for Use. STIFF, 181, Goswell Road, E.C.
*A notorious fraudster who swindled thousands of investors out of their life savings.
8/6/1895

LORETTA MOONEY, who also calls herself "Addis" in the variety theatres of California, is now Lady Sholto Douglas, daughter-in-law of the Marquis of Queensberry. She has a slender ring of gold, which she demurely exhibits when she is asked if she is really the wife of Lord Sholto George Douglas. Vicar-General Prendergast, it appears, recently granted a special dispensation, by virtue of which any priest under his jurisdiction might make Lord Sholto and Miss Mooney man and wife. They were married in San Jose by Justice of the Peace Deman. Lady Sholto Douglas's wedding-ring is a plain gold band, lettered on the inside "S. to L., May 30th." She and Lord Sholto will keep house in San Francisco. She will continue to dance and sell drinks at a resort, earning $25 a week. She is just eighteen years old. She has dispensed liquors for several years in variety theatres in California, especially in Bakersfield, where Lord Sholto became her adorer.

MR T. MORTON POWELL'S latest venture, *The Greed of Gold*, is having a gratifying reception in the provinces, the "beam engine" sensation causing a perfect furore. The opium den scene, in which a child is placed by a Chinaman upon a couch and is drawn slowly towards the cage of a mad gorilla while the animal is endeavouring to break loose, evokes intense enthusiasm, especially when the child is rescued and the Chinaman himself falls upon the couch and is torn to pieces by the insane brute.

WANTED, to Sell, a Small Half-horse Power Boiler. Very pretty. In good condition. Cost £18, take £8. Box 5,631, "The Era" Office.
15/6/1895

DURING the performance at the Empire Palace, Edinburgh, on the 15th inst., Miss Loie Fuller had administered to her in error by her mother a dose of cocaine instead of another drug. The mistake was almost instantly discovered, and Miss Fuller was driven without delay to the Royal Infirmary, where she was successfully attended to, and was subsequently taken to her hotel. No further bad effects are anticipated.

A PATHETIC story was told before the Birmingham coroner on Wednesday at an inquest on John William Workmar, a professional acrobat of middle age, who cut his throat in the public street. He was the leader of the Angelo troupe, consisting of his two sons and two daughters. They had found work slack for some months. Being at the end of their resources, they endured considerable privation, and on

Sunday deceased set out to walk from Tamworth to Birmingham without anything to eat and almost shoeless. Next day while going along Lancaster Street he pulled out a razor and inflicted a fatal gash. The verdict was "Temporary insanity, induced by poverty and want."
22/6/1895

WHAT is popularly called "a cock-and-bull story" has appeared in certain "society" papers to the effect that a once-popular prima-donna is now shelling peas for a living in Covent Garden Market. We have made many inquiries for the pea-shelling vocalist, but have not found her. It is obvious, however, that a popular prima-donna would not be nameless. We therefore feel compelled to echo the sentiments of Betsy Prig in regard to Mrs Gamp's imaginary friend Mrs Harris. "Sairey Gamp," said she, "I don't believe there ain't no sich a person." What we did discover in response to our queries was that a young woman who was for a time in the chorus had for a year or two worked in the market. Her story was an operatic romance. Originally employed as a barmaid in the neighbourhood of the market, she became acquainted with a young Italian orchestral player who was attracted by her good looks and love of music. She accompanied him to his native country only to find him faithless. Turning to account her knowledge of music, the poor girl sang in the chorus at some Italian theatres, and, after much privation, reached the sea coast and got back to London. This story is, we understand, quite authentic, and is far more probable than that of the "pea-shelling prima-donna." Eminent and popular vocalists can generally make enough in a few years to shield them against poverty, as the salaries paid by Sir Augustus Harris will go far to prove.

AN explosion of a peculiar nature took place at the People's Palace, Sunderland, on Wednesday morning. It appears that a youth named James Forster was entrusted with the preparation of the batteries used in the spectacular display, *The Battle of Trafalgar*, given by the Fothergill Family, supported by a number of local children. Whilst engaged in his work he was joined by a youth named Chas. Sloan (who appears in the performance), and he, picking up a fuse, held it to the gas to examine it. The result was an explosion, followed by the ignition of some coloured lights, and Sloan was severely injured about the hands and his eyebrows blown off. Forster had a narrow escape, his hair being completely singed off. The explosion caused the door to close, and the panel was broken by a lad named Miller, and the escape thus effected. But for the promptitude of Mr James Passmore (of the well-known Brothers Passmore, eccentrics), a big conflagration, involving great destruction to property, might have resulted. He extinguished the flames after a spell of very hard work. His pluck may be appreciated when it is borne in mind that powder and other explosives were on all sides of him when he was coping with the flames. Only powder sufficient for the night's performance was in the property room at the time of the accident, it being a custom of the Fothergills not to have more than requisite at the hall at one time. Young Sloan, who is a juvenile boxer, will, it is expected, be all right in a day or two. The damage was mostly confined to the wigs and dresses used in the spectacle.
13/7/1895

MR BEERBOHM TREE has been telling an emissary of *The Englishwoman* about a dog named Argus who used to regularly accompany him to the theatre, and particularly objected to sensational scenes. When Mr Tree was playing in *Captain Swift* Argus used to take his place in the wings and follow his every word and look until the suicidal situation was reached. The moment Mr Tree felt for his pistol Argus used to rush into the darkest corner he could find, and, burying his head between his paws, listen for the thud of the actor's fall. After that the dog would crawl to meet his master with a howl of joy at Mr Tree's apparent return to life.

TO THE EDITOR OF THE ERA.

Sir, – While seeing the charming representation of *A Midsummer Night's Dream* at Mr Daly's theatre the other morning, I remarked that the lion in the interlude is permitted more freedom than the late Mr Phelps approved of for that noble beast. I played Snug, the joiner, at the Prince's Theatre, Manchester, in 1874, and I remember that, as the lion, I was instructed to keep quite still, my tail, with a string attached to it, being wagged up and down two or three times, from the wings, by no less a personage than Mr Phelps himself. This incident is impressed upon my memory from the fact that, on the first night, at my exit, the string got twisted round Mr Phelps's venerable legs, somewhat delaying his entrance, and calling forth several remarks which, on referring to my Shakespeare, I found were not in the part of Bottom.

Yours truly, RUSSELL CRAUFORD.

Green Room Club, July 15th, 1895

20/7/1895

AT Mrs Robert Crawshay's Baby Exhibition the other day, Mrs Beerbohm Tree's infant came out at the top of the list, under the head "Sound and Sufficient Teeth," and won the prize, beating Lady Ashburton's Mildred, who had fourteen teeth at the age of eighteen months. The prize winner is evidently a chip off the old block, or, perhaps we should say, a slip from the old Tree.

27/7/1895

ON Bank Holiday the Leyton Fire Brigade held their annual fête at the grounds of the Essex County Cricket Club, Leyton. The principal attraction was the announcement that Miss Alma Beaumont, the parachutist, would make one of her descents. Owing to a mishap, the balloon escaped without the fair lady, to the disappointment of the crowd. On the following afternoon, however, Miss Beaumont made a most successful ascent and descent. Within half an hour she was brought back to the grounds in a cab safe and sound. Miss Beaumont stated that she had landed in the garden of a private house in Leytonstone. After the occupants had recovered from their surprise at her unexpected appearance, they made her a cup of tea and showed her every kindness.

10/8/1895

IT is not "all honey" to have to play the villain, especially when the very excellence of your impersonation puts you in danger. At the Princess's, Glasgow, last Saturday, during the performance of *Jack-in-the-Box*, the occupants of the gallery were thoroughly incensed at the wickedness of the villain of the piece, and someone shouted "Throw a brick at him." Donald Sutherland, one of the "gods," replied, "I haven't a brick." "Well, then," was the rejoinder, "strike him with a bottle," and Donald, overcome with excitement, hurled a beer bottle on to the stage. It missed the "bold, bad man," but nearly struck one of the ladies of the company on the head. The local Bailie, in passing sentence of a guinea or twenty-one days' imprisonment, remarked that the character of the acting at the Princess's must be of a high order of merit, since it evoked such displays of sympathy.

17/8/1895

MISS OLGA NETHERSOLE, but for the intelligence of her servant, might have lost the whole of her valuable and very artistic jewellery. On Saturday last a man who said that he came from a firm of jewellers with whom Miss Olga Nethersole transacts business, called at her residence in Walsingham House and stated to her maid that he had come for Miss Nethersole's jewels, which he said his firm had instructions from Miss Nethersole to clean up and attend to prior to her playing at the Grand Theatre on Monday. The man was of gentlemanly appearance, and about thirty years of age; but fortunately the maid was sufficiently wide-awake to refuse to give up the jewels without an order from her mistress, and so the gentleman departed with the awful threat to her "that the jewels would not be ready to be worn on

Monday night." On subsequent enquiry, it was discovered that no such message was sent from the firm, and that it was clearly an attempt to steal the actress's magnificent jewellery.

Telegrams, "Phasey, London." BALLET, BALLET, BALLET. Youth and Beauty. Graceful Dances Arranged. Sparkling Music provided. Pantomime Season, 1895 and 1896. WANTED, Managers to please state how many Ladies they require. Describe the Dances you wish them taught. Send on Words and Music of your Choruses. Your Ladies will be sent out perfect in every item. ANGLO-ITALIAN TRAINING SCHOOL. 3, LAMBETH PALACE ROAD, LONDON, S.E. Over 200 Young and Pretty Girls were Engaged from this School last Christmas.
24/8/1895

WANTED, a Travelling Tub for Seal; also Paintings for Seals. State Lowest Price, on approval. Whale Museum, Skegness.
31/8/1895

AT Bow Street Police Court, on Thursday, two youths, apparently about twenty years of age, were summoned by Mr Hales, theatrical costumier, of Wellington Street, for wilful damage. About 1.20 on the morning of Aug. 15th the complainant was standing at the corner of Wellington Street, when he saw the two defendants come up to his shop. There was a sun blind, supported by two iron bars, let down over the window. As the defendants passed the window each seized a bar and began to swing on it, as if they were in a gymnasium. As a consequence the bars were bent, the sockets were broken, and the blind was torn from its rings. The repairs cost £2 10s. Complainant caught one of the defendants, and the other was subsequently found. The defendants, who had nothing to say, except to ask why the blind was down at that time of night, were fined 5s. and £1 5s. costs for the summons, or, in default, fourteen days.
7/9/1895

MISS LETTY LIND last week met with an accident which might have been, but happily was not, "attended with serious consequences." She fainted, and her sister, Miss Adelaide Astor*, held a bottle of smelling salts to her nose. But Miss Astor did not notice that the fluid from the wide-necked bottle was going down the sufferer's throat. Dr Miller, of Windsor, was immediately summoned, and so serious was the case that at one moment he thought he should have to perform the operation of tracheotomy. Happily, after three hours' intense agony and partial suffocation, Miss Lind recovered, and is now doing well.
**Miss Astor may have been preoccupied with thoughts of her forthcoming marriage to Mr George Grossmith Jr, which took place later that month.*
14/9/1895

WANTED, to Sell, Pretty Tame Singapore Monkey, been Children's Companion in a Gentleman's Family for Nine Months. Impossible to make it Bite People of either Sex. Would suit a small Showman either for Show inside or for Parade. Price 30s. Write TAYLOR, 52, Lillie Road, Earl's Court.
21/9/1895

REALLY, some restraint should be shown by our American visitors when they arrive on the shores of slow-going old England. It was the hasty, ill-considered, and ill-mannered action of a New Yorker that caused the disturbance on Thursday evening, soon after the raising of the curtain at the Duke of York's Theatre on *Her Advocate*. He disputed the right to his stall of a well-known London solicitor, and though that gentleman produced his voucher this did not prevent the Yankee from taking the lawyer by the coat-collar and hustling him out. An appeal to the box-office at the conclusion of the act showed that the aggressor was in the wrong. The American had made the mistake of appropriating a seat in a

different row to the one printed on his ticket. Of course, explanations and apologies were forthcoming, and we do not anticipate international complications.
28/9/1895

THE "human horse" Alpha and thought-reading pony Beta will make their first bow to an English audience at the Aquarium today. Alpha is a handsome light-chestnut thoroughbred, with a wilful temper. He is six-and-a-half years old, stands sixteen hands high, and has been trained since infancy. He is said to have a marvellous memory. Beta is an English-bred miniature pony easily standing underneath Alpha. The two animals are devotedly attached to each other, and both follow their trainer like a dog. It is stated that the horse correctly plays the harmonium, and writes his own name on a slate. The two animals conclude their entertainment with a comical and amusing scene, the larger equine celebrity driving his companion in a perambulator.
12/10/1895

MR GEORGE EDWARDES'S *Artist's Model* company had an alarming experience on Monday whilst proceeding in a special from Leeds to Birmingham on the London and North-Western Railway. The train was approaching the level-crossing near Alrewas, between Burton and Lichfield, when the driver perceived that the gates were closed. Not withstanding the prompt application of the vacuum brake, it was found impossible to avoid a collision. The obstruction was completely demolished, but the engine kept the rails, and was only slightly damaged. The gate-keeper's wife, apprehending the danger, had made an unsuccessful attempt to open the gates, and saved her life by leaping out of the way as the smash occurred.

THE Uniforms Act, which was passed last year after it had had inserted a clause exempting stage performances from the scope of its prohibitions, was put into force at Clerkenwell, on Tuesday, against a street performer who had dressed himself as a Jolly Jack Tar to enable him to dance a hornpipe with effect. The magistrate put him to a compulsory outlay of twenty shillings, and as this amount undoubtedly exceeded his profits he will have to do his hornpiping either as a coster or a curate, whose dress does not come under the provisions of the Act.
19/10/1895

ONE of the principal incidents in the drama *Robbery Under Arms*, which is being played by Messrs Drew and Auld's company at the Prince of Wales's Theatre, Southampton, this week, is the daring robbery of a stage coach by a band of desperadoes. Considerable commotion was caused on Monday night when the leading horses dashed across the stage at great speed and crashed into the scenery on the other side of the stage, but fortunately little damage was done, and so admirable were the arrangements that the curtain had only to be lowered for a few minutes to put everything in order. On the curtain being raised again the coach with the four fine horses drove on amidst great enthusiasm.

WANTED, a Clever Child to Play Puck. An Orphan Preferred. BEN GREET, Theatre Royal, Middlesbrough.

WANTED, to Sell, Kitten, with Four Eyes and Two Mouths, suit Freak Show, Good Painting included. Would exchange for Small Barrel Organ. VINCENT, Hannah Street, Porth, Glamorganshire.
9/11/1895

THE Plymouth police are now engaged in attempting to unravel the mystery surrounding an assault upon and attempted robbery of Miss Gracie Leigh, one of the principal artistes in *The Water Babes* company. Miss Leigh, who was lodging in Mulgrave Street, Plymouth, during the visit of this company to the town, states that she retired to bed at about four o'clock in the morning, having sat up reading. Between the hours of five and six she awoke to find a man in her room, who, in a rough voice, demanded her watch and chain, which, it appears, she habitually wears when in bed. Miss Leigh alleges that in the encounter which followed the man struck her in the face several times, damaging one of her eyes and cutting her cheek. The miscreant ultimately escaped by the window.

AT Beckenham, on the 8th inst., a theatrical company engaged the Public Hall for the purpose of giving a performance of a melodrama in four acts. The posters which had been freely displayed on the various hoardings in the town represented a very tragic scene, and a large audience assembled to witness the entertainment. But neither the acting nor the scenery gave satisfaction. The audience hissed the performers repeatedly, and when the curtain dropped at the close a large number of them made their way to the pay-box and demanded the return of their money. The demands were peremptorily refused, and the audience, now thoroughly roused, were compelled to go out into the street. But a large crowd of them determined to wait for the actors, and when the latter made their appearance they were greeted with yells and groans, and some of the bolder of the crowd pelted the members of the company with mud, the disturbance being only quelled on the arrival of the police. The company ran back into the hall for shelter, and remained there until the crowd had dispersed.
16/11/1895

THE LATE MR AND MRS DACRE.
THE startling news which at the beginning of the present week was received by cable from Sydney, New South Wales, caused quite a shock in theatrical circles, and has since formed the subject of conversation wherever members of the profession have met. The tragic deaths of Miss Amy Roselle and her husband, Mr Arthur Dacre, could at first scarcely be realised by their friends in this country, but the terrible intelligence was confirmed, and there could be no longer reason to doubt that Mr Dacre had shot his wife dead, and then committed suicide by cutting his own throat.

Miss Amy Roselle, who will be remembered as among the most esteemed of London actresses, had a perfectly unique experience. Hardly had she reached her teens when she was a star actress, playing a repertory which would have appalled many a more experienced artist. This is how it came about. Her father, originally a schoolmaster in Glastonbury, where she was born in 1854, had an overweening predilection for the stage. Stories ran in the family of him having paid handsome fees for the privilege of supporting this actor and the other. "I have often," Miss Roselle has related, "heard him tell of his paying ten pounds to the elder Wallack for the privilege of playing Horatio to the more famous actor's Hamlet."

It was the remarkable talent of her brother Percy that drew the family into professional life. Percy, who was a tiny creature, was a born actor and elocutionist. He had a career almost as successful as that of Master Betty, whose pieces he was wont to perform. Eventually it was decided that a girl about his own age would be a suitable support, and so it was that Miss Roselle became an actress. Her brother's diminutive stature added a charm to his impersonations, but as he grew older his slender physique unfitted him for the career of an actor, and he withdrew from the stage to become an artist. It was then that the elder Roselle's interest centred in his daughter. She had been used in the first instance as a convenience, but it began to be perceived that there was something in her, and when she took to the profession seriously she developed an intense love of it. When her father took to training her in earnest he became the lessee for three months of the Cardiff, and then of the Swansea Theatre. There the clever girl played the whole round of leading parts in rapid succession. Her father was a careful tutor and most exacting critic. Miss Roselle's first professional engagement of the ordinary kind was at Plymouth, where a stock company still flourished under the direction of Mr Newcombe. It was the last of the stock companies, and no doubt she was one of the last actresses to obtain the advantage of such an experience. […]

Her marriage with Mr Dacre took place in 1884, and in 1887 they went on a long provincial tour, for which two or three pieces were specially written for them. On once more settling down in London, Amy Roselle made brave attempts to come to the front. She delivered recitations at the Empire with rare elocutionary force, but this feature did not prove a lasting attraction for audiences accustomed to ballets and laughter-moving varieties. [...] One of the last chances Miss Amy Roselle had of distinguishing herself in London was when, as understudy to Miss Ellen Terry at the Lyceum in 1892, she played for a few nights Queen Katharine, in Sir Henry Irving's imposing revival of *King Henry VIII*, while her last actual appearance in London was in Mr Pinero's play *The Second Mrs Tanqueray*, in which, on its production, she played Mrs Cortelyon in admirable style. To a good presence and a fine voice she added thorough command of her art. [...]

Of her association with the Lyceum Miss Roselle always spoke with keen satisfaction. She had an interesting story to tell of a performance of *Macbeth* under difficulties. Miss Terry was ill, and Miss Roselle was hastily summoned. The doctor could break the news of Miss Terry's illness to Mr Irving with a lighter heart if at the same time he might convey the assurance that Miss Roselle was well acquainted with the part. "Rely on me," said Miss Roselle, with a double meaning, for curiously enough Lady Macbeth was the one heroine of Shakespeare with whom Miss Roselle had not even a bowing acquaintance. But she was a marvellously quick study, and was able to come to a rehearsal next day letter-perfect, making, as events proved, one of the greatest successes of her career.

Mr Arthur Dacre, whose real surname was Culver James, was about the same age as his wife. He threw up the medical profession, for which he had qualified and which he had practised for a while, and determined to adopt that of the stage, finding an opening in one of the late Dion Boucicault's companies. [...] When Mr Beerbohm Tree produced *Hamlet* at the Haymarket at the beginning of 1892 he selected Mr Dacre for the role of Horatio. It was in the hope of obtaining more thankful engagements than had lately fallen to him and his wife that they left England for the Antipodes a few months ago with the best of wishes from their numerous friends. [...]

Their season at Melbourne was an unlucky one, and was attended by some very unpleasant events. They tried Adelaide, and here too the results were disastrous. They then opened at Sydney, but failed to draw. A tour in New Zealand was made, but here again the business was very poor. A return to Sydney followed, and they succeeded in getting an engagement at the Theatre Royal at a joint salary of £30 per week, for the season, but unfortunately for them, the season only lasted for three weeks.

The Dacres at this time had an offer to go to South Africa, and their prospects seemed to be somewhat brighter. The lack of success they had experienced and the troubles they had gone through preyed on Mr Dacre's mind, and he became very gloomy and despondent. He had sometimes spoken to friends about the ill-luck which constantly followed him, and told them that he saw no way out of his difficulties but by suicide. He also stated that he had talked over the situation with his wife, and that they had decided when the end came that they would die together. Mrs Dacre also said that they would die together, and that when the time came she would meet her end bravely, as a British woman should.

The day before the tragedy both seemed cheerful. Dacre spent the Sunday in writing letters. In the afternoon Mrs Dacre took a soporific. How soon after this the tragedy occurred is a matter of conjecture. She was found shot twice through the left breast, a subsequent examination showing that the heart had been pierced, and Dacre was found with his throat cut, evidently by his own hand. The carotid artery was severed. The wounds showed medical knowledge. An alarm having been given, the people in the house where they were staying burst open the door. They discovered Amy Roselle lying dead on the bed, apparently smiling happily and peacefully.

Arthur Dacre was still alive. He gasped out, "Oh! My God, what agony!" and died. A doctor was at once sent for, and on arrival saw that Dacre had been struggling to throw himself on the bed beside the body of his wife. [...]

Mrs Dacre always carried about with her a small packet of English earth, so that she might be buried in English soil. This was reverently sprinkled about the coffin in the grave. A clergyman of the Anglican

Church officiated, and read part of the service. Among the papers the unhappy man left was one containing a wish that the following words should be inscribed on the tombstone of himself and his wife: – "They loved each other. In death they were not divided."
23/11/1895

THE terrible news of the death of Mr and Mrs Dacre in Australia caused a shock that was felt through the whole of the profession. Both artists were so justly popular, and their affection for each other and their art was so well known, that the distress caused by learning their fate was redoubled by the pleasant memories of the Dacres which had been cherished by many artists and private friends. Since their sad bereavement in the loss of their beloved and only child they had never been the same, and the trials and troubles they had to undergo, added to this, doubtless proved unendurable.

TO THE EDITOR OF THE ERA.
Sir, – Thank you very much for your notice of my recent appearance as Lady Macbeth at the Wimbledon Theatre. The notice given me to play the part was very short, and I had only a few hours to get ready to enact not only Lady Macbeth, but also Desdemona and Ophelia. The difficulty in which I placed myself by accepting this engagement was increased by the fact of my not having been able to play for over two years, having one arm broken and one leg fractured, which misfortune was followed by brain fever, and my age is only twenty-four. Another difficulty was that I had never played Ophelia before, and the other two parts only twice, and I had to go through these performances without even a stage rehearsal.
Yours truly, ADA LUTINA.
106, Great Russell Street, Bedford Square.
Nov. 3rd, 1895.

AT a meeting of the Salford Board of Guardians, yesterday, it was reported that among the occupants of the tramp ward on Thursday evening were seven members of a theatrical company, who, it is alleged, had been left destitute by a "bogus" manager. They were respectably dressed, but only a penny was found among the whole of them.

LORD SHOLTO DOUGLAS, son of the Marquis of Queensbury, has adopted the theatrical profession. He made his first appearance at the Alcazar Theatre, San Francisco, in *The Guv'nor*, in a very small part. Later in the evening, at the same house, Lady Sholto obliged with a song and dance.
7/12/1895

THERE was a very eccentric personage in the stalls of the Princess's Theatre on Saturday last. He sat with the collar of his great coat up and with his hat on, smoking a cigar. On being spoken to by the attendant, he extinguished the latter, and took his hat off, but replaced it soon afterwards. When Stephen Norton, in *A Dark Secret*, said he had no "oof", the gentleman threw half-a-crown across the footlights. Further developments were, however, arrested by a pressing invitation from the management to an interview in the vestibule.

IN the Westminster County Court, on Thursday, Mr Goodwin, an artist, sued Mr Lowenfeld for services rendered in designing dresses for *Gentleman Joe*. Seventy sketches were prepared, and the price charged was £1 per sketch. The defendant's counsel, in cross-examining Mr Goodwin, said: – You were to draw Lord Donnybrook true to life, and you dressed him making a call with a greyish morning coat and a bowler hat. Is that true to life? Witness – Yes. Counsel – Does an earl make morning calls in a bowler hat? Witness – I have no experience of earls making morning calls. His Honour – Does an earl who pays visits up the river wear a coronet? Witness – I don't know. In further cross-examination Mr Goodwin said that he gave quite a fortnight to the work. After hearing expert witnesses his Honour gave a verdict for 40 guineas, including the £20 which had already been paid.

WE had hoped – and believed – that clerical intolerance had vanished from our land. But this appears not to be the case. In Carlisle there is a vicar, not so pleasant a vicar as that Mr Gilbert introduces in *The Sorcerer*, who tolerates

The gay Sally Lunn
And the rollicking bun,

and does not disdain to sing of the days when he was a "pale young curate." Not so genial a representative of the Church is the Rev Mr Shepherd, of Carlisle, who has dismissed from his saintly choir a young lady named Gibson for the dire offence of taking part in an amateur performance of the charming Gilbert and Sullivan opera *Iolanthe*, a work which we emphatically declare is as pure an example of the lyric drama as ever was placed upon the stage. Yet no sooner does this Shepherd learn that one of the lambs of his flock at St John's had committed the awful offence of appearing as a fairy in *Iolanthe* that he sends her the following fierce and unjustifiable communication:

Dear Miss Gibson, - I can hardly tell you how grieved and shocked I am to hear that you have been appearing for several nights on the stage of the Carlisle theatre. It has grieved me more than anything that has occurred in connection with St John's during many years past. You have also afforded, I hear, merriment among the young men of the choir, who freely commented on your appearance on the stage. You will quite understand how impossible it is for me to ask you to continue to be a member of St John's choir.

It is the first time we have ever heard a word breathed against the moral influence of a Gilbert and Sullivan opera, a kind of production we had always thought impeccable. Indeed, we have often seen clergymen – perhaps as holy men as the Rev Vicar of St John's, Carlisle – enjoying the harmless mirth of Mr Gilbert and the delightful melodies of Sir Arthur Sullivan evidently without a thought that they were faithless to their cloth in doing so. Probably if the Carlisle vicar would look a little closer into the state of St John's he would find many more serious flaws in its religious and moral condition than that of innocent Miss Gibson, who has our sincerest sympathy in what we consider an intemperate and unreasonable attack by a reverend critic who evidently condemns *Iolanthe* without knowing anything about it.

A CATASTROPHE at Koster and Bial's, New York City, on Friday, the 29th ult., resulted in the death of old Tom, the pet cat of the house, known to every foreign artist who has visited the establishment since the opening. A rehearsal of Kilanyi's glyptorama was in progress, and Tom was playing about the immense frame from behind which the pictures are shown. Without any provocation whatever he bounded in between the heavy rollers and the canvas, and with one parting howl his catship was flattened out. What was left of poor Tom was consigned to a box and thence to a grave underneath the stage of the hall.

WANTED, Useful Young Lady for Ghost Sketches. Must mind own business. Long Engagement to suitable party. No vacancy for blonde hair novice. BURNETTE, Ghost Shop, Commercial Street, Newport, Mon.
14/12/1895

7
1896
A POUND OF SAUSAGES ENCLOSED IN A DAINTY BOX

TO THE EDITOR OF THE ERA.
Sir, – While standing in the pit entrance of Boxing Night I noticed a couple of fishermen applying for tickets, and as they were – well, not exactly sober, I instructed our pay-box man not to sell them any; this more especially as we have a full licence attached to the theatre, and I was afraid they would want to be "keeping Christmas" up in our bars inside. Being refused admission seemed to grieve them very much, and, after some little deliberation between themselves, one of them turned to me and said, "Say, ole feller, you know what it is, we're a bit drunk; but let's come inside, *we want to get sober*!" and after promising to stick to soda water I passed them, rather tickled by their quaint request, and glad to see they were sensible enough to know that they would have more chance of "getting sober" in a theatre, although fully licensed for refreshments, than they would in knocking about from pub to pub outside.
Yours Truly, A. LOVEDAY,
Assistant-Manager, P.O.W. Theatre, Grimsby.

PANTHERS STRICTLY PROHIBITED.
TO THE EDITOR OF THE ERA.
Sir, – A great deal of surprise has been manifested since the publication of your last issue specifying the presence in the cage of death of a large boarhound, made up to represent a panther. As it was generally understood that the real animal was to have been introduced, and as my early advertisements clearly specified the importation of the genuine article, I trust you will allow me to explain my reasons for the alteration. The play, as you are aware, was produced in Bury for copyright reasons, with the full sanction of the Licenser of Plays to introduce a panther, but within a fortnight after said production I received a notice from him that his attention had been drawn to a certain rule (no. 21, I believe) applying to the licensing of theatres, prohibiting the appearance of any wild animal upon the stage.

Needless to say, this caused me a considerable amount of anxiety, and we had a very lengthy correspondence on the subject, but without avail; and I finally hit upon the idea of importing a magnificent boarhound, and, having succeeded in training the animal – which, with the skin, &c., has cost me in the aggregate far more than the genuine article would have done – I have been able to put before the public an imitation which it is almost impossible for any except experts to distinguish from the real thing.

There is nothing "gruesome" whatever in the situation, as when the panther is in the act of springing from the first cage to the second, into which the lady is thrown, a division door between the second and third cages is instantly dropped, and the lady is saved by the comedian dressed as a bear.
Yours truly, ARTHUR JEFFERSON.
Eden Theatre, Bishop Auckland.
4/1/1896

FAIRIES IN CABS

A VERY extraordinary instance of animal instinct occurred at the Theatre Royal, Middlesbrough, on Tuesday last during the Palace scene of Louis La Rondelle's pantomime, *Babes in the Wood*. Mr John G. Brett introduces a miniature circus with ponies, baboon, and a donkey. Whilst putting the baboon through its paces the trainer noticed how eagerly it sought the footlights and scanned the first row of the stalls. A seafaring man, who was evidently the object of interest to the baboon, uttered a peculiarly distinctive cry, when instantly the baboon sprang across the footlights into his arms. An immediate inquiry on the part of Mr Henry Tweedie, the acting-manager, elicited the extraordinary fact that the seaman had originally brought the baboon from its native land, but that was several years ago.
11/1/1896

MISS CARLOTTA HUFFEY, professionally known as Miss Adelaide Lutina, sued a Mr Harcourt Master for breach of promise of marriage on Friday. Miss Lutina, who is twenty-four years of age, met the defendant in a vegetarian restaurant in 1892, and he subsequently proposed marriage to her. She gave him her jewellery, valued at £50, to keep, and never saw it again. In 1894 he wrote saying he was not worthy of her, and asking her to forget him. Miss Lutina fainted and fell, breaking her arm and leg, and afterwards discovered that the defendant was a married man with four children. The jury found a verdict for the plaintiff with £400 damages.
This is clearly the "Ada Lutina" who defended her performance as Lady Macbeth in 1895.
25/1/1896

SIR AUGUSTUS HARRIS, ever resourceful and adaptive, has at last solved the difficult problem, how to prevent members of the Drury Lane pantomime company from standing in the "prompt entrance" during the performance, and so encumbering the stage. He has placed on the floor of that entrance a grating, to which electric wires are fixed, so that a very unpleasant "current" is induced through the body of any person standing on the "grill" in question. After a few "shocking" experiences, the extra ladies at Drury Lane have given up lingering on the "P." side of the stage, and have taken to marching quietly off to their dressing rooms by the narrow path still left for their access to and from the footlights; and one of the most irritating annoyances of Mr Arthur Collins, the excellent stage-manager at Drury Lane, has thus been entirely removed, and he has no occasion now to implore the artists not to stand in the wings of the prompt side.

ON Wednesday night, at the Grand Theatre, Stalybridge, Mr Edwin Hugh, who is playing Spike in Hardie and Von Leer's *Plunger* company, met with a severe accident. Whilst hurrying to his dressing-room for a quick change, he accidentally pushed against his dulcimer, and a piece of steel attached to it ran into his leg and resisted all efforts to remove it. By a surgical operation the steel, which proved to be an inch and a half in length, and had become embedded in the bone of the leg, was removed; and Mr Hugh is progressing as favourably as can be expected under the circumstances. Of course, he will be unable to work for some time.

IN the course of the successful engagement of Mr Kiddie's pantomime *The Babes in the Wood*, at the Eden Theatre, Bishop Auckland, Mr Arthur Jefferson, the lessee, invited the children of the local workhouse to a morning performance, after which they were regaled on milk and buns, each being presented with a new penny piece.

WANTED, Known, Miss Rosin, Indo-Japanese Juggler and Equilibrist, the Original and Only Artist using the Acetylene Illuminant, and Johnny Sharman's Great Troupe of Australian Worrying Dogs, the most Comic, Exciting, Knockabout, Funny and Only Act of its kind. Always a sure success. National Hall, Croydon.
1/2/1896

PROFESSOR WESTERN and DIANA (lady and gentleman) promise an exceptionally fine shooting act on Monday next at the Aquarium. Diana will commence the performance by extinguishing twenty-five candle lights which form the initials of her name. From a running deer Professor Western will pick off small objects in rotation, and also shoot through a finger-ring which the lady holds between her fingers, and break an object at the back of the ring. He will split cards and shoot two objects from the lady's head with two pistols, breaking them at the same time. The lady will then don a bullet-proof cuirass and face the Lee Metford rifle which is fastened into a stand, and discharge it by firing against the trigger with a shot from her revolver, receiving a bullet in the cuirass. She will then open the cuirass and show what it contains. Professor Western will introduce the bullet proof tricycle, invented by himself. Riding around the stage, he will shield himself while the lady fires at him, breaking objects which hang on the shield. The whole shooting will be executed with quick-firing rifles and revolvers with a slight report.
8/2/1896

MR FRED LLOYD and MR FORBES DAWSON were in a certain telegraph office on Tuesday, and the first-named gentleman wired to a manager: – "Bank Robbery; can do March 9." They left the office, and were about to take the train westwards when they were detained by a person who turned out to be a detective. They had been "shadowed" at once, and it was only by presentation of their cards and by their explaining that *The Bank Robbery* was the title of a piece that an unpleasant contretemps was averted.

ON Monday night, at the close of James and Marie Finnie's aquatic performance in the Scotia Music Hall, Glasgow, the drop scene would not come down. A gasman mounted the edge of the tank to assist the scene in its course, when he fell backwards into the water. He could not gain his feet, and was seen by the excited spectators to be struggling under the water. Several stage hands tried to rescue him, but failed, when Finnie rushed upon the stage, jumped into the tank, and saved the unfortunate gasman, amidst loud cheers.

MISS BESSIE BELLWOOD experienced quite a disappointment on Jan. 29th. It was her intention to sail from New York on the *S.S. Teutonic*. She arrived on the pier accompanied by her maid just as the gang-plank was hauled back, and, seated in her carriage, she witnessed the ship glide away with all her luggage on board. After severely reprimanding the cabman she hastened to the office of the company to demand her money back, but, receiving no satisfaction, she went away sorrowful.
15/2/1896

MR ZANETTO, of the Zanetto troupe of Japanese jugglers, gave an extraordinary exhibition at Clifton on Wednesday last in the presence of several thousand people. A turnip was thrown from the Clifton Suspension Bridge to Mr Zanetto, who was on the path below, and he caught it on a fork held in his mouth. £3 11s. 5d. was collected on behalf of the Bristol and Clifton Children's Hospital.
22/2/1896

ON Thursday night, with a "clear stage and no favour," the twenty-seventh anniversary of "Sausage Night" was celebrated at the Surrey Theatre. As usual, the closing week of the pantomime was the time selected for the festival, and immediately after the conclusion of the performance every employee, to the number of nearly 300 persons, was marshalled on the stage, where Mr W. Harris, of West Smithfield, the originator and founder of the annual feast, with a kind word and hope of future meetings, presented each with a pound of sausages enclosed in a dainty box. At the conclusion of the distribution a vote of thanks to the founder and donor of the gifts, together with best wishes for the health of himself and family, was duly passed with musical honours.

COUNT MAGRE, the little man who married Tom Thumb's widow, and who is thirty inches high, has just ordered a bicycle for his own use. It is to cost sixty guineas, though it will be the smallest "bike" on record. The dimensions include a fourteen-inch wheel and a twelve-inch frame, and the weight is not to exceed ten pounds. His wife, who still retains the name of Mrs Tom Thumb, pays for it, and shows indications of being herself tempted to indulge in the universal craze for wheeling. She still drives about in the tiny carriage drawn by Shetland ponies given her by Queen Victoria. The little lady is now fifty-five years old, and her Italian husband is forty-seven. They live in Indiana, U.S.

WANTED, Full Company for Stock. Must Know the meaning of the word Stock and be able to Act, not Drink. Address, stating lowest terms and latest references (if unknown), to MARK H. LINDON, Victoria Theatre, West Stanley, Durham.
29/2/1896

"CARRIAGES AT 10.30" was the announcement which appeared in the provinces the other day on one of the programmes of Mr Drinkwater's company, and which intimated to the carriage folk that that was the time to have their conveyances ready to convey them home after the performance. A country girl, who had enjoyed the play, said to Miss Isabel Grey, a member of the company, "I loiked your acting, Miss, very much; in fact, everything I saw was first class, but I didn't see them carriages what was to come on at 10.30, and which was down on the programme."
14/3/1896

"THE LADY SLAVEY" reached its fiftieth performance in New York on Thursday evening. A perplexing question lately arose among the members of this company at the Casino. Some eggs that were used in the previous production were left in an obscure corner of one of the dressing-rooms. The next tenant, Miss Marie Dressler, on discarding an old skirt threw it in the corner where lay the innocent eggs. A weak "cluck-cluck" was the first intimation that she and her maid were not the only occupants of the apartment, and upon investigation they discovered three tiny chickens, evidently just hatched by the warm flannel skirt, which had acted as an incubator.

LAST nights of pantomimes in the provinces are often marked by an unchecked rowdyism which we trust will not be extended into the metropolis. On Saturday evening, during the final performance of *Robinson Crusoe* at the Prince of Wales's, Liverpool, the audience became very disorderly, and commenced throwing things on the stage, such as sweetmeats, toys, and biscuits. At length one young blackguard threw a lump of confectionery that hit Mr Fred Williams, the popular Mrs Crusoe, on the face and cut him. The comedian uttered a well-timed rebuke, and something like order was restored on the removal of one of the offenders from the theatre. Mr Williams has suffered no ill effects from the contretemps, and will commence his engagements in town on Monday at Collins's.
21/3/1896

A DISGRACEFUL disturbance took place on Monday night at the Variety Circus, Middlesbrough-on-Tees. After Bella and Bijou had sung four sketch songs a portion of the audience insisted on an encore, making such a prolonged disturbance that the manager, Mr Norman, had to appeal for order. The uproar continued, however, the audience refusing to hear the next turn until Bella and Bijou responded to the encore. This the manager refused to allow, as the artistes named had already done four turns, and other performers were waiting to go on. As the hooting and yelling continued, the band played the National Anthem, and the lights were turned down. Mr Norman then called upon the police to clear the hall. This was immediately received with the cry "Mob the police!" and at one time a collision seemed imminent. The police, however, ultimately managed to effect a clearance, and the doors were closed for the night. The ringleaders of the disturbance, it is stated, are to be proceeded against.
28/3/1896

MR FENTON WALSH, the assistant manager of the Avenue Theatre, and William McFee, commissionaire in the same house, will think twice before they play the Good Samaritan again to a person who goes to sleep in the stalls, as they did on Wednesday to Arthur Neville Eyre, of Gilslead Hall, Brentwood. Mr Walsh and McAfee carried the sleeper into the bar, where he slumbered for about twenty minutes. On awakening he charged his benefactors with having robbed him of 19s. 6d. and other moneys. When the case came on at Bow Street on Thursday, Eyre did not appear, and Sir John Bridge said the prisoners had endeavoured to do the prosecutor a good turn, and in consequence had been charged with the offence. He hoped that it would not prevent them doing kindly actions in future, but it would be better on other occasions to remove drunken men from the premises. There was not the slightest ground for the accusation against the prisoners, and they would be discharged. Sir John added that the prosecutor ought to be summoned on his own recognisances.

THE dead body of a woman, recovered last Sunday from the Mersey, at Didsbury, and removed to the mortuary at Withington Workhouse, has been identified as that of Miss Mary Ann Donsworth, forty-four years of age, who resided at Moss Side, Manchester, and who was, until recently, the box-office keeper at the Theatre Royal, Manchester. Miss Donsworth left home the previous Thursday night, and was not afterwards seen alive by any of her friends. Some time ago her landlady died. The two had been very deeply attached to each other, and this loss appeared to have preyed on the mind of the survivor to such an extent as to cause despondency, and there is little doubt that while so suffering she committed suicide. Miss Donsworth was for twenty years in the box-office of the Prince's Theatre, Manchester, and for seven years occupied a like position at the Royal.
11/4/1896

ON the 10th. inst., at Her Majesty's Opera House, Blackpool, during the performance of *Patience* by Mr D'Oyly Carte's opera company, a strong smell of something burning caused someone to raise a cry of "Fire," and many of the audience rose to rush outside. The emergency doors were promptly flung open by the attendants, but happily the audience became composed, the performance was not interrupted, and excitement soon subsided. It appears that a man in the pit had thoughtlessly put his pipe with the tobacco still alight into his pocket, with the result that his coat caught fire, and thus caused the alarm.

MR BEERBOHM TREE'S VISITOR.
James B. McAvoy, alias Marchant, a tall, well-dressed young man, of good address, who falsely represented himself as a member of the Carl Rosa opera company, was charged on remand before Mr De Rutzen, at the Westminster Police Court, on Tuesday, with stealing Mrs Beerbohm Tree's purse, containing about £2 in gold and a cheque for £14 15s., under circumstances which have been reported.

Sergeant Harris, of Scotland Yard, said the prisoner was very well-connected, and he had himself stated that he had run through a fortune. He had been identified as a person wanted for alleged cheque frauds at Margate two years ago, and there was a warrant in existence from that town for his arrest.

The prisoner said he had a perfect answer with respect to these charges, but with regard to Mrs Tree's purse he pleaded guilty. He wished to emphasise the fact that he called on Mrs Tree with the genuine intention of soliciting some assistance, he (prisoner) having been connected with the press and stage, both in England and America, for many years. He thought Mr Tree might have used his influence for him, and had no idea of felony when he was shown into the study. Seeing the purse on the table, he regretted to state that he yielded to sudden temptation. As he did not call at the house with the remotest idea of robbery he trusted that his worship would see fit to deal with the case.

Mr de Rutzen said he would not assume any guilt in the cases at Margate, and his sentence on the prisoner of two months' hard labour was solely in respect of the robbery from Mrs Tree. It was very common – far too common – for rogues to call on well-known people either to beg or steal, and such an offence as this could not lightly be passed over. *18/4/1896*

MR C.W. SOMERSET'S dogs saved a boy's life at Brighton, on Easter Tuesday. A lad eight years old, named George Martin Laylard, was walking with his nurse on the new pier, and descended the steps to the landing beneath. The boy slipped and fell into the sea, and would have inevitably been drowned had not Mr C.W. Somerset, with his two magnificent St Bernard dogs, which were nightly performing at the theatre in *The Honour of the House*, been on the pier. Before Mr Somerset had time to divest himself of his coat, the two dogs sprang from a height of nearly twenty feet into the water below, and in less than two minutes had landed little Master Laylard safely at the feet of his nurse. His mother testified her appreciation of the gallant deed by presenting the dogs with two solid silver collars, with the following inscriptions: – "To Bob and Mona, in grateful memory for saving the life of her dear son, April 7th, 1896." This, by-the-way, is the third life Bob has saved in twelve months.
25/4/1896

AT Marlborough Street Police Court, on Tuesday, Charles Connelly, thirty-five, described as a French polisher, of Gosfield Street, Tottenham Court Road, was charged, before Mr Hannay, with having assaulted Mr Walter Beaumont, an actor, living at Castle Street, Oxford Street, by striking him on the head with a coal hammer.

The prosecutor said that shortly after midnight on Monday he was with a friend in an hotel in Castle Street, Oxford Street, when the prisoner came in minus hat, coat, waistcoat, and boots, and called for a bottle of soda water. He was served with the soda water, and took off his braces, which he handed to the proprietor as security for payment. The braces were handed back to him, and he was told that he could pay in the morning. He then turned to the prosecutor and said, "Will you pay for it?" The prosecutor declined good humouredly, thinking that the man was possibly one of the Princess's stage hands a "little bit sprung" and wishing to be funny. Connelly also asked his (prosecutor's) friend to pay, but again receiving a refusal, "accused" the prosecutor of keeping a horse and his friend of having ridden it. He also said that the prosecutor's mother owed his (prisoner's) mother money for furniture, and that the prosecutor was indebted to him over a betting transaction. The prosecutor turned to speak to another person when he received a violent blow on the left cheek from behind, and observed the prisoner holding a coal hammer in his hand. The police were called and Connelly was given into custody. He had never seen the man before.

Mr Hannay (to the prisoner) – Do you wish to ask the witness any questions?

The prisoner – He is a very fine actor, but he has told lies. I won't ask him any questions.

Mr Charles Henry Giles, the landlord of the Princess Victoria, corroborated the evidence given by the prosecutor, and said that the prisoner struck the prosecutor with the blunt part of the hammer. He took the hammer away from the accused and sent for the police.

Constable 254 D said he took Connelly into custody. He was quite sober, and when charged he said nothing.

The wife of the prisoner here stepped into the witness-box, and on seeing her Connelly exclaimed, "Cheer up, Sal; keep your head on." Mrs Connelly said that her husband had been "queer" two years ago. He got into the same condition on Saturday morning last, and a doctor told her that so long as he did no harm he would be all right.

Mr Hannay said that the prisoner's conduct was quite unaccountable if he were sane. He would be remanded for the state of his mind to be inquired into.

The prisoner – Can't you allow bail? I can find security for any sum you like. As Marlow, the gaoler, led him from the dock he exclaimed "Thank you, sir, you have done your best."
2/5/1896

MISS BESSIE BELLWOOD met with an adventure in the early part of this week. She had arranged to travel by the night mail from Nottingham to Middlesbrough, and so that her sleep should be undisturbed she had the door of her compartment locked. Early in the morning she found herself at Newcastle-on-Tyne.

WANTED, to Sell, Monster Spider Crab, 12ft. across, Caught in Japanese Waters. A Fortune to Showmen. Price 30 Guineas. MITCHELL, 167, Girlington Rd., Bradford.
9/5/1896

NO more appropriate playhouse could have been secured for the revival of *Jo* than Drury Lane Theatre. Next door, Wych Street Way, is the site of Tom All Alone's graveyard, and the sympathetic having at a matinée wept with Miss Lee* at the churchyard gate in the theatre, may go out and have a look at the real thing, or what remains of it; for the County Council have swept away the foul slums, and a paved playground for the children now occupies the place of the graveyard so well described by Charles Dickens in "Bleak House." All is gone but the iron gate, but rumour has it that this, too, will disappear to make still more realistic the scene in the theatre where Miss Lee "keeps movin' on."
Jennie Lee, who played the little crossing-sweeper for many years.

REMARKS from the audience are often smart – to wit, at the Gaiety, Brighton, last week, in the second act of *The War Cloud*, the old Colonel invites Major Norland to take off his coat and receive a thrashing. The Major hesitated and was lost, for a woman shouted from the pit, "he daren't take his coat off, *he ain't got no shirt on!*"
16/5/1896

THERE was an unrehearsed incident at the Leeds Grand Theatre the other evening. Miss Rosie Boote, a lively dancer with a facility for high kicking, was executing some vigorous steps when the shoe of her right foot flew high up into the auditorium, and it is supposed reached the dress-circle. The lady discontinued her dance, and was carried off the stage by an actor. The audience, however, uproariously demanded a reappearance, and Miss Boote, with one foot still shoeless, came hopping on to smile her acknowledgements. Doubtless some lucky fellow is treasuring the shoe of the fair Boote as a memento of an unusual experience.
In 1901 Miss Boote married the 4th Marquess of Headfort.

A SERIOUS accident occurred to the Great Wheel at the India and Ceylon Exhibition. While travelling round on Thursday night between eight and nine o'clock it came to a sudden stop, and officials were totally unable to move it either one way or the other. About sixty persons were thereby imprisoned in the upper carriages until noon on Friday, when they were released. They all got a hearty salutation from the crowd, and were provided by Messrs Spiers and Pond with with a breakfast at the nearest buffet. The imprisoned passengers, after the first excitement had calmed down, took things philosophically. Sleep, for various reasons, was out of the question, but there was no ground for fearing personal injury. As early as possible in the morning an attempt was made to reach them and give them provisions. Among those employed on the wheel, most of whom are old bluejackets, is a man who, reckless though the procedure seemed, volunteered to climb round the wheel. Taking with him a length of thin cord, he commenced his perilous journey, watched with the greatest agitation by the crowd below. When he reached a car with someone in he let down his cord. This was made fast by those below to a thicker cord, and finally to a basket. He motioned to those below the number of people in the carriage, and there was sent up in the basket whisky, lemonade, and buns, which were passed through the windows, and gratefully accepted by those in the carriages, who had been absolutely without food during their incarceration. One of the comic incidents of the situation was occurred when the rope attached to one of the provision baskets broke in mid-air and a whisky bottle was smashed to pieces in consequence. During the early morning of Friday the wildest rumours were afloat. Among other things, it was said

that some of the people had died of fright, and especially that two women were dead in one of the carriages. There was no foundation at all for these statements. There were no casualties at all, either to the passengers or those engaged at work for the company.
23/5/1896

A VERY funny incident occurred to Carl Hertz (who is now touring South Africa) at Vereenigin, near Johannesburg. He carries a large wooden cannon in one of his boxes, which he uses in one of his illusions, and as the officials are very particular about allowing firearms into the country since the late war (everyone being thoroughly searched) there was quite a scene and scare when they saw the cannon, and it took about ten official signatures, a lot of examination, and plenty of red tape before he could get it through, and each time he was looked upon suspiciously. Before departing one of the officials asked Mr Hertz for a light for his cigar, and as Mr Hertz carries a trick match-box, which explodes a cap every time it is opened, he handed the gentleman the box, which detonated as usual. The official jumped into the air, and threw the box away as if it was dynamite, while the rest of the crowed simply yelled themselves hoarse. That settled it; Mr Hertz was not allowed to depart, but had to explain matters first, and the train was delayed two hours.
30/5/1896

SERPENTELLO, the contortionist and neck dislocator, who left Manchester for Plymouth on his bicycle on Monday last, has arrived safe and sound, with a hearty appetite.

MR CHARLES BERTRAM, in his amusing book "Isn't it Wonderful?" – after referring to an annoying accident that happened to M. Houdin – relates the following anecdote of his own platform experience: – "A similar occurrence happened to myself at St James's Hall, but ended for me a little more disastrously. I had borrowed a ring from a lady in the audience, and jokingly requested her to place a value on it. This she did, and valued it at £4. I then tied a piece of ribbon to it, and placed the ring on a plate in full view of the audience, and then proceeded to make an omelette. Having mixed the ingredients, I threw the ring and ribbon into them, and pouring a little spirits upon them, went through the make-believe of cooking the omelette in a pan. On setting fire to the spirit there is a blaze, and a lid is placed upon the pan. When the lid is removed, instead of an omelette, a dove is found with the identical ring attached to its neck by the ribbon. All went well until I removed the cover of the pan. There was the dove surely enough with the ring tied to its neck, but during the applause of the audience the dove flew up, round the hall, and out of an open window into Piccadilly. I never saw it or the ring again, and I had to make the best of a bad bargain, and pay the lady £4 as a compensation for her loss."

NOTICE. – ORLANDO MACCOMO (the original) begs to inform friends that he is not married, and never was, so cannot possibly have a wife in Boston, Lincolnshire. Thanks to kind friend who has circulated that report.
6/6/1896

MR C.A. JAMES, the proprietor of the Waxwork Exhibition, Dublin, gave his annual outing to 200 newsboys of that city on Thursday. Special cars were provided, and the youngsters had a trip to the seaside, where balloons were sent up, and all kinds of amusements and refreshments were provided. Before returning home each boy was presented with a cap filled with toys. The weather was delightful, and a very enjoyable day was spent.
20/6/1896

THERE was a slight accident on Tuesday night at the Avenue Theatre, Sunderland, during the performance of *Signal Lights*. In one of the acts a dog pulls a cord to change the lights of the signals on the line. The signal-post toppled over, breaking the lamp and spilling the oil. This caught fire and burned for some little time on the stage. The audience took the incident with perfect calmness, and there was no stoppage in the action of the play.

AT the Bradford County Court, on the 26th ult., Charles Garry, an actor, was sued by Sam Haigh, of the District Bank, Bradford, for £5 damages for a dog bite. The defendant had recently been playing the part of Svengali, in *Trilby*, at the Bradford Theatre Royal. On May 14th Mr Haigh was cycling down Manningham Lane, Bradford, when a dog flew out from the causeway and tried to bite him. Mr Haigh attempted to kick the dog away on one side, and the animal then ran round the machine, and bit his leg on the other side. The defendant had offered to pay £3 3s. His honour gave judgement for plaintiff for the amount claimed.

QUEEN VICTORIA is the heroine of a drama now being acted at the leading Siamese theatres. The plot is as follows: – Victoria is about to be married in Ceylon to the King of Siam, when that monarch breaks off the match, and Victoria invades his country. She is repulsed with great loss. The Duke of Cambridge does his best to turn the fortunes of the day by wielding a battle-axe against three Siamese fairies, but the English are getting the worst of it when the King of Siam relents and bestows his hand on Victoria, who has been madly in love with him from the first.
4/7/1896

JOHN OJIJATEKHA BRANT SEEO, Prince of the Mohawk Tribe of North American Indians, and at one time actor and member of the Go-won-go Mohawk company, recently broke the record in Preston by being converted, christened, confirmed and married according to the rites of the English Church all in the merry month of June.

DURING the high wind on Tuesday afternoon a large captive balloon, owned by Mr J.B. Mulholland, of the Metropole Theatre, Camberwell, advertising *Morocco Bound*, which is being played there this week, suddenly broke away, and disappeared. It has not yet been heard of.
8/8/1896

SAD FATALITY AT THE NOVELTY.
EARLY on Tuesday morning a shocking fatality occurred at the Novelty Theatre, Great Queen Street, resulting in the sad death of Mr Temple E. Crozier, one of the actors engaged in the representation of Frank Harvey's play *Sins of the Night*. In this piece Mr W.M. Franks played the part of a revengeful Creole, whilst Mr Crozier represented the villain of the piece, a Spaniard. The Creole falls upon the Spaniard and stabs him, with the words, "Now my sister is avenged," and with these words makes his exit from the stage. The audience on Monday night had no time to realise that a fatal blow had been struck when Mr Franks left the stage. When the curtain was drawn up for the purpose of the tableau, another member of the company, remarking the pallor that had come over Mr Crozier, drew the dagger from his companion's breast, and in answer to an anxious question received the reply: "It's all right; don't worry." These were the last words spoken by the dying man, and the audience passed out into the streets ignorant of the pitiable reality of the scene they had witnessed. Behind the scenes, however, all was excitement and apprehension. Four doctors were quickly brought in, but their assistance was unavailing, and they were shortly joined by the divisional surgeon of the police as a formal witness of the scene. Mr Franks, thus placed in a distressful position, was arrested by the police upon a charge of manslaughter. The dead body of Mr Crozier was left through the night on the stage of the Novelty Theatre, and was on Tuesday morning placed in a shell and carried to the St Giles mortuary. The body was still dressed in the Spanish costume, with the paint yet upon his cheeks, and thick in raddled lines on the white face. The weapon used by Mr Franks was his own property, being a gift from the late Miss Ada Cavendish, with whom he is connected by family ties. […]

In the course of an interview, Mr Tyrrell, the manager of the Comedy Theatre, said: – "This affair has naturally caused great distress to everybody in the theatre, for both the young men were exceedingly popular in the company. They were on very friendly terms with one another. Of the accident itself I can say very little, for there is really very little to be said. It was all over in a few minutes, and poor Crozier himself hardly seemed to realise that he was mortally wounded. It happened like this. The fatal mistake was that Mr Franks, instead of going to the property-man for a dagger, used a dagger of his own. When the curtain had fallen Crozier became faint, and we tried to pull him round with brandy, whilst messengers were sent in all directions for doctors. Dr Gould at once pronounced the case hopeless, for the dagger had penetrated deep, although the wound seemed so small that it was almost imperceptible. When the police arrived and asked how it had happened, Mr Franks said, "I did it. It was an accident. It is a terrible thing," and, almost stupefied, the poor, distracted fellow left the theatre with the police.

Miss St Lawrence, the lessee of the theatre and the leading actress of the company, was not a witness of the affair, and was in her dressing-room when she was called to the stage. When the alarming news was brought to her she fainted, and Dr Gould was called from the dead man to attend to her. Acting upon advice, she appeared on Tuesday night as usual, when *Sins of the Night* was repeated. The affair seemed to have caused curiously little excitement in the neighbourhood, and there was no sign of exceptional interest, either inside or outside the theatre, on Tuesday evening. An unfeeling report, circulated in the afternoon, that Mr Franks, who had been released on bail, would take up his part, was without foundation, as might have been expected. As a token of respect for the dead actor the opening farce was not given, and the final scene of the drama was so modified that the stabbing of the Spaniard was omitted. At the commencement of the play Mr Walter Tyrrell, the manager, addressed a few words to the large audience present, intimating that in consequence to the fatal accident to Mr Crozier the part which he had filled would be played for the rest of the week by Mr Harold Child, while that sustained by Mr Franks would be entrusted to Mr Robert Smith. He asked the indulgence of the audience, not merely for the new comers, but for the entire company, who still suffered from the shock and the sorrow which the performance of the previous night had brought to them.

Mr Franks, who had acted together with Mr Crozier for some years past in the provinces, has received numerous sympathetic messages from well-known members of the theatrical profession.

After the inquest the coffin containing the body of the unfortunate young actor was removed from St Giles mortuary and conveyed to Melton Mowbray, of which town the deceased was a native. The coffin was met at the station by the father and brother of Mr Crozier, and the interment takes place this afternoon in the parish churchyard. He will be buried in the same grave as his mother, who died a year or two ago. In Melton Mowbray the utmost sympathy is felt for the bereaved father at the untimely death of his son. Several beautiful floral emblems were sent from the Novelty Theatre, and one, a cross, from "A dear friend," was placed at the head of the coffin.
The coroner's jury later returned a verdict of death by misadventure, and Franks was discharged.

WANTED, by Will Dalton ("Trousers"), Funny Knockabout Comedian, concluding Portsmouth, Gravesend, Dover, Sandgate, Brighton, and Margate. One Week, Sept. 7th, or Oct. 5th and 12th. Clean, Funny Turn. "Trousers", "Trousers", "Trousers." Address, WILL DALTON, Pier Pavilion, Herne Bay, Kent.
15/8/1896

AN accident, which might have proved very serious, happened to Mr E.L. Garside on Saturday night last, during one of the sensation scenes in *Life's Shadows*. Mr Garside, as the villain of the piece, places a young lady upon a machine to be hacked to pieces by a number of revolving knives. When this scene was reached one of the audience, more excited than the rest, threw a bottle, which struck Mr Garside on the head, causing blood to flow freely. The offending party was promptly marched round to the stage, but Mr Garside, regarding the incident as a compliment to the realism of his acting, refused to charge the culprit.

IN Messrs Dottridge and Longden's latest drama, *The Serpent's Coil*, which is being played to exceptional houses at Crewe this week, one of the many exciting incidents is that of the heroine being attacked by a huge Indian serpent. This scene is wrought up with such intense realism that that the other day a young "super" lady who had been listlessly standing on the O.P. side of the stage, seeing the reptile gliding towards its prey, uttered a wild shriek, and, rushing through the stage-door, could not be induced to return for any consideration. Excitement also prevailed in the crowded audience, a heroic gentleman standing in the stalls with a heavy stick upraised to strike the reptile in case it came his way.

WANTED, Known, Leo Zylva, the Eighth Wonder of the World, from the Land of the Moa, the most Wonderful Tattooed Man on Earth, who is Tattooed from the base of the neck to the soles of the feet, a perfect Work of Art; Tattooed in the most superb colours, representing every Bird, Beast, and Reptile which entered the Ark, and Foliage of all descriptions in all its Grandeur and Splendour, and Marvellous Maori Clubs Performer; also with a Japanese Umbrella, &c. A Sure Draw. 150, Old Street, Ashton, Lancashire.
22/8/1896

AT the Skibbereen Petty Sessions on the 19th inst. John William Holland, of Mardyke, Skibbereen, was charged with throwing Mr Frank Burdette, acting-manager of Mr Calder O'Beirne's Opera Company, over the balustrade of the Skibbereen Town Hall, on the night of Saturday, Aug. 15th, thereby endangering his life. The particulars set forth in the deposition made by Mr Burdette were to the effect that on the night of Aug. 15th he was standing at the head of the stairs in the Town Hall, his duty being to see that every person entering the hall had a ticket. These tickets were issued halfway up the stairs. He saw the defendant come in about a quarter to nine o'clock and asked him if he had a ticket, and he replied, "No." The deponent then said, "You can't go into the hall; go and get one, there's a good fellow." The deposition continues, "I thought he went; he moved away, and I went over to the balustrade. He made a rush at me, caught me by the legs below the knees and 'chucked' me over head foremost. I fell on my right side, partly on my face and chest, at the foot of the stairs by the entrance-door. I remember being carried home. While I was talking with the prisoner before he threw me over, Mr Calder O'Beirne and another gentleman, whose name I do not know, were standing at the door leading into the hall talking. The prisoner did not appear to be under the influence of drink. I gave him no provocation, and nothing passed between us save what I have said."

The defendant, on being asked if he had any questions to ask, replied, "No, sir; I'm guilty. I was drunk."

The head constable said he saw the injured man in the hospital that morning, and he said that he was very much better, but had a little pain still in his chest.

Mr Burdette's counsel said it was one of the most brutal assaults that was ever committed in the town. He applied for a remand for a week.

The prisoner was accordingly remanded to Cork Gaol.

TO THE EDITOR OF THE ERA.
Sir: – The other evening I was at one of our theatres, and, with many near me, suffered from that pest, the man who talks. In this case it was evidently a young military man. However interesting it might be to him and his companions, a conversation carried on in a tone almost as loud as the actors on stage – indeed, far louder than some of our young actors think fit to adopt – was an unmitigated nuisance to all near him.

Would it not be well that these ill-mannered young "swells" should be given public reproof?

I can remember being in front at the Haymarket the night when some people in the royal box made themselves very objectionable during *His First Champagne*. Mr Compton, after a time, stepped to the front and read the offenders a short and sharp lecture. At the end of the performance Mr Buckstone received a visit from a furious youth, who complained that an actor had been allowed to insult him, "an officer in Her Majesty's service, and the son of the Lord Chamberlain." Mr Buckstone's reply was to the effect that he did not care a damn whose son he was, he should not insult – with impunity – his audience or his actors.

On another occasion I heard the late Charles Mathews at the St. James's Theatre cope with similar bad breeding. Quietly stepping up to the stage box, he took out his watch and looked at it for a few seconds, then, turning most politely, said, "We shall only be ten minutes longer. May the audience listen to us first?"

A story is told of one of the actors of bygone times, George Frederick Cooke. After bearing for some time with the interruptions of a young officer, he went up to him, and effectually quieted him with this: "The King (God bless him), can make any damned fool an ensign, but it is only the Almighty can make an actor."

Yours truly, "A.B. AT THE COFFEE HOUSE."
Aug. 24th, 1896.
29/8/1896

TO THE EDITOR OF THE ERA.

Sir, – I should like to call the attention of the profession and the public generally to a not unusual occurrence to those cabbing it from the Strand district to London Bridge Station. Several times lately my partner and self have been raced by rival cabs at top speed from one end of Southwark Street to the other, chosen, I suppose, on account of its suitability for hard driving. On Sunday night, while with two lady members of our company, the inevitable race took place, ending with a collision, on which both horses bolted, our vehicle only being saved from a tip-up by the rude, though not unwelcome, shock of contact with the railway arch, a fortunate ending to what promised serious, if not fatal, results. To say the ladies were "seriously upset" is to put it feebly, and it is to be hoped the police will take action to prevent a recurrence of such "accidents."

Pros. should make it a rule to suppress the least sign of "sporting instincts" on the part of the "London gondolier."

Yours truly, HY. MAXWELL, Milton and Maxwell Comedy Combination.
Grosvenor Park, S.E., Sept. 1st, 1896.

ON the morning of the 31st ult. two Liverpool detectives apprehended, at Lime Street Station, three young girls, between thirteen and fourteen years of age, who ran away from home at Rhyl with the intention of going on stage during the pantomime season. They each carried parcels containing theatrical costumes and other stage accessories. On the arrival of their parents, who were communicated with, they were conveyed home none the worse for their adventure.

AT King's Heath, Birmingham, on Wednesday, Christopher Parker, travelling showman, was summoned for producing plays without a license at a place of entertainment at Bournbrook. On the evening of the 22nd ult. Police-sergeant Rudnick and Police-constable Mullard visited the show in the High Street, Bournbrook, the building being constructed of wood with a canvas roof, and two caravans forming the front. A large playbill was exposed setting forth the information that a new company would that night perform the great sketch entitled *Sweeney Todd, the Demon Barber; or, the String of Pearls*, with comic songs and a new farce. The officers took front seats, paying 3d. each, and the entertainment immediately began. There were 150 persons present, a large number being children. On being spoken to by the sergeant Parker said that he did not know that he required a licence. Defendant repeated his plea of

ignorance, and said he had given similar entertainments in Birmingham, and had not been interfered with. They did not play from books, but "out of their own heads." They merely gave "tabloos" and "sketches." William Henry Rawlings, Grace Rawlings, John Bishop, Nellie Child, John Warren, and George Fulford, who were charged with being actors in a patent theatre which was not licensed, all said they did not know Mr Parker was not licensed. The Bench fined Parker 20s. and costs, and each of the actors were mulcted in a nominal penalty of 1s., including costs.
5/9/1896

AN opposition is being organised to the proposed new theatre at Hinckley by a Puritanical section of the local population. Already an objection has been handed in, and it is reported that the objectors are preparing a petition praying that the magistrates will exclude from their midst such an evil agency as a theatre. The Hinckleyites are evidently a most ignorant and uneducated lot of bigots.

MR JOHN T. STORER, business-manager for Mr Sidney Turner's *Dorcas* company, has received the following letter from an aspirant to stage distinction, aged seventeen: –

Dear Sir – just a line or two for to ask you if you have enough of girls on the play house, and if not I would like to be taking on. I can dance very well, and hornpipes, wazles, reills. Only wants a little traning. I can sing seuons very well, and is very active on the limbs, and very smart, good apperances, five foot ¼ inch tall, dark eyes, dark hair, tawney skin. Can play the drum and tamberine, as I was on the Royal Theater before it was burnt down. I have a friend of mine can sing very well, so if you have roome for us we would be very thankful, or even for myself it will do. I was very young when I was able to dance. Please write by return of post if I would do or not. Don't disappoint me. I have no more to say at present.

A DUTCH journal gives some extraordinary information respecting the musical tastes of our Royal family. This oracle of Holland gravely declares that the Prince of Wales is seeking to rival the Emperor of Germany as a composer. It even states the kind of music the Prince has composed. Cantatas for choral societies are said to be the Prince's chief aim. But English readers will inquire why we have heard none of them. Just now the provincial festivals are taking place. Why, then, does not the Heir-apparent figure among the composers? This imaginative Dutchman says further that the Duchess of York is remarkably skilful as a banjoist. But the most curious information the Hollander supplies is to the effect that the Royal family give concerts on a large scale, and that the proceeds are devoted to the support of the German bands which may be heard in so many London squares. Dwellers in the Modern Babylon evidently knew nothing of all this. But where did the Dutch chronicler get his information? We fear the bulk of it must be taken with the customary grain of salt.
12/9/1896

PROF. MACCANN'S White Pomeranian has been trained to sing "Annie Rooney" in the key of C. She is accompanied by her master on the English concertina. The canine prima-donna is one of the handsomest of her breed, and won the first prize in her class at the Crystal Palace in 1894.

PERSONS in Spiritual Difficulties may see by appointment, and in strict confidence, helpful friends who are sincere Christians, at 17, Beaumont Street, Marylebone (five minutes' walk from Baker Street Station). There need be no reference to Church or Creed. Certainly there will not be any attempt to obtain money or to proselytise. Everything will be done to lead such inquirers to the living Christ. All letters to be addressed to Rev. W. DARLOW SARJEANT, 17, Beaumont Street, Marylebone, W.
3/10/1896

A WELL-DRESSED man, who gave the name of William Shakespeare, and described himself as a phrenologist, was before Mr Sheil at Westminster Police Court, on Tuesday, charged with being drunk and annoying passengers in an omnibus at King's Road, Chelsea. The prisoner's appearance and make-

up presented an extraordinary resemblance to portraits of the "Immortal Bard," and occasioned considerable amusement in court. Constable 462 B was called to eject him from a 'bus, in consequence of his refusal to pay his fare and annoyance to other passengers. He told the officer not to put hands on him, as he was a descendant of the Bard of Avon. Force had, however, to be employed to remove him from the vehicle. Defendant said he had only been a fortnight in this country from America. Mr Sheil – You ought to have stayed there. You are fined 10s. or seven days. As the half-sovereign was not forthcoming the defendant was removed to the cells.
10/10/1896

A SERGEANT of the Bootle police, when passing, the other day, the Muncaster Theatre, Bootle, where Mr Charles Majilton's *Round the Clock* company was appearing, noticed a poor little waif, in evident suffering, on the theatre step. His legs looked frozen, and one of them was stiff and numb. The officer stopped, and spoke kindly to the lad, but he uttered a cry of pain and rolled over, unable to use his limbs. Mr Dean Majilton, a member of the company, came up, and was touched by the boy's condition, and then Mr Rex Kyburn, who plays old Gewgaw, the miser in the piece, carried the little fellow to his own quarters. As the sufferer had neither shoes nor stockings, Mr Tedd Naylor, who assumes the character of the cabman in the play, offered to give him a pair of the latter. Young Mr Majilton took the boots off the Scotch dummy, one of the *Round the Clock* properties, but they would not fit the lad, so the actor removed his own boots, and placed them on the boy's feet. When warmth had been restored to his limbs, the little fellow was sent home in a tramcar, it having been previously ascertained that he was an orphan.

WANTED, Thirty or Forty Suits of Children's Armour, to Fit Children between the Ages of Nine and Twelve. Also Spears and Shields. Box 6,646, "The Era" Office.
17/10/1896

THE giant Welsh baby, which had been on view at the Panopticon, Cardiff, died on Saturday last. It was to have been at one of the London music halls this week.

WANTED, Lady Boxers. A Grand Boxing Contest will take place on Monday, Oct 26th, at Alvo's Empire Palace, Middlesbrough, between Miss Mitchel and Miss Sulivan. Not under the Marquis of Queensberry's Rules, but under Professor Le Fleur's Rules. These Dogs will Box Three Rounds for a Sack of Spratt's Dog Biscuits. The Winner Promises to Equally Divide the Stakes with Brother and Sister Artists. Educated Dogs, Donkeys and Mule at Liberty Nov 2nd.
24/10/1896

MR F. STONE, manager of *Jane Shore* company, had a novel experience of a gratuitous advertisement in Lancaster. Whilst walking down one of the principal thoroughfares a placard outside a grocer's shop caught his eye. On it was written in chalk, in large letters, "Have you seen the great historical drama *Jane Shore*? Why should Jane Shore eat dry bread, when she could have our best butter at 1s. ½d. per pound?"
7/11/1896

THE repentant playgoer has been revived, this time in Liverpool, where on Monday last, at the Dale Street Police Court, a young girl named Beatrice Rendell, aged seventeen, was brought up on remand charged with stealing jewellery and a prayer-book from her employer, Mr J. Fitzpatrick. On the 3rd inst. the girl went to the Adelphi Theatre, Liverpool, and during the performance was so carried away with emotion caused by the acting of the leading lady that she cast the jewellery and prayer-book from the gallery at the feet of the artist. The articles, however, were missed in the meantime, and the girl was taken into custody for stealing them. It was stated that the articles had been recovered, and the magistrate bound the prisoner over under the First Offenders' Act.

MR CHARLES HAWTREY has sent to Paris for a life-size model of a baby elephant, coloured white, which he intends to place in front of the Comedy Theatre. The figure will contain machinery, which will keep the head and trunk in constant motion, and at night will be lighted up by electricity. It certainly will form a striking advertisement for Mr R.C. Carton's clever piece.*
*A White Elephant.

TO THE EDITOR OF THE ERA.
Sir, – I, like Mr Permane, when ordinary expenses are paid, have to give all, and very often more than all, of my income to the railway to travel my troupe of dogs, and trust you will kindly allow me to ask the association* if, while this good movement, to which all pros. must lend their hearty support, cannot consider this subject and assist the professionals who travel animals by adding a clause to the effect that professional performing dogs, &c., should be allowed to travel by weight. An ordinary passenger is allowed to travel one dog weighing 1cwt. for one dog fare; if 1½ cwt., a fare and a half. Therefore they could travel four dogs, weighing 1cwt. each, for four dog fares; while I, who am travelling every week with a troupe of eight dogs, weighing 4cwt., cages included, have to pay double the amount, and am only carrying exactly the same weight. My journey from St Helens to Bournemouth, Sunday, cost me 25s. for my fare, 25s. grooms, and £2 8s. for dogs. Owing to the train being half-an-hour late arriving in at Euston I lost the connection at Waterloo, and, as they will not book dogs all night at the station, I had, through the railway, the expense of putting up in London.

This will give you some idea of the enormous amount owners of animals travelling each week spend in the year on railways. If the association thinks this worthy of consideration, I shall be only too willing for each of my canine performers to pay their annual subscription, and I should think all owners of troupes would be glad to do the same, as it must be acknowledged without doubt that animals are performers, and should benefit because they are so if possible. Wishing the association a speedy success, Yours truly, FLO EVERETTE.
*The Music Hall Artistes' Railway Association

MR PERCIVAL CRAIG has been in the habit of using donkeys for advertising purposes. Recently he was informed that one of his animals had shown obstinacy, and had established himself for a comfortable nap in the middle of the road, being no doubt "bored" by his duties as a booming medium. With one of his most genial smiles Mr Craig immediately said, "That shows you how depraved even a donkey's nature becomes when connected with the advertising business. He has not had those boards on a week yet, and is already commencing to lie." By the way, Mr Craig, whose photograph in his laughing song is a very successful one, has had two curious applications made to him by enterprising firms in Lancashire, one a firm of dentists for the use of the photograph to advertise their false teeth, and the other a firm of hat manufacturers, requesting Mr Craig to have his laughing photograph taken in one of their big sombrero hats for exportation to South Africa.
28/11/1896

TO THE EDITOR OF THE ERA.
Sir, – With regard to last Saturday night's souvenir of *Teddy's Wives* at the Strand Theatre, it was advertised that the gentlemen of the audience would receive 100 gold-tipped cigarettes, and the ladies a morocco-bound-leather box of sweets; and, instead of this, the ladies got a cardboard box, and the gentlemen an ordinary box of 100 cigarettes, which were *not* gold-tipped. This excited much dissatisfaction, and at some part of the performance the audience called loudly for *no fees* and *gold-tipped cigarettes*. Yours truly, DISGUSTED.
5/12/1896

WANTED, a Few Good Aquatic Pantomimists, Floaters preferred, for Continent. DURRELL, Swimming Baths, King's Road, Chelsea.
12/12/1896

MR AUGUSTE VAN BIENE has been greatly pained by the comments bestowed on his hair and person by the New York critics. On the evening on which he ended his engagement at the American Theatre he took occasion to answer those gentlemen. He said, "I have only one fault to find with my reception here, and that concerns the newspaper critics, who have taken exception to my personal appearance. I came to America as an actor and a musician, not as a professional beauty. Had I posed as the latter I do not believe that your Government would have allowed me to land."
19/12/1896

MR STANLEY COOKE, who plays the elderly relative in *Charley's Aunt*, on tour with Mr Penley's No. 1 company, was presented on the 18th inst., at the Royalty Theatre, Glasgow, with a box of cigars by the students of the Glasgow and West of Scotland Technical College. The presentation was made in a novel manner, the box, which was largely labelled "nuts," being sent down a wire attached to the stage from the gallery. Afterwards Mr Cooke was compelled to make a short speech, and finally the students, numbering about 500, dragged him in a horseless carriage about two miles round the city, and eventually brought him to his hotel.
26/12/1896

8
1897
THE WAY IN WHICH IBSEN ARRANGES HIS HAIR

MR THOMAS W. KEENE, the American actor, once starred in *Virginius* in the early days of his career. As the venture was not largely capitalised no properties were carried by the show, and the local theatres were called upon to furnish everything. On one occasion at a "one night stand" no urn could be found in which to place the ashes of Virginia, so that they could be shown to Virginius at the end of the play. Nothing daunted, the stage-manager seized upon a large water cooler, painted a label over the words "Ice Water", lugged it on in the last scene, and tendered it to the dying Roman father. He had forgotten, however, to let the water out, and as Virginius reached his hand forward to stroke the urn with poetic and paternal tenderness, he accidentally turned the faucet. A small stream of cold water trickled down upon the actor's thinly-covered legs. The "shiverings and shudderings of Virginius in his death moments" were spoken of as "extremely natural" by the local press the next morning.

A NOVEL form of advertising has been adopted by that astute resident-manager, Mr F.C. Sutcliffe, of the Tyne Theatre, Newcastle-upon-Tyne. In one of the large establishments of Grainger Street, in that city, he has on view an excellent wax model of the heroine of Messrs Howard and Wyndham's thirteenth pantomime of *Sleeping Beauty; or, the Mystic Yellow Dwarf*. The figure on view is a full life-sized wax model of the Beauty Allfair, as she appears in the fourth scene. By a mechanical effect the figure is made to appear to breathe in a most natural manner, and is attracting much notice.
9/1/1897

MR REGGIE P. RUTTER met with an unfortunate mishap at the matinée performance of *Sinbad the Sailor* at the Metropole Theatre, Gateshead, last Saturday. In the Diamond Cave scene, Mr Rutter, the Tinbad of the pantomime, makes an entrance on a machine which is supposed to represent a motor-car. At the same time, Sinbad – Miss Hetty Peel – soars aloft in the clutches of the great eagle; but, on this occasion, the machine came in contact with the outspread wings of the property bird, and the motor-car, on which Mr Rutter occupied a somewhat elevated seat, was upset, and the occupant was thrown with considerable violence on the stage. The audience were naturally alarmed at the occurrence, but were quickly reassured when it was found that Mr Rutter had happily escaped with a few bruises and a wrench to one of his ankles, which, however, did not incapacitate him from continuing to play his part.
23/1/1897

THERE was a strange scene at Wallack's Theatre, New York, the other evening. A revival of *Cymbeline* on an elaborate scale by Miss Margaret Mather had been announced, and at eight o'clock a crowded house sat waiting patiently at Wallack's for the curtain to go up. The orchestra had played one, then two, and then a third selection, when the audience grew uneasy and at last began to show it was impatient. At nine o'clock the curtain rose, disclosing an effective scene, with an assorted company of players in the foreground. But in the centre of the stage stood a gentleman in modern evening dress, the stage-manager, who, in a shaky voice, explained that "owing to the non-appearance of the Iachimo there would be no performance".

The missing actor, Mr E.J. Henley, had, it appeared, been arrested at the stage door by a policeman on a charge of obtaining $50 under false pretences of a peculiarly vindictive lady who had advanced him that sum for purposes for services rendered in an intended production of a play called *Adele*, an adaptation of the elder Dumas's *Antony*. This lady, Mrs Hoffman-Martin, had already been exceedingly conspicuous in her native town of San Francisco, where she was some time ago acquitted of poisoning her husband, once Governor of California. Incensed at Mr Henley's careless methods, which had prevented the production of *Adele*, she locked him up one day last week in his dressing-room, and refused to release him until he had given her an order on Miss Mather's manager for the small sum which had been paid him on account of salary. This order was dishonoured, and, now more enraged than ever, Mrs Hoffman-Martin swore to have revenge.

She had it, unmistakably, and, what was more, she had the delight of observing the excitement which her action had caused from a convenient place in the front row of the balcony. Mr Henley was bailed out – too late, however, to allow of the performance of *Cymbeline*. Miss Mather fainted when she heard what had prevented her from keeping faith with the public. She had already been unpleasantly disturbed on the previous evening by the behaviour of one of the leading members of her company, who, during a rehearsal, had gone to sleep in the middle of one of his speeches.

AT the Theatre Royal, Stockton, on Monday night, at the conclusion of the third act of *The King of Crime*, Miss Violet Vivian, who was playing the part of Mére Crochard, responded to a vociferous call from the audience. To avoid the risk of catching fire from the footlights, the space being limited, she had to walk upon the apron of the curtain, which was unexpectedly raised, throwing her headlong on to the shoulders of two of the members of the orchestra. The fall was thus fortunately broken, and what might have proved a fatal accident prevented. Miss Vivian, although suffering from a nervous shock to the system and acute pain, pluckily finished her part. We are pleased to learn that the lady is rapidly recovering from the effects of the accident.
6/2/1897

A PRETTY instance of the care with which every property is supplied in our modern productions is the live lamb which Mr Wilson Barratt carries in his arms on his first appearance as Lemuel, in *The Daughters of Babylon*, at the Lyric Theatre. The animal had evidently been well rehearsed, and submits to the mock surgical operation on its foreleg with great philosophy and calmness.
13/2/1897

THE other afternoon an amusing scene took place in the Court Theatre, Warrington. While *One of the Bravest* was being rehearsed a cow, which was being driven to the saleyard close by, became frightened and dashed through the door of the theatre into the pit. The orchestra beat a hasty retreat under the stage, and the actors also made a precipitate flight. The pit was in darkness, the gas not having been lighted, and it was only by the noise of the struggles of the cow that its whereabouts were discovered. A butcher, aided by several of the theatre officials, attempted to drive the beast out of the building, but their efforts met with little success until the gas was lighted, when the animal was quietly put out, but not before some damage had been done to the seats.

MR JOHN LE HAY has just had an amusing experience. As everyone knows who has visited the Palace, he is a capital ventriloquist, and his antics with a white-haired doll, who is perpetually complaining of

his "rotten cotton gloves", always provoke laughter. One of the doll's readily excused impertinences is to ask some prominent member of the audience to kindly return the sixpence he borrowed. Mr Le Hay was recently giving his entertainment before a large party of the guests of Mr Alfred Rothschild. The usual request was made concerning the sixpence, and to Mr Le Hay's great surprise and delight the coin was a few days after was sent him, but mounted in the form of a pin set with diamonds and rubies. Needless to say that Mr Le Hay values the gift very highly.
6/3/1897

MR ERNEST ROBINSON, otherwise Seymour, a professional vocalist, had furnished apartments in the house of Mrs Elizabeth Parker, of Princess May Road, Stoke Newington, and his landlady alleges that he brought home with him some professional acrobats, who practised their tricks over her furniture. The result was that one chair and one pier glass were broken, and when she asked the defendant to pay for the damage he said he didn't do it, and wouldn't pay for it. The case accordingly came before Mr D'Eyncourt at the North London Police Court on Tuesday. In reply to Mr C.V. Young, who defended, the complainant said that she did not see the defendant do the damage, but she heard the noise of the broken glass, and went up to his room and asked what was the matter. The defendant told her to go and mind her own business. Mr D'Eyncourt advised the complainant to withdraw her summons for "wilful and malicious" damage, and take her action to the county-court. This suggestion, she said, she would act upon.
13/3/1897

MR JOHN WILMOT, a member of Miss Isabel Bateman's company, which appeared last week at the Paisley Theatre, went mad on Saturday night on the stage. The presence of mind of the other artists kept the audience ignorant of what had occurred, and there was no halt in the performance. The police were called in, and Mr Wilmot was examined by a doctor and removed to an asylum. The cause of his mental breakdown is supposed to have been overstudy.

"MARY ANDERSON" is a name which should save even a poor ballet girl from ill-usage. A young woman giving that name, and saying that she had been for years employed at the Pavilion Theatre, Whitechapel, was on Monday, at North London Police Court, complaining of her husband's brutality. He was a glass-beveller, living at Regent's Row. The end of it all was that the husband got seven days' imprisonment, and the wife was granted a separation order, with custody of the child. The dramatic way in which Mary said "I don't want to hurt ya, Bill; but ya have knocked me abaht, and ya knows it," would have made an excellent peg for Mr G.R. Sims or some other emotional writer.
20/3/1897

THE rage at the American schools and colleges for amateur performances of burlesques in which lads appeared made-up and dressed as women has been carried to such extremes that the entertainments have been forbidden at many such establishments. To such a height had the craze grown that a high-school boy was recently discovered wearing side combs in his hair during school hours.
27/3/1897

SIR HENRY IRVING'S extraordinary transformation into Napoleon, in *Madame Sans-Gêne* at the Lyceum Theatre has created much wonder and admiration. Sir Henry is nearly six feet in height, but by increasing the bulk of his figure by means of a cleverly constructed sheath, and by an ingenious abbreviation of small clothes, an optical illusion of shortness of stature is most effectively obtained.
17/4/1897

ONE of the performing elephants belonging to Sanger's Circus, now touring in South Wales, has just accomplished an excessively vigorous vindication of the respect due to his race. Mr Jones, of Cefn

Farm, Llwynhendy, was driving to Llanelly in a trap containing several large cans full of milk, and when passing the elephant the wheels of his conveyance accidentally passed over its toes. The animal, snorting with rage, immediately picked up the trap with its trunk and threw horse, trap, and driver with great force into the hedge. The unfortunate farmer was badly cut on the head, the trap was much damaged, and the milk cans were smashed. The horse was not injured.

TO THE EDITOR OF THE ERA.
Sir, – I am glad to see the activity employed in opposing this bill.* Had I been in England, I should have assisted the opposition to the utmost of my power.

There is a similar law here in Belgium. Consequently, on our arrival at Furnes last Wednesday, the Mayor gave me a copy of the Act. I assured him there was no one in my troupe under the stipulated age. Now, I know of no acrobats or gymnasts who are really Belgians; so I said: "How comes it, man, that you attend to strangers before your own family? Only this morning I saw the most brutal sight I ever saw in my life. Three girls, the eldest not more than fourteen years old, were yoked to a canal barge, large enough to carry the whole of my circus material, for the transport of which I employ one hundred horses. On the barge sat a man smoking, and a woman who was steering, while the children were making steps of about six inches at a time." This was the degrading sight my company all witnessed six kilometres from Furnes. England, like Belgium, has many classes requiring the attention of Parliament before the very few acrobats and gymnasts under eighteen are interfered with. How seldom accidents occur to acrobats and gymnasts, either under or over the stipulated age. Do we not almost weekly hear of serious accidents in the football field, on the cycling track, and the race course? Are youths under the age of eighteen to be debarred from taking part in these sports? If not, why not, as well as acrobats? I can hardly imagine what our acrobatic troupes would be like in a few years if this law should come into force. How many really good artists should we get if they had to be recruited from youths over eighteen years of age?

Let our members of Parliament be shown that the present Bill is as big a mistake as was the Moveable Dwellings' Bill, when it was proved that the showmen were considerably more comfortable than the average middle class.
Yours truly, GEORGE GINNETT.
The proposed Dangerous Performances Bill, which sought to prohibit children under the age of eighteen from being employed as gymnasts and acrobats.

WANTED, Known. £200 Reward for Detection of Confederates. Thought-Reading Extraordinary. Profoundest Mysteries. Spiritualism Exposed by Mystic Irene and Dr Collin. Mephisto Up to Date, Sixteen Midget Arc Lights on the Person. Electrical Venus, 90,000 Volts. MANAGER, 18, Albion Street, Liverpool.
24/4/1897

MR DAVID DE BENSAUDE, the husband of Miss Violet Cameron, died recently at Mogador, Morocco, aged forty-five. It will be remembered that Mrs De Bensaude brought a suit for divorce against her husband, who, according to the evidence of Lord Lonsdale, tried to cut his wife's throat at Porto Bello, and in New York threatened to maim or disfigure her on or off the stage unless she gave him £1,500. We congratulate Mrs De Bensaude upon being rid of a troublesome and distasteful connection.

"WONDERLAND" in Whitechapel has a strong attraction in Sylvester's Grand Circus. A novelty is introduced in the course of the entertainment by Mdlle Rosina, the well-known equestrienne juggler. By an invention of her own, used in connection with Edison's patent, the lumina, her horse and her costume are most brilliantly illuminated by incandescent lights, and, the arena being covered with a black carpet and all lights turned low, the effect is most pleasing. Mdlle Rosina juggles and manipulates different objects while the horse is galloping, the motion of the horse acting as a motor and keeping the electric force up to the power required. There are no wires or batteries brought into use either inside or outside the arena.

Queen's Jubilee. What is to be the Leading Feature in the Show Business? Why, 2 ENORMOUS SERPENTS, 20ft. Long, capable of crushing a bullock. Quite a Show by themselves. Everyone that has seen them is paralysed. With the case, not a heavy one, they weigh 4cwt. Some money could be taken in a large town with these. Over 400 serpents in stock. CROSS, Liverpool.
1/5/1897

MR GEORGE EDWARDES, the energetic manager of the Gaiety and Daly's Theatres, has been seriously indisposed for two or three days past. He dined at a well-known restaurant, and there was served with some peas, which proved to be tinned, and poisonous. Mr Edwardes suffered severely from the effects; but is now, we are glad to say, completely recovered.

WANTED, Address of Mr Tom Beverley, Husband of Miss Jenny Valmore. Very Important. Address, KNOWLES, 22, Halford Street, Leicester.

WANTED. – Those People who are so anxious for my Address, please Note, it is care of Arthur Sharrow, Esq., Solicitor, Leeds, whose Office Boy will promptly Destroy all Undesirable Letters and Telegrams. Signed, TOM BEVERLEY.
8/5/1897

WHAT was nearly a fatal accident happened during the performance of *The Sledge Hammer* by Mr Frank Lindo's company at the Theatre Royal, West Bromwich, on the night of the 14th inst. In the last act there is a terrific fight with sledge hammers between the two villains, played by Messrs Ronald Bayne and Arthur W. Skelton; and in the excitement caused by the enthusiasm of the audience Mr Bayne struck with such force at his opponent as to completely smash the hammer, which rebounded from the anvil, where it fell on his forehead. Luckily, beyond a nasty bruise over the left eye, Mr Bayne is none the worse for the experience.

WANTED, Comedians for Water Pantomime in London, Whit Monday. Must not object to go in Water. Box 7,211, "The Era" Office.
22/5/1897

WANTED, Couple Coloured Gentlemen, and Couple Coloured Ladies, in the neighbourhood of Newcastle, for Lifeboat Tableau. June 12th. Wire, Lowest Terms. WELDON WATTS, Grand Theatre, Newcastle-on-Tyne.
5/6/1897

TO THE EDITOR OF THE ERA.
Sir, – During our visit to the Gaiety Theatre, Hastings, last week, with *The American Belle* company, I found my private basket, which was placed under the stage with the other luggage, had been broken into, and a new evening dress suit stolen; I might also add that a box of cigars was taken from another member of the company's basket. The matter is now in the hands of the "police", but as there is no stage-door keeper, and it is quite possible for anyone to walk in from the street, by inserting this it might serve as a warning to others visiting this theatre. Yours truly, FELIX LEAMAN, Musical Director.

A CORRESPONDENT who signs himself "Attentive Listener" complains that audiences in the Manchester theatres are the most inattentive to be found in the kingdom. When a peaceable citizen, he says, goes to the theatre to enjoy a first-class performance of a popular work, and finds certain parts of the house crowded with young persons of both sexes, whose sole object seems to be to keep everybody from enjoying themselves, it is about time a stop was put to it. He goes on to state that "at one of the theatres, during the progress of one of the most charming of musical comedies, the rude remarks passed by certain members of the audience were disgraceful, and this was especially so when any young lady attempted to get a high note. This seems to be the signal for these ignorant persons to howl and shout, at the top of their voices, like so many savages." This is certainly unpleasant, not only for the listeners, but for the performers.

"ROCCO'S LITTLE CHAMPIONS" are two tiny Yorkshire Terriers, which have been taught to perform no less than thirty-eight tricks. The time occupied in their training has been three years. They go through their act on a specially made miniature fit-up stage. At present they have been appearing at society "At Homes", Lord De Rothschild's amongst the number; but presently they will be seen in the London music halls.
19/6/1897

WANTED, Two Artistic Ventriloquial Figures. Old Lady and Old Gentleman. Must be new and thoroughly good. Something superior; not too grotesque, yet with comical expression on old man's face. Invisible Jaw Openings preferred. Well Dressed and Portable. Must see them before purchasing. Address, VICTOR ANDRE, St George's Hall, Kendal, Westmorland.
26/6/1897

MADAME SARAH BERNHARDT, on Thursday, went to Portsmouth to open her provincial tour there with a matinée of *La Tosca* at the Theatre Royal. It had been arranged that when she reached the town in the forenoon she should cross over to the town hall and visit the Mayor, who awaited Madame Bernhardt surrounded by many of his municipal colleagues, with twenty of the borough magistrates and a body of police. At the station Madame Bernhardt accepted a bouquet of flowers and bowed to the applause of the people. But when she reached the town hall and saw that she was expected to climb a flight of steps, she declined to alight from her carriage, and drove on to her hotel, leaving the local dignitaries astounded by her incivility. She afterwards made a kind of apology to the effect that was ill and "could not climb all those steps". Mr Daniel Mayer and Mr J.W. Boughton, lessee of the Theatre Royal, called upon the Mayor with explanations; but the behaviour of Madame Bernhardt was not what we generally expect from a Parisian lady.

THERE was an unrehearsed incident during the performance of *Mankind* at the Leeds Theatre Royal on Monday night. When Miss Grahame, in the course of the play, told her stage husband that he was going to the dogs, her pretty toy Pomeranian walked on to the stage, to the great amusement of the audience. It had just escaped from the dressing-room, and, of course, made straight for its beloved mistress.
17/7/1897

CONSIDERABLE excitement was caused at the Portsmouth Town Station on Sunday last by the discovery that the chief baggage van of the special train conveying Mr George Edwardes's *Circus Girl* company had caught fire through an over-heated axle. Expensive costumes were hurriedly thrown out on to the platform, and the principal properties were saved. The ladies were very much upset, and Miss Millie Hylton and Miss Lydia Flopp both fainted. Messrs Page, Horace Mills, and Charles Stevens were conspicuous in their activity in saving the property of the company.

MR ARTHUR BERTRAM'S *New Baby* company left Ilfracombe at 7.0 a.m. on Sunday last for Buxton, where they should have arrived the same night, but the journey proved to be a chapter of mishaps. On

arriving at Exeter they found the truck with the baggage had become uncoupled and was left on the line. This necessitated a wait at Exeter while a special engine was sent in search of the missing truck. Eventually the truck was found, and the company proceeded to Birmingham to find the connection to Buxton gone, and they were obliged to put up at the Midland Hotel for the night. On Monday morning the company left Birmingham for Buxton with the runaway truck. On arriving at Derby it was discovered that the truck had caught fire through a heated axle, which necessitated another wait for the properties to be transferred. The company eventually arrived at 2.0 p.m., the journey having taken thirty hours.
14/8/1897

TO THE EDITOR OF THE ERA.
Sir, – After eighteen years on the stage, I fancy my latest experience is one of the best.

I was playing at a fashionable watering place last week in a so-called theatre. We had *one* man to work all the scenery; *one* "orchestra", who seemed a stranger to the piano. This one might expect at a seaside theatre, but here comes the joke:

The gas in the theatre goes low, the *one* man on the stage leaves in a hurry, rushes over to a neighbouring public-house, and asks in a worried voice for *"Six pennorth o' coppers, the heaviest you've got."* Gets them, capers back, and the gas goes up. Result – semi-illumination of the stage. Enquiries prove the fact that the gas-meter is on the penny-in-the-slot system. Has the drama come to the state of being dealt out at a penny a time?
Yours truly, THESPIAN STREET.

JULIAN'S CIRCUS visited Seaton, on the Devon coast, on Monday, and some of the employees went with their horses to the sea, for the purpose of washing them. One of the men rode his horse a considerable distance into the sea, when a school of mackerel at once played around them, and, strange to relate, the man caught one of the mackerel in his hand while on horseback and brought it to shore with him. There were a large number of persons present who witnessed the curious proceeding.
28/8/1897

THE beautiful Opera House at Crouch End has been filled nightly with an audience eager to witness Miss Minnie Palmer and her talented company in the charming comedy-opera *The School Girl*. A large crowd collects to watch Miss Palmer arrive in her motor brougham. She leaves her residence at Buckingham Gate at 6.30, and arrives at the Opera House at 7.15; and does the return journey at an even quicker rate. Miss Palmer is so delighted with this mode of travelling that she has ordered a luxurious motor brougham to be built for her, which she will take with her round the provinces.

AN instance of unconscious humour occurred in the performance of *The Sign of the Cross* at the Grand Theatre, Fulham, on Monday last. In the scene where Nero's myrmidons interrupt the Christians' devotions in the Cestian grove, and massacre the worshippers, one lady super was stabbed three times, more or less fatally. But such was her endurance that she took no manner of notice, beyond a slightly harrowed expression, and continued to chant the hymn comparatively unmoved.

A YOUNG lady recently applied at the Cardiff railway station for a "Sixpenny return ticket to Blackpool." She had been reading the leading lines in a bill issued by the *Sons of the Sea* company, announcing that for sixpence invested in admission to the theatre to see Mr Matt Wilkinson's clever and breezy nautical drama, the investor's amusement and benefit would be equal to a trip to Blackpool. She had not, however, read the context of the bill when she applied for her ticket.

DURING the performance of *A Guilty Mother* at the Regent Theatre, Salford, last week, a man in the audience was so carried away at the end of one of the acts by the villainies of Mortimer that he presented that gentleman with a bottle of "pop". The present was not given in the usual way, but was hurled with so much violence on to the stage that it burst with a report like a pistol, deluging those nearest with its contents. Fortunately the man's aim was not quite as good as his intentions, or a serious accident might have resulted.
4/9/1897

AN accident, happily not of a serious nature, happened at the Widnes Theatre on Tuesday evening, when Mr Robert Barr's company was appearing in *The Football King*. In the fourth act Miss Mildred Eversleigh is on the railway line, and is supposed to rescued by Mr Claude Aymond, just as an express train is coming up. Miss Mildred Eversleigh was in her usual position, but, unfortunately, the rescuer did not accomplish his task, being only a few seconds too late, and the "express train", which weighs about 2cwt., "dashed" up, striking Miss Eversleigh in the side. The lady fainted and had to be carried off, but the accident appears not to have been serious. Some amusement was caused in the front of the house when it was seen that Mr Claude Aymond lifted the lady away with one hand, whilst with the other he pushed the "express" back off the stage.

WHILE Mr Beerbohm Tree's company were playing at the Prince of Wales's Theatre, Birmingham, last week, the ceiling of one of the dressing rooms fell with a crash, burying Miss Frances Ivor and Bullyboy, the *Dancing Girl* dog, beneath nearly a ton of débris. Miss Ivor, who was dressed ready for her entrance on the stage, was seriously hurt, but courageously went on, notwithstanding her highly disordered condition. The lady is now in the doctor's hands.

HANNAH WEBBER, for some years a music-hall artist and male impersonator in the United States, landed on Tuesday at Liverpool, having worked her passage to England, disguised as a cattleman, on the Johnston liner *Templemore*. Miss Webber, discharged from hospital in New York without means, wished to rejoin her relations in Sheffield. Her disguise was not discovered until the vessel was nearing Liverpool, when the woman, who had worked as well as any of the others of the crew, injured herself by lifting a 2cwt. bale of hay. Her fare to Sheffield was paid by the owners of the steamer.
11/9/1897

MISS ELLEN TERRY, while on a driving tour in North Berkshire, and staying at Faringdon, in the Vale of White Horse, came across a milkman in a clean white smock frock. The actress at once became anxious to purchase the smock, but the milkman would not part with it. However, he consented to state where he bought it, and Miss Terry at once went to the shop, and was quickly the owner of a smock frock similar to the one which had taken her fancy.

TO THE EDITOR OF THE ERA.
Dear Sir, – I am pleased that someone has struck a blow against the annoying practice of blackmailing by stage employees. They hold out their hands for tips on Saturday as if it was part of their existence, and Heaven help the artist who fails in giving should he or she be there a second week or come back later on. The system of tipping is a "crying shame", or, as Gus Elen remarks, "a great big shame," and should be put down by all managers.

At one music hall in the East End of London the stage hands sit in a double row, so that as the artist passes out he must run the gauntlet. The stage hands should tip the artist for keeping them in employment, as the artist can do without the stage hands better than they can do without the artist, who could work on a bare stage; where would the employees be then? I am one of the rank-and-file artists, receiving an average salary of £5 weekly, and my weekly expenditure is as follows: –

Weekly Tips: – Stage Manager, 2s. 6d.; gasman, 1s.; scene-shifters, 1s. 6d.; book boy, 1s.; total, 6s. Other weekly expenses: – Agent's com. on £5 salary, 10s.; railway journey (average), 10s.; apartments, 10s.; board, £1; luggage in and out, 5s.; total, £2 15s.

I have put all at lowest possible figure, and what with weeks out and a permanent home to keep up and other expenses very little of the £5 comes to the pocket of,

Yours faithfully, TOM NORMAN (Character Vocalist).

18/9/1897

M. AUGUSTE VAN BIENE, who arrived in New York recently, in speaking of his new play *The Wandering Minstrel*, remarked that the music is made to fit into the action of the play, and is not "dragged in by the hair" as it sometimes the case. He said, "I once saw a raft scene in an English play. One of the shipwrecked party suddenly exclaimed, 'What's that I see floating towards us on the waves?' 'A grand piano,' shouted another. Then the piano was hauled up on to the raft and one of the famishing castaways played a 'Rhapsodie Hongraise' by Liszt. That cured me of 'dragging in music by the hair.'"

THE great fight for $50,000 between Fitzsimmons and Corbett, one of the greatest fights that has ever taken place in America, is to be shown today in all its vivid reality on the stage of the Imperial Theatre, adjoining the Royal Aquarium, London. Every movement of the men from the time of leaving their dressing-rooms to entering the ring, and until the winding-up scene, when Corbett was counted out and carried to his corner, will be shown in every detail. The fight will be exhibited on films measuring over two miles in length, upon which are photographed upwards of 165,000 moving living pictures.

25/9/1897

TO THE EDITOR OF THE ERA.

Sir, – Three times lately I have noticed in the list of letters awaiting actors and actresses in *The Era* post-office the name of Charles Sugden. Each time I have sent a stamped envelope, and, having duly received a letter addressed to Charles Sugden, on opening it I have been disappointed in finding, instead of a flattering offer of an engagement from a wealthy syndicate or a substantial manager, a demand for money – in one case from a lodging-house keeper in Middlesbrough; another from a tailor in Bradford; and another from a baritone singer, who had evidently been engaged by Charles Sugden, and had not been paid his last week's salary.

I have never been in Middlesbrough, and, although I have committed several indiscretions in my life, I have never been guilty of having my clothes made in Bradford, and I certainly have never engaged a baritone singer.

Although it was rather annoying I did not much mind these letters, and I sent them back to their respective writers; but this morning on going to the Vaudeville stage door for my letters, I was informed that two ladies had been waiting for me for two hours, but had gone away disgusted. Whether they had been told to call and see me I could not ascertain.

I was not aware that there was another actor or singer called Charles Sugden, but if there is, I should consider it a great favour if you would publish my letter, in order to say that the gentleman who has not paid his landlady at Middlesbrough, his tailor at Bradford, and has failed to pay a baritone his last week's salary, is not

Yours faithfully, CHARLES SUGDEN.

Vaudeville Theatre, Strand, W.C.

2/10/1897

MR J.M. BARRIE met on Monday last with an accident while directing the rehearsal of a play founded on his book "The Little Minister", at the Haymarket Theatre. He was sitting on a platform when the handrail around it, against which Mr Barrie's chair was leaning, gave way, and he fell backwards into

the orchestra stalls. Medical aid was summoned immediately, and, although Mr Barrie was unconscious for a time, he soon recovered.
9/10/1897

FIVE-POUND notes cleaned by machinery. This is not exactly what Mr Harris, the manager of the Chemical Cleaning Company, advertises to do, but he does undertake to clean from a single handkerchief to 1,000 pairs of tights. Mr Harris tells a good story to prove the thoroughness yet harmlessness of the chemicals used in his cleaning process. An actor sent a suit of clothes to be cleaned. In the pocket was a worn and dirty £5 note. The clothes were placed in a huge centrifugal drum, and after they had been cleaned the note was discovered in the pocket of the coat, but instead of being worn and dirty it was beautifully crisp and clean.
16/10/1897

MR EDWARD LANGTRY, the husband of Mrs Langtry, died at the Cheshire County Lunatic Asylum, at Upton, near Chester, on the night of the 15th inst. On Sunday week Mr Langry was found wandering about the streets of Crewe in a dazed and aimless fashion. Subsequently he was twice escorted off the railway there by the officials. Detective Perkins, finding that Mr Langtry's face was badly bruised, took him to Dr Stainsby, of Crewe. On Monday he was again found in Crewe in a condition which necessitated more serious attention, and he was taken before the justices. Dr Bailey certified that Mr Langtry was not responsible for his actions, and the magistrates ordered his removal to the county asylum. His condition was alarming from the first, and on Tuesday it became extremely critical. During the whole time the asylum authorities were in daily communication with Mr Langtry's friends, and they were duly informed of his death.

At the inquest, which was opened on Monday, Dr Lawrence, medical superintendent of Chester Asylum, stated that Mr Langtry was admitted on Oct. 4th. His mental condition improved towards the third or fourth day. Next day he was rather worse, and on the evening of the 15th he died somewhat suddenly, the cause being effusion of blood on the brain, resulting from injuries. The coroner adjourned the inquiry till Monday next.

The funeral of Mr Langtry took place on Tuesday afternoon, at Chester General Cemetery. The ceremony was very quiet, the chief mourners being Mrs Hollis (sister of the deceased) and her husband, Dr Hollis; Mr Christopher Collins, of Southampton; and Dr Renton, representing the authorities of Chester Asylum. A large crowd assembled, in the hope of seeing Mrs Langtry, but they were disappointed, she being represented only by a beautiful wreath of violets, tied with purple silk ribbon, and bearing the words, "In Remembrance. – LILY LANGTRY." Wreaths were also placed on the coffin by Dr and Mrs Hollis. The Rev E.A. Farrar, of Chester, conducted the service.

Sir George Lewis, on behalf on Mrs Langtry, states with reference to the report that her late husband was found with only a few coppers in his pocket, that Mrs Langtry has, since her separation from her husband, regularly made him an adequate allowance. As soon as she heard of his condition she at once forwarded to the authorities at Chester sufficient money for his immediate wants. The allowance paid by Mrs Langtry was quite irrespective of the income which Mr Langtry derived from his Irish property.

Mr Langtry's chief claim to fame was as the husband of Mrs Langtry. When the tidings reached this country in May last that Mrs Langtry had obtained a divorce from him in California, he was interviewed on the situation. He denied the charge of desertion, and declared that he did not intend to take any action in regard to the decree. Mr Langtry was born in Ireland, stood 5ft. 9in., was a fine specimen of robust manhood, and was fifty years of age. He was well-known on the London Stock Exchange. In 1875, when he married Miss Emilia Charlotte le Breton, the daughter of the late Dean of Jersey, he was in the diplomatic service.

WHILE Gustavus Adolphus Elen was quietly seeing that that the plants in his front garden at Clapham were growing the way they should grow, he was forcibly reminded of the penalty which attaches to popularity. Two young urchins stopped in front of the coster warbler. One said to the other, "Don't-cher-know who him is?" "No," said the other. "Why, it's 'Enery Erving." "No it ain't," said number one, "it's the cove what imitates the dustman."
23/10/1897

A CLOWN in a German circus called La Cirque du Nord, which recently arrived in Christiania, impersonated – or rather caricatured – Ibsen. The dramatist strongly objected to the travestie, but without avail. We dislike personality, especially upon the stage; but the way in which Ibsen arranges his hair certainly offers an almost irresistible temptation to irreverent imitators.

RIOT AT THE SURREY.
ON the 13th inst., at Southwark Police Court, James Salter, fifty, an attendant at the Surrey Theatre, was charged before Mr Slade with assaulting Edward W.S. Rowlands, of 34, Trinity Street, a medical student at Guy's Hospital, by striking him on the right eye at the theatre on Friday evening. Mr Beard appeared for the prisoner.

Dr Howell, house surgeon at Guy's, said the prosecutor was too ill to attend the court. He was admitted to the hospital at half-past twelve a.m., suffering from concussion of the brain, and was bleeding from the mouth, and had a severe black eye. He was in a very serious condition.

Mr Beard said he wished to apply, on behalf of Mr Conquest, proprietor and licensee of the Surrey Theatre, for summonses against the last witness and six medical students. They caused a disgraceful uproar at the theatre, and entirely stopped the performance of the drama *Sporting Life*. They abused the company, threw things on the stage, shouted at the top of their voices, went round the boxes, kissed their hands to ladies in all parts of the building, and altogether carried on a most shocking and disgusting disturbance. Mr Conquest desired to have summonses against them for refusing to quit when requested, and for disorderly conduct; and at the hearing ample evidence would be forthcoming from the actors on the stage and members of the audience as to the outrageous behaviour of the accused persons.

Dr Howell protested that a mistake had been made with regard to his participation in the disturbance. Mr Beard had just taken his name outside the court, but as a matter of fact he was on duty at the accident ward of the hospital at the time of the alleged proceedings at the theatre.

Mr Leonard, acting-manager of the theatre, deposed that the actors complained to him about the conduct of the students, and the attendants informed him that the students endeavoured to force their way into a box occupied by Mr Conquest's daughter and niece. Witness requested the offenders to leave the house, and they refused to do so. There was a big scuffle. The students brandished their walking-sticks, and there was much difficulty in ejecting them.

Mr Nairn (chief clerk) – Do you want summonses for riot?

Mr Beard – Well, the affair amounted to a riot, but I am asking for summonses for disorderly conduct. We only desire to stop this sort of thing being continued. We don't want these students at all in the theatre.

In reply to the magistrate, Mr Leonard said he was not certain whether or not Dr Howell was at the theatre.

Mr Slade expressed his willingness to grant summonses against the students, and remanded the prisoner Salter on £60 bail.
20/11/1897

SIR HENRY IRVING has lost a faithful friend in Fussy, his favourite fox-terrier. Fussy was devoted to his kind master; and heavy must have been the poor dog's heart on one occasion, when, left behind by accident at Southampton on one of Sir Henry's American trips, he had to "tramp it" back to London, where he arrived weary and travel-stained at the stage-door of the Lyceum. Fussy was suffering from various ailments of canine old age. His eyesight was failing, and he was becoming feeble and asthmatic. But Sir Henry was spared the distress which Mr and Mrs D'Oyly Carte had not long ago to endure, of seeing a beloved dog die slowly and painfully. Fussy, blind and infirm, fell down a stage-trap at the Theatre Royal, Manchester, last week, and broke his neck. Sir Henry feels the loss of his favourite very deeply.

A LAUGHABLE incident took place on Monday last at the Coliseum, Leeds, where the Corbett and Fitzsimmons fight was being shown by aid of the Veriscope. During the excitement in the last scene, where Corbett is counted out, the crowd (in the scene), climb into the ring, with the result that the audience could not see anything of what was going on in the ring. A great many of them stood up in the body of the hall to try to see over the heads of the crowd (in the picture) and yelled for them to get down. Then they seemed to realise what they had done, and a peal of laughter rang through the house.

THE one sad and absorbing topic of today is the cruel and dastardly murder of William Terriss by the wretch Prince. Words are unavailing to express the sorrow which we, in common with the whole of the dramatic profession, feel at the loss of the warmly admired and deeply beloved actor who has been cut off in the very prime of his popularity and success. He will be buried at Brompton Cemetery on Tuesday at one o'clock.

To a representative of *The Era* Mr C. St John Denton has communicated some interesting particulars of the man Prince. "Years ago," says Mr Denton, "when I was acting, I was engaged at the Adelphi, and appeared in a small part in *Harbour Lights*. Prince was in the same position. I understood he had been there some time; indeed, we looked upon him as a 'standing dish.' He dressed in the same room as me, and I had ample opportunity of noting his eccentricities. I see he is described as a 'Scotchman.' He had a brogue that you could cut! He was of foreign appearance, and had a cast in one eye. Prince was a weird, secretive creature. He may have been a wastrel of a decent stock. He possessed a great histrionic ambition, and was, in fact, a dressing-room butt. We were always chaffing him about his ability and aspirations, and he was easily angered. He would say, 'I'll startle a few of you some day.' He could not bear to see any young fellow promoted, as he thought, over his head to a better part. He used even then to express animosity to Terriss, and it was common chaff to say, 'No doubt you ought to occupy his position,' for we put it down to the foolish jealousy of a disappointed man. I do not know how long he stayed at the Adelphi; in fact, I have no recollection of seeing him for years. About a month ago he turned up at my office in a deplorable state, and reminded me of our old association. I had him in my private room and talked to him. He told me vaguely he had been with travelling companies, but he was an obvious failure in life. I was sorry for him, and tried to get him employment. In the meantime he has come in and out, as many a poor actor will. I thought I had engaged him as a pantomime chorister, but when the manager saw him he refused to accept him because he had a cast in his eye. Then I told him he might go play Lord Mount Severn, in a small production of *East Lynne* in which I was concerned; but he pleaded that he could not, for want of a frock coat. I had practically pledged myself to find him employment, however humble, this Christmas; for he was in a deplorable state, and one could not help feeling sorry for him. He was in these offices at half-past five on the night of the murder."
18/12/1897

9
1898
THE PATENT PNEUMATIC TAIL

THE *nom de theatre* of Lord Rosslyn when he makes his first appearance as a professional actor at the Court Theatre in Mr Pinero's new play will be Mr James Erskine. As Lord Rosslyn's mother was a Fitzroy, he is a descendant of Charles II and Barbara Villiers, Duchess of Cleveland, a lady who was in her day distinguished for her marked preference for the stage. Lord Rosslyn is not the only descendant of Charles II now on the stage, for Mr Cosmo Gordon, a son of Lord Alexander Gordon Lennox, now acting under the name of Mr Cosmo Stuart at the Comedy, is a descendant of Charles Lennox, Duke of Richmond, the illegitimate son of Charles II and the famous Duchess of Portsmouth.

ON Monday evening, during the second palace scene in the pantomime *Aladdin* at the Elephant and Castle Theatre, the attention of the audience was riveted on the plumed headdress of Miss Fanny Erris, the talented young lady who so dashingly sustains the part of Pekoe, the Vizier's son. For a moment the spectators imagined they were witnessing an electric effect, but almost instantly flames shot a foot or more upwards, and it was seen that the plumes were on fire. A chorus lady standing behind snatched at the plumes and extinguished the flames. Miss Erris was standing beside the highly inflammable wings and cut cloths, and there can be no doubt that the coolness and promptitude displayed by both ladies were the means of averting a serious accident. Miss Erris evinced no alarm, and continued to speak her lines. It appears that in entering the scene the plumes passed between the wire guards of a gas bracket in the wings. The affair was over so quickly that the audience had scarce time to become alarmed, and none left their seats.
1/1/1898

MISS MARIE LOFTUS was the complainant in a case heard at Manchester on the 14th inst., the defendant being a cab proprietor named George Beaumont, whom she charged with using abusive language to her. A second summons charged Beaumont with assaulting Miss Loftus's maid, and a cross-summons was taken out by Beaumont against Mr Ben Brown, Miss Loftus's husband, for assault. Miss Loftus is the principal boy in the pantomime, *Jack and Jill*, now running at the Palace of Varieties, Manchester, and the circumstances which led to the issue of the summons arose through a mistake made by Beaumont on driving her home on New Year's Day after the pantomime. Beaumont had a contract to drive the two sisters home to Brunswick Street from the Palace every night. On New Year's Day he drove up to the stage door. The attendant put Miss Loftus and her maid into the cab, and the driver went to Brunswick Street. They protested, explaining that they had told him Grafton Street, whereupon he became abusive, and pulled the maid out of the cab. Then he drove to the mews. Afterwards Mr Brown went to the mews and tweaked his nose. Beaumont was fined 10s. and costs for using abusive language, and 40s. and costs

for the assault on Miss Bullen (Miss Loftus's maid), and Mr Brown was fined 21s. and costs for assaulting Beaumont.
22/1/1898

WANTED, Known, if Things left at 28A, Great Chapel Street, Westminster, by Winona, Lady Rifle Shot, are not claimed within Seven Days from this Date, they will be Sold to defray Expenses.

MASTER PERCY MARSHALL, the Little Willie of Mr Ben Greet's *East Lynne* company, is lost. He was last seen at the Theatre Royal, Shrewsbury, at a quarter to seven on Wednesday evening. At half-past seven he was missed, and the staff of the theatre searched the town, but without result. A "local" boy was placed in the bed, in the last act, and Willie's dying speeches were spoken in an assumed voice by one of the ladies of the company, to the complete satisfaction of the audience. Up to Friday afternoon no tidings of the child had been obtained.
29/1/1898

Twelve-year-old Percy turned up two days later:
The boy was found outside the hall where the piece was to be played. He was seen there crying by someone connected with the company. For two nights he had been out, and in all probability had had lodgings on the cold ground, for his clothes were stained with mud. He stated that he had not intended to go away; he only took a tricycle with the intention of going for a little ride, but rode so far that he found he was too late to get back to Shrewsbury in time to take his part in the play, and therefore dared not return. He decided to try to get to London to his sister, and ask her to write to the company explaining his escapade. At Trench-crossing he said someone got him to give his tricycle up to the police, so he had then perforce to attempt to return to his company on foot. Some thirty miles the boy had to walk, and his sufferings must have more than sufficiently punished him for his error.

MR ALFRED MOUL has arranged for a series of Cinematograph pictures of the test matches now going on in Australia to be presented at the Alhambra. They will be shown for the first time on Monday, and not only will the views include incidents in the match itself, but also pictures of the popular "Ranji" taking a turn at the practice net.

WANTED, by a Coloured Man of Fine Physique, height 5ft. 10in., Situation in any capacity at Club, Theatre, or Hotel. Speaks English and French, and can give good references. Address, Box 7,956.
5/2/1898

MR MARK SHERIDAN has sent us, and we have forwarded, two guineas to the Music Hall Benevolent Fund and two guineas to the Actors' Benevolent Fund. About two months ago the message-boy of the Theatre Royal, Edinburgh was leading Mr Sheridan's dog out for exercise, when an Irish terrier came along and the pair began to fight. A policeman approached, drew his baton and struck Mr Sheridan's dog, with the result that the animal lost the use of its right eye. The constable expressed his regret, and Mr Sheridan let him off with paying the vet. and giving four guineas to the above funds. The dog – barring his eye – is all right, and made his reappearance on the stage on Monday, when he had a cordial reception from a sympathetic audience.

TWO chorus ladies of D'Oyly Carte's opera company, Miss Alice Erskine and Miss Maud Carey, arrived in Oxford on Saturday evening, after fulfilling an engagement at Basingstoke, and obtained lodgings in Mill Street, Oseney. During the evening they did some shopping, and after returning to their lodgings had supper and went to bed. On Sunday morning Mrs Harris, the landlady, took some tea upstairs. Miss Carey, after receiving the tea, turned toward her companion, whom she thought was asleep, and said, "Wake up, Alice, here's the tea." Miss Erskine did not move, and was found to be dead. At the inquest on Monday Mr A.R. Wilson said the body was well nourished, and death was due to natural causes. Deceased had valvular disease of the heart. The immediate cause of death was syncope from pressure caused by an over-distended stomach from undigested food. The jury returned a verdict accordingly.

AT BOW STREET, on Tuesday, Joseph Callaway, aged sixty-four, was charged with being disorderly. On Monday night the prisoner stood in Villiers Street, Strand, and exclaimed in tragic tones, "Lead on, Macduff, lead on! I'm the only real and genuine Sir Henry Irving. Lead on, Macduff, lead on!" The prisoner had a stick in his hand, and waved it about so energetically that several people narrowly escaped being struck. Police-constable 103 E took him into custody, and as he was being led away he exclaimed, "Lead on, lead on! I'm Sir Henry Irving." The prisoner was fined 7s., in default ten days.

WANTED, it Known, that Henri, the Boss Musical Act, has been doing his usual at Miners' Theatre, Ashington. This is a Turn that can go well anywhere, as it is not made up of Antediluvian Chestnuts and Shelved Melodies and Worm-eaten and Obsolete Instruments. Address, next Week, HENRI MASSEY, Theatre, Seaham Harbour, Durham.

WANTED, to Sell, Fine Fox. Does a whole performance by Himself. Does Fifteen Tricks and Somersaults. Cheap. ATHERTON, 228, Silwood Street, Rotherhithe, London S.E.
12/2/1898

MR CHARLES E. MACHIN wishes to contradict the report that has been circulated that the Avenue Theatre, Sunderland, has been sold to a firm of brewers for a bottling store. The idea, of course, is absurd.

WANTED, for a Medicine Company, Two Sioux American Indians. Address, Box 7,997, care of "The Era" Office.

MANY of our readers will learn with regret of the death of Mdlle Le Grande, who was associated for some years with the celebrated champion ornamental swimmer Professor James Finney, with whom she worked the "halls" and from whom she learned the art. Miss Le Grande married a few years ago Mr F. Galloway, musician, of Bradford, Yorks., but carried on her profession up to a few months ago, her last appearance being at the Aquarium, Scarborough, where she completed a most successful summer's engagement. She died on the 14th inst. from complications following confinement, and was interred at Underhill Cemetery, Bradford, Yorks., on the 16th inst., amidst a large gathering of sorrowing relations and friends.
26/2/1898

ALDERMAN ROBERT GIBSON, Lord Mayor of Manchester, and party occupied the Royal Box at Olympia last Wednesday night, and made a tour through the Palmarium to inspect the freaks and the menagerie. The entire party was in levée dress. At the close of the performance the Lord Mayor and his guests repaired to the Palmarium to preside at the christening of a new arrival to the menagerie. Flora, one of the large camels, had given birth to a little one early in the evening, and it was decided by Mr Bailey to name it "Gibson", in order to commemorate that gentleman's visit. After the Lady Mayoress of Manchester had broken a bottle of wine over the head of the little camel, and formally given it its name, it was suggested that the three little lions, now five weeks old, be supplied with names also.

WANTED, to Sell, Seventeen Sensational Torture Paintings, and one Automatic Machine. Best Offer to save Storage; or Exchange Cinematographe films. All Models sold. FRANCIS, 14, Clonliffe Road, Dublin.
5/3/1898

MR HALLETT'S "IRON MAIDEN" TOUR.
WANTED, for the above, Powerful, Young, Emotional Actress, good Natural Scream essential. Open April 11th, Rehearse Week previously. Address, W.H. HALLETT, 25, Queen's Street, West Bromwich.
19/3/1898

AN amusing incident occurred in Manchester last Monday afternoon. Mr George Robey, who is appearing as Idle Jack in the pantomime of *Dick Whittington* at the Comedy Theatre, has been in the habit of riding from his apartments to the theatre every day either on the back of a young elephant or on a bicycle. On Monday, shortly after 2 o'clock, the animal's keeper, on returning from the theatre, called at the "Oxford Grill" for refreshment. The quadruped coolly followed its keeper into the corridor of the inn, where it was supplied with a pint of ale and two pork pies, which it evidently relished, for it bellowed and thrust forward its trunk, but as no more refreshments were forthcoming the animal was requested to withdraw. But here a difficulty presented itself; the beast could not turn round in the passage in consequence of the inadequate space, and it steadfastly declined to go out backwards, as the outer doorstep was evidently more than the elephant would venture upon. No amount of persuasion proved effective, and a few planks had to be secured and a bridge made from the top step to the pavement. By this means the animal was got out, without the temporary bridge being broken by the weight.
26/3/1898

THE Earl of Rosslyn, at a Masonic function at Burnt Island the other day, in replying for the Provincial Grand Lodge of Fife and Kinross, made some statements connected with his appearance as Lord Arthur Gower, in *Trelawney of the 'Wells'"*, at the Court Theatre. He said: – The strange feeling comes over me that for once in my life I have not got to paint my face and put on strange clothes. I came here with a feeling of sadness and wonder as to how you would all receive me – the feeling of one who has by his own stupidity fallen from a high estate, and who is compelled to earn his own living." It is, indeed, sad to have to earn one's own living, whether by the result of one's own stupidity or from natural causes; but his Lordship really need not be so deeply depressed at being obliged to paint his face and put on strange clothes. Many ladies of the highest rank and fashion do both things, and think nothing of them. For a young man of no particular histrionic ability to earn an acceptable salary on the boards on the strength of his rank, and then to go down into the country and talk of his connections with the drama with sadness and false shame seems to us far from creditable.

ON Easter Monday the Theatre Royal, Maidenhead, was crowded, and all went well until the drama *Streets of London* finished and *Aladdin* was well on its way. Then some foolish person raised a false alarm of "Fire!" and the audience rose *en masse*. Actors and actresses in all descriptions of dress and undress came on the stage and shouted that it was all right, and Mr J.B. Jackson, the manager, begged of the people to keep their seats, assuring them that there was no danger. Meanwhile hundreds had forced their way out, while many ladies were half-led, half-carried away in a fainting condition. But the rush on the left section of the gallery had proved too great a strain, and with a tremendous crash it gave way, carrying with it about 200 people. The shrieks were appalling; men from all parts of the building, including actors from the stage, went to the help of the people who were entangled in the broken woodwork, and to the intense relief of all it was found that no one had received any serious injury. The marvel was how such a crowd could be precipitated to the ground without many broken limbs, and the

only explanation is that all were on their feet when the crash came, and that after the first sway the whole structure settled down straight, simply dropping the people to the floor. Mr Ryder announced from the stage, "Thank God, no one is hurt," and asked the people to disperse quietly. Temporary arrangements have been made for seating the gallery people, and the performances are given as usual. Miss Evelyn has offered a £10 reward for information as to the person who raised the false alarm.
16/4/1898

WANTED, Lady Lion Tamer, or one that has a slight knowledge of such. Address, Box 8,172, "The Era" Office.
23/4/1898

ON Monday last, at the St George's Theatre, Walsall, the crush to see Mr T. Morton Powell's *Greed of Gold* Company was so great that two persons were pushed over the balcony into the pit. They were not injured, although a lady upon whom one fell was severely shaken.
30/4/1898

FROM the States we hear that Mr W.H. Barnes of Sioux City, Iowa, has two enormous elk, weighing 800lb., that can not only be driven in harness, but can make a headlong plunge of 50ft. into a tank of water. They do the act entirely of their own free will, no force of any kind being used.

WANTED, a Person to Share in Purchasing Two Small Elephants, find Half the Cash. The Advertiser will guarantee to Break them in a very short time, and also guarantee to find an Engagement for them that will Pay their entire Cost in Four months, perhaps less. Address, Box 8,218, "The Era" Office.
7/5/1898

A VERY handy little work is "Little's London Pleasure Guide," published by Simpkin, Marshall, and Co. Amongst many other things it contains full information respecting the London and suburban theatres and music halls, mentioning the names of the lessees and business-managers of each house, the hours during which the box-offices are open, the telephone numbers, the prices of the seats, the cab fares from certain well-known points, the nearest stations, the customary attractions at each house, and the omnibuses that pass the doors. A plan of the interior, with the reserved seats numbered, accompanies the notes upon each of the West End theatres, and of several of the larger music halls.

THE members of the Ben Greet company "B" will probably never forget their visit to Hawarden just about a year ago, when Mr and Mrs Gladstone witnessed for a second time *The Sign of the Cross*, the play which impressed the right hon. gentleman so much. This was the last occasion on which he attended any entertainment. Mr Gladstone thanked the company as he left the institute for their charming evening. A peculiar incident happened, which might have put a sudden stop to the proceedings. During the second Nero scene the "fit-up" gave a lurch. Mr Ben Greet was playing the part on the occasion, and saw from his throne Marcus, all the ladies, and the scene shifters clinging on to the poles to prevent the structure from falling upon the illustrious visitors, who, seated in the front row, were fortunately unaware of their narrow escape.

THE following extraordinary letter has been sent to Mr Will Hebden, the well-known descriptive vocalist and comedian: "Sir, – I witnessed your marvellous impersonation of a convict twice this week. Two or three little things you say have convinced me that you, like myself, have had the misfortune to be put away. I should very much like to have a talk with you, as I think I know your face, and that you were away with me. If you are *still on*, I know of a job here in Brighton that is absolutely safe, and would mean cutting up £200 between us. Come down stairs when you get this and talk it over. I will be there at 10.30. – Yours, A. JONES. I have plenty of money, and can afford to stand a bottle. P.S. – Have

you got any tools with you? If not, it doesn't matter, as I have plenty of the latest. *Burn this at once.*"
21/5/1898

AN alarming accident happened about 6.30 on Monday evening to Madame Albina, the Australian lady parachutist, who made an ascent from Wembley Park. The ropes attached to the parachute apparently became entangled, and she lost control over the machine, which descended before she was ready. Madame Albina was precipitated into a tree, and thence fell into the roadway close to the Spotted Dog public house at Willesden Green. She fortunately escaped with a severe shock and slight injury to her side and one of her thumbs.
4/6/1898

MISS LILY HANBURY possesses a "miniature Collie" about the size of a Japanese spaniel. Its name is Wobbles. Another dog of hers is a very large Yorkshire terrier called Mopsie. Mopsie will sit up all night awaiting Miss Hanbury's return, and have hysterics in the front hall on her return. Miss Hanbury had once a Yorkshire terrier named Juju, which formerly belonged to Miss Julia Neilson. She now possesses a small grey kitten named Mr Jelf and a green parrot named Solomon.

AN inquest was held in Sunderland on Friday afternoon upon the body of Rowley Harrison, a well-known Tyneside comedian, who died in the local hospital. Rowley, who for thirty years had been a leading character comedian in the North, made his last appearance on the boards during Easter week. He became depressed in spirits, and at dinner-time on the 29th. ult. his son discovered him in the act of hacking his throat with a razor in front of a looking-glass. He was removed to the hospital, and lingered until this morning. On the last night of his public performance he exclaimed to a fellow-artist, "I hope I will get over the show tonight, because a queer feeling has come over me." The jury found that death was due to injuries self-inflicted during temporary insanity.
11/6/1898

APROPOS of Madame Sarah Bernhardt's matinée of *La Dame Aux Camellias* at the Grand Theatre, Croydon, on Thursday next, Mr Abud tells the following story: – During his last tour with Madame Sarah Bernhardt, the overflowing audience in Glasgow one night were watching Dumas' famous play with palpitating hearts, when suddenly the "divine Sarah" became aware of warning shouts from the front, and simultaneously found herself in the grasp of two strong arms. At first she thought it was Darmont a little overdoing his part, but judge of her horror to find that it was the lime-light man, who, carried away by the scene, had rushed on to protect her, and with his face bathed in tears shouted to her lover's father, "Ye maunna hairm her; she's a guid lassie." Happily Darmont himself came to the rescue, and led the excitable lime-light man to the region of the flies.

WANTED, to Buy, Some Really Funny (Refined) Banjo Songs. Something without the usual Mother-in-law or Pawnshop Verses. H.J. EBSWORTH, 32, Drayton Park, N.
18/6/1898

EPP'S COCAINE. – Cocoa-Nib Extract (Tea-like). – The choicest roasted nibs (broken-up beans) of the natural Cocoa, on being subjected to powerful hydraulic pressure, give forth their excess of oil, leaving for use a finely-flavoured powder – "Cocaine," a product which, when prepared with boiling water, has the consistence of tea, of which it is now, with many, beneficially taking the place. Its active principle, being a gentle nerve stimulant, supplies the needed energy without unduly exciting the system. Sold only in labelled tins. If unable to obtain it of your tradesman, a tin will be sent post-free for nine stamps. James Epps and Co., Ltd., Homeopathic Chemists, London. (ADVT)

WANTED, to Sell, Paintings of Female Boxers, Fat Woman, for Picture Gallery. SMITH, 21, Ossilton Street, King's Cross.
9/7/1898

AT the St John's Schools, Miles Platting, the other night a concert was held. The curate of the parish was present, and intervened when one of a nigger troupe was singing a comic song, remarking that they were on the "shady borderland between virtue and vice." The singer was stopped from completing his song. A little later, when a young lady dressed in male attire came on the stage the curate peremptorily put a stop to the performance. Considerable disturbance was caused in consequence of the audience demanding their money back.

DURING a procession at Lancaster on Tuesday of Sanger's Circus a pair of large ostriches got away. One was immediately captured and put back, but the other eluded capture for the time being and stalked proudly through the town, eventually making a dash for the open country. A stern chase ensued, policemen and civilians mingling in one common cause, and the bird was brought to bay in a back yard. It was at last secured, but not before it had given a startling football display and "downed" three constables.
16/7/1898

IT gives some idea of the overcrowding of the dramatic profession at present to state that more than 200 actresses applied for quite a minor character in Mr G.R. Sims's new drama at the Adelphi.
23/7/1898

MDLLE CHARMION, who has been making a sensation in New York, made her first appearance in England at the Alhambra last Wednesday. A trapeze is suspended above a large net on the stage. Mdlle Charmion enters in smart walking costume, and expresses, in pantomime, her intention of ascending to the trapeze. She is raised to it by the usual means, and then, seating herself on the bar, she deliberately divests herself, in succession, of her skirt, bodice, stays, boots, garters and stockings, and chemise, appearing at last in the flesh-coloured tights and other items of the costume of a female gymnast. She next does some well-known feats on the trapeze and on a horizontal ladder. Whether English audiences will be attracted by the spectacle of a muscular and shapely young lady undressing in public remains to be proved.
6/8/1898

LEONIDAS'S cat and dog circus, now showing at Proctor's Twenty-Third Street Theatre, New York, is said by our American correspondent to be the cleverest collection of canine and feline performers he has ever encountered. It includes St Bernard, Siberian, Dane, setter, collie, and poodle dogs, besides a tiny toy terrier and half-a-dozen cats, whose intelligence is nothing short of marvellous. One of the cats stretches herself between two chairs and forms a hurdle, over which the heaviest dogs jump until the poodle, who plays a circus clown, dislodges the cat, and wins the clown's share of applause. One of the largest dogs then takes the cat's place, and the jumping proceeds until the poodle, undaunted by superior size, upsets the big dog and appropriates more applause. Another of his tricks is to remove a chair from which his trainer has just risen, and walk off the stage with it. The trainer, of course, sits down hard and shakes his fist at the poodle. Then he places some food on the table, and after putting an iron collar around the poodle's neck, and chaining him up, leaves the stage. The poodle immediately slips his collar over his head and makes for the table. He makes away with the food, but leaves some for the cat, who is reposing on a chair. Trotting towards her, he draws her attention to the food on the table, returns to his place and slips the collar over his head again, and looks on with an innocent air when puss is caught *flagrante delicto*. When the trainer fires a pistol at the poodle the animal emits a yell and pretends to be *in extremis*. At this the biggest dog in the collection emerges from the wings on his hind legs dressed as a policeman, and placing his paws on the trainer's shoulders, arrests him and walks him off the stage.

A screamingly funny trick is done by the collie. Dressed in female costume he pushes a small carriage, bearing several of the dogs, across the stage, and slips his skirt in the process, exposing a pair of undergarments of generous cut, from which his tail protrudes in the most mirth-provoking fashion.

The cats are wonderful, too. The dogs go through a steeplechase, with the cats in baskets in their mouths, and take all sorts of liberties with them. One of the cats concludes the performance by climbing a thick rope to the ceiling of the theatre, while the spectators crane their necks and watch his progress. A basket is suspended from the ceiling, and into that the cat leaps. The trainer gives a warning shout, and then fires a pistol, whereat a large parachute of gay colours is released and expanded, and falls over the heads of the orchestra, while the cat lands safely in the hands of the trainer.
13/8/1898

ON Monday night, just as the doors of the Grand Theatre, Glasgow, were about to be thrown open, a loud explosion of gas occurred. It would appear that a gas jet had been left open from Saturday night, and upon the main meter being turned on the gas in the pay-box escaped. William Clayton, aged forty, the ticket-taker, who was carrying a light, opened the pay-box, and a loud explosion resulted. Clayton was dashed against the wall, and badly bruised and burned about the head. He was taken to the infirmary. Another man, named Walter Williams, aged twenty-five, who was standing on the stairs, was also burned about the face. A large plate-glass window was blown out, and some of the glass fell upon John Conway, standing in the street. He was badly cut, and will lose the sight of one eye. He was also removed to the infirmary. A large crowd was waiting to gain an entrance at the time. Subsequently the performance was conducted as usual, there being no indication of either panic or fire.
20/8/1898

MRS POSSEL, the lady who met her death on the 21st ult. by a fall from a cliff at Sorrento, in circumstances which involved the arrest and detention for four days of her husband, Mr Joseph Possel, who shot himself on Wednesday, was a Miss Nellie Beckett, and was a member of the chorus at one of the London theatres.

MARTHA JANE BOSTON, a middle-aged lady of substantial proportions and respectable appearance, who said she belonged to Penzance, was charged at Chester, on Tuesday, with stealing an opera cloak which had been temporarily left on a seat at Chester station on Sunday week by Miss Amy Long, a member of Mr George Edwardes's *Circus Girl* company. Miss Amy Long attended on Tuesday, and identified the cloak, and the prisoner, who said drink was the cause of her delinquency, was committed for trial at the quarter sessions.
27/8/1898

WE regret to record the decease, under very melancholy circumstances, of Mr Scott Fisher, the actor. He had been very ill with consumption for several months, and during the last few weeks the malady had taken a very serious turn, although he had the very best medical attendance that could be obtained. The unfortunate gentleman gradually grew weaker and weaker, and the doctors at length found it necessary to break the news to him that his recovery was practically hopeless. The news, it is understood, very greatly affected the unfortunate gentleman, and on several occasions he lost his reason for short intervals. A week ago, however, he was somewhat better, but complained to his mother, who, with a trained nurse, had been staying with him night and day, that he continually suffered from a choking sensation. "Sometimes," he said, "I feel it is impossible to breathe. I cannot stand the horrible sensation much longer, and if I have any more attacks I shall certainly end it all." He made a similar remark to one of the doctors who was attending him, and upon this the strictest orders were given to Mrs

Scott Fisher and the nurse to watch the deceased by day and by night. This they did, taking great care that no opportunity should be given to Mr Scott Fisher to make away with himself. Mrs Scott Fisher found a revolver in her son's room, and this she took away and locked up in a drawer in her bedroom. On Wednesday morning the deceased was somewhat delirious, but in the evening he appeared considerably better, although he complained once of the choking sensation which he had previously described. He somehow managed to elude the vigilance of his mother, and slipping out of his room in the evening he got possession of the revolver, which he hid in his pocket. He waited until Mrs Scott Fisher and Mrs Wilkinson were in the room with him, and in their presence shot himself, and death was almost instantaneous. Mrs Scott Fisher was terribly shocked, and was yesterday lying almost prostrated with grief. She has been the recipient of many marks of condolence from members of the theatrical profession, among whom Mr Scott Fisher was a great favourite. The funeral will take place on Monday, at Chiswick, at half-past two.
Fisher was twenty-seven years old and a member of the D'Oyly Carte company.
3/9/1898

WANTED, to Sell, Genuine Novelty, Röntgen X Ray. Seeing Bones in the Hand or anything. Living for Life for anyone. Taking Money in the Street Nightly. Must be Sold. A Bargain. Would make Grand Side Show. Particulars, ELLIS, 1, De Beavoir Road, N.
17/9/1898

THE following appeared a few weeks ago in a prominent American newspaper: – "Mr Leonard Boyne in the Police Court. – The Runaway Horse and the Damage it did. – A Building Devastated. – Gunpowder and Sweetmeats. – Last week at the Old Bailey, London, England, Mr Leonard Boyne, the well-known actor and proprietor of a play called *Sporting Life*, surrendered himself to stand trial for breaking two large panes of plate glass and breaking down the partition between a sweetstuff shop and an emporium for the disposal and distribution of the savoury fried fish and chips. It appeared from the evidence that a two-horse dray, hired by the prisoner, was standing at the stage-door of the Theatre Royal, Manchester, when the sudden discharge of a number of cannon and guns used in the drama of *Sporting Life*, frightened the horse, which bolted down Well Street and did the damage referred to. The jury found Mr Boyne guilty, and he was fined $250. We should advise Mr Boyne to be more sparing of his gunpowder in future." All this reads very nicely; but there is no Well Street near the Theatre Royal, Manchester; there are no cannons or guns used in *Sporting Life*, and no gunpowder; and last, but not least, had any accident happened, the case would have been tried in Manchester, and not at the Old Bailey.
24/9/1898

VIOLET, the youngest daughter of Mr J.B. Elliott, made her debut as a bicycle rider at the Empire Theatre, Blackpool, on Wednesday, September 21st, 1898. Her age is two years and ten months.
1/10/1898

MISS ELLEN TERRY, being at Birmingham last week, took an opportunity of paying a visit to Coventry on Saturday, her object being to discover if possible her birthplace in that city. In Market Street there are two houses, and the occupant of each asserts that his residence is the place where the distinguished actress first saw the light. They are both tradesmen, and one, Mr Judkins, a butcher, has up a brass plate inscribed, "The birthplace of Miss Ellen Terry;" while the other, Mr Needle, haberdasher, across the road, exhibits the inscription, "The original birthplace of Miss Ellen Terry." The well-known actress remained for some time in Mr Needle's shop, and asked several questions about the history of the dwellings in Market Street. The news that Miss Terry was inside the house spread rapidly, and when she reappeared the crowd which had assembled gave her a hearty cheer. Fifty years ago there was a theatrical lodging-house in Market Street, and Miss Terry's father was playing at the old theatre in Smithford Street at the time of her birth, in 1848. There lives in Coventry today the old lady who was

Miss Terry's casual nurse. Miss Terry has long contemplated the visit to Coventry which she made on Saturday, for, writing to a citizen in November, 1892, she said, "I think of running down to see her (the old lady) some day, and when I visit Coventry I shall look for the registration of my birth." As a matter of fact, however, no entry of the event can be found in the local registers.

MR CHARLES COBURN'S latest acquisitions are from the pen of Mr George Thorn, author of "Should Husbands Work?" They are "When I Wants to See Myself I Looks at Him" and "The Joyful Infant." In the latter item the comedian will appear as a baby, woollen boots and all, who has escaped the Vaccination Act. The melodies are by Mr Coburn himself.
8/10/1898

H.R.H. PRINCE NICHOLAS OF GREECE is evidently desirous of achieving fame as a dramatic adaptor. He has sought permission of Mr W.S. Penley to translate *Charley's Aunt* into modern Greek.

MISS MAUD ROUDES, who was one of those saved from the wreck of the *Mohegan* in Falmouth Bay on the 14th inst., is an American artiste, who made her debut at the Royal Opera, Covent Garden, as Gerhilde, in *Die Walküre*, in June, 1897. Later in the year she appeared there with the Carl Rosa company, taking the part of Venus, in *Tannhäuser*. At Covent Garden last season she undertook the roles of Mercedes, in *Carmen*; Lady Clarence, in *Henry VIII*; and Flora, in *La Traviata*. Miss Roudès's mother, Mrs Graudin, lost her life by the disaster. Miss Roudès was placed, with her mother and other passengers, in a ship's boat. In lowering, the boat overturned. Miss Roudès clung to the seat, and kept her head above water and below the bottom of the boat. She remained in this dreadful position for about an hour before she was rescued by the lifeboat. Mrs Graudin had one foot nearly wrenched off in being removed from the boat, and soon after being landed she expired.

THE chief sensation in Paris variety circles just at the present moment is the entertainment given by Miss Lona Barrison, one of the Sisters Barrison, who were seen a year or two since at the London Alhambra. Miss Lona comes on to the stage of Olympia in what may be called masher evening dress, with opera hat and eye-glass. While singing she divests herself of coat, waistcoat, collar, and tie, and by a clever device slips her trousers. We cannot say with the song, "There she stands and waves her hands," but while running about in a shirt just reaching her knees her affectation of shy reserve fetches the audience immensely. She eventually gets rid of the garment, the tail of which is embroidered with a large coronet and monogram, and after taking off her hat stands revealed in pink tights and scanty corsage. While in this undress she goes through a clever equestrian act, in which she rides astride. We wonder if we shall see Miss Barrison in London.
22/10/1898

"QUEEN'S EVIDENCE" still retains a firm hold on popularity, and the business done by Mr Stewart Cleveland's company on tour is excellent. The walking of the blind heroine towards the open lock gate raises the audience to a pitch of great excitement, and shouts of "Don't go!" "For God's sake turn back!" from the women in the audience, are mingled with hisses and volleys of execration from the men.

MISS ADA WARD, at a recent Salvationist meeting at the Drill Hall, Colchester, gave an account of her "awful and terrible past." She actually had a play written for her, went to Paris, spent "enormous" sums of money on her dresses, and contemplated making a long tour in the provinces. She is now living in a quiet little cottage, with a black pug dog, a parrot that cannot talk, and a canary that was given to her in America, in a bouquet, on her benefit night.
29/10/1898

THERE are some marvellous stage effects and sensational acts in *The Klondyke Nugget*, which goes on tour the first week of December. In one act of Mr C.F. Cody's drama the villain saws a wooden bridge through, and when the hero rides madly up the pass on horseback the bridge breaks and precipitates animal and rider into a deep ravine. The horse ridden is specially trained for the business. Another set is worked by a double stage. The top scene represents a snow-capped mountain, and underneath is a gold mine, with all the grimy miners hard at work digging out the nuggets. The play, which is humorous as well as dramatic, is in five acts and seven scenes, and a number of genuine Indians and miners will appear. Mr C.F. Cody is now fast booking this tour.
5/11/1898

THE matinée hat question took quite a serious turn last Saturday morning at the Lyceum Theatre, when *Pelleas and Melisande* was performed, and when, it must be confessed, the ladies' hats and bonnets took a most aggressively outrageous form of structure. Taking time by the forelock, a pittite anticipated the trouble to come, and before the curtain rose made a little speech of request and reproof to the fashionable folk in the stalls. Several ladies, and there were many of high degree present, acceded to the desire of the people in the pit, though here and there a few refused to remove even a bonnet pin. A lady nearby suggested to us that for some to remove their hats meant a temporary loss of golden locks and curls.
12/11/1898

AFTER Mr Jesse Colling's speech at the meeting of the Classical Drama Committee at the Council House, Birmingham, on Monday, Mr C. Harding read the following letter, which Mr Benson had received from a resident in the city: "Dear Sir, – An elderly lady, who takes a great interest in your work, will attend your matinée performance tomorrow – that being the only day she is able to come. As it is very desirable that she should be in no way depressed, I write to request you to allow all persons who have been killed in the play to appear before the curtain, in order to remove all unpleasant impressions from her mind." The reading of the letter elicited loud laughter.
19/11/1898

A MAN appeared at Newport Police Court on Monday last, at the close of the magisterial business, and made a curious application to the Mayor and other justices. He said that he threw two shillings on the stage at the local Lyceum last week during the performance of *The Silver King*, and he was afterwards "chucked" out. The man, it seemed, had been overcome by the distress of Nellie Denver in the eviction scene, and threw the money on stage out of commiseration; and the attendants, mistaking his intention, turned him out of the theatre. He now sought to have the cash back. The magistrates' clerk recommended the applicant to see the police about the matter.

A NEW matinée hat has been invented, and it is to be hoped it will be generally worn. The hat illustrated is composed of black "crin" with jet embroidered design, and is arranged in becoming draped fashion. A very handsome "fantaisie" is lightly, but securely, fixed on the left front in the most approved method. When the wearer reaches her seat in the theatre she has merely to raise her hand and remove the aigrette, which she can use as a fan during the performance, and at the close slip the feathers into the hat as before.
26/11/1898

THE Wallenda Sisters, who have been very favourably received at the Alhambra, are three comely and well-shaped ladies, who appear in a tank placed upon the stage, and brilliantly illuminated. They write on slates, eat and drink underwater, besides swimming very skilfully, their movements being particularly easy and graceful. A sensational part of their performance is a long dive, which is very prettily arranged. After they have been submerged for some time in reclining attitudes, a sister rises and then descends,

and appears to awaken one of her companions, who soon stands up, and brings her head above the surface. The last of the "sleepers" is not so easily aroused, but eventually she, too, assumes an erect position, the length of her submersion* evoking hearty applause. The Wallenda sisters supply a pretty and popular turn, and are already great favourites at the Alhambra.
*This was later timed at four minutes and nine seconds.

WANTED, to Inform Old Friends, Through the Heavy Fall of Snow, my Theatre was Crushed to the Ground, and now Lies in a Heap of Ruins. Would be Most Happy to Hear From a Few Sympathising Friends. JOE HODSON, Hebden Bridge, Yorkshire.
3/12/1898

PARISIAN playgoers had presented to them at the Palais-Royal Theatre on Tuesday last one of the most indecent farces ever submitted to the visitors to that very lively house. A double-barrelled adultery supplies the plot of *Chéri!* and leads up to a scene in which three men scamper about in their night-shirts before ladies in a burlesque of Miss Loie Fuller's dance. But the most disgusting details are in the second act. A chambermaid named Felice, who has been criminally assaulted by a savage at a fair, has thus become quite dumb, and the doctors have declared that a similar fright can alone restore to her the power of speech. An old rake leads the girl out of the room which is the scene of the third act, and a few minutes afterwards she returns, throws open the door, and cries loudly, "Dinner is served!" The Parisian public is delighted with the refined and modest humours of *Chéri!*

AN amusing incident recently occurred at the Theatre Royal, Halifax, during the performance of *The Penalty of Crime*. In the first act the villain seized his opportunity to rob a gentleman with whom he was staying of a large sum of money which was kept in a safe. The lights were lowered and the thief entered, exclaiming, "Now is my time!" when a voice from the "gods", evidently that of an elderly female, shouted out in angry tones, "I shall tell him if tha does." The audience laughed heartily, and it was several minutes before the uproar subsided.
17/12/1898

M. FRANCISQUE SARCEY, writing in the Paris *Figaro*, approves of the Duke of Manchester's intention to go on the stage. "Why," says Sarcey, "should not a Duke who has spent or lost his fortune work like other people who have never had a fortune? There is no reason why the Duke of Manchester should not become an actor of genius. Why should not the Duke receive promotion and become a king, by right of genius, like Garrick?" Such a result is, of course, possible; but judging by the Duke's performance at the Strand matinée on Monday, it is "a long way off."
24/12/1898

MISS EVA LYNNE, the young lady who is now playing the part of the Princess in the Adelphi pantomime, *Dick Whittington*, some short time ago, accompanied by her father and sister, made the ascent of Mount Etna, a far higher and more dangerous volcanic mountain than Vesuvius. It took two days and a night to get to the top and back. Part of the journey was accomplished on mules, but the last 200 yards, through the streams of lava, had to be done on foot. The mouth of the crater was reached by crawling on hands and knees. The people of Catania, whence the party started, never expected to see the "mad English girls" back alive, for not more than half-a-dozen ladies have ever attempted the ascent of Etna beyond Mount Rosa. Miss Eva Lynne has also travelled extensively in Spain, Italy, and has visited India and the Soudan.

WANTED, Known, Anyone Using my Patent Pneumatic Tail on any animal costume will be prosecuted to the full extent of the law. (Signed) W.G. HURST.   *31/12/1898*

10
1899
MR SHAW'S EXTRAORDINARY JOCULARITY

THE REV J. DUNK, a Wesleyan minister at Wolverhampton, in his sermon last Sunday, uttered the sentence, "You have seen the clown in a pantomime on the boards of a theatre." One of the congregation shouted out "I have not been to the theatre." The preacher begged the speaker's pardon, and the latter explained, "You have referred to this matter at two services, or I would not have mentioned it." A little later the preacher said, "You all know what a clown is?" The former interrupter then excitedly called out that he did not know what a clown was; that he objected to the word; and that Mr Dunk, as a Wesleyan minister, had no right to stand in a Wesleyan pulpit and assume that members of the congregation went to the theatre.

HERCAT was engaged on Wednesday evening to give his conjuring and ventriloquial entertainment at Highclere Castle before the Earl and Countess of Carnarvon and a large party of guests, which included H.R.H. Prince Duleep Singh. Hercat's pianist having missed the train, His Royal Highness volunteered to play Hercat's music, and proved himself to be an excellent pianist and accompanist.
7/1/1899

ON Saturday night last in the course of the concluding scene of *The Belle of New York* at the Cardiff Theatre Royal Mr Lionel E. Lawrence, who was playing Ichabod Bronson, suddenly stopped in the middle of one of his songs and said, "Ladies and gentlemen, I refuse to go on with my song, as there is a man right in front of me who has been reading a newspaper all the evening. It is most disgusting, and I must ask you to excuse me from singing any more." The gentleman continued to peruse his paper, and said he had a perfect right to read a newspaper if he liked, and would not be stopped by anyone. He continued to do so, and the performance went on without any further incident.
14/1/1899

AT the Grand Theatre, Fulham, after the interval between the parts of the pantomime, Madame De Dio gives her dance lumineuse, in which various devices, representing flowers, butterflies, and portraits, are reflected. She is comely and shapely, and scores a success, especially in the fire dance, as "She", which terminates with her appearance as a heap of glowing ashes.
21/1/1899

VISCOUNT HINTON, of organ-grinding notoriety, had some experience of the stage. He married when not yet twenty, an actress named Sheppy. He eventually got an engagement as "responsible utility" at the Garrick Theatre, Leman Street, Whitechapel, under the management of Mr Smythe and Miss Ellington, and appeared as Sweeney Todd, in *The Fleet Street Barber*, at a salary of 25s. a week, under the stage name of Willie Deane. For four nights he played with success, but on the fifth he fell down a stage trap and was so much injured that for three months he could not eat anything, but was fed with a

spoon. After his mother's death the Viscount lived with his wife near Kennington Lane, she fulfilling an engagement at the South London Music Hall. In 1872 some dowagers raised for him a capital of £100, and with that he started a theatrical company, which he named Lord Hinton's Burlesque and Comedy Company. It consisted of eight players, himself and his wife included, with an orchestra of three – a cornet, pianist and a fiddler. He opened at the Public Hall, Bishops Stortford, with *The Haunted House* and the burlesque of *Beauty and the Beast*. On the first night the curtain rose to an audience of seven. Sanger's circus was at Bishops Stortford at the time, and on the Friday a storm blew down the tent. Mr George Sanger asked Lord Hinton if his troupe might have orders for the play, and every performer from the circus assembled in the hall. That night the box-office took 3s. 6d., and at the end of the week the gross receipts amounted to £1 17s. Lord Hinton, however, was no "bogus manager". He paid a fortnight's salary all round, settled for the rent of the hall, sold his scenery for £5, and came back to town. Mr Horace Wigan, who was then managing the St James's Theatre, engaged Lord Hinton, at 35s. a week, to play Maurice, in *All For Her*, in which the leading part was sustained by John Clayton. Lord Hinton's stage name was Harry Dormer. After playing four nights at the St James's, Mr Wigan decided to close the theatre. When shortly after Mr Wigan reopened the Princess's with *All For Her*, he once more cast "Harry Dormer" for the part of Maurice. The drama ran for three weeks, and Lord Hinton played in it every night.
28/1/1899

THE authorities at Peterborough Infirmary have under their care a remarkable case. An itinerant conjurer was admitted to that institution in great agony. Part of his entertainment included the swallowing of pebbles ranging in size from a pigeon's egg downwards. The man said he had done this for years without inconvenience, but he has found himself in difficulties. Under skilful treatment, some sixty stones have been recovered, weighing altogether twenty-four ounces. It is expected that the man will be well enough to leave the hospital in a day or two.
18/2/1899

WANTED, Lion Tamer, Male or Female, Black or White. Write or wire, Biddalls Brothers' Menagerie, Skating Rink, Southampton.
25/2/1899

THEATRICAL managers have queer experiences of persons with an ambition for the dramatic art. A lady recently made a curious application to Mr F.W. Purcell, the proprietor of the Alexandra Theatre. The letter is written on fancy notepaper, on which are depicted, in gay colours, roses and other pretty flowers, and runs as follows: – "Dear Sir, having sought the advice of a phrenologist, I was told to make an application for to enter as an actress. I should be very much obliged to you if you could engage me at the Alexandra Theatre. If any particulars are required I should be very pleased to answer them."

MRS PATRICK CAMPBELL had a rather trying ordeal to go through on the first night of her appearance at the Grand Theatre, Birmingham, this week. Whether it was that the audience had not got the pantomime out of their minds or not, it is difficult to say. Certainly they did their best to regard *The Second Mrs Tanqueray* as a comedy. Whenever they could construe Mr Pinero's pungent philosophy into an excuse for merriment they did so. Probably for the first time on the stage the relations of Paula and Ellean were found to be a fit subject for laughter. But Mrs Campbell sternly kept on her way, bating no jot of her earnestness. Her reward came. As the passion and the grim tragedy of the play grew in intensity, a quiet fell on the house. The thoughtless were awed to silence, and the last two acts were played before as well-behaved a house as could be imagined. It was the conquest of the Philistines by sheer force of genius. But the battle was a hard one.

WANTED, Known. Burns wears a 6½ Hat, and underneath there is a Brain that Concocts the Most Wonderful Clog Dancing ever seen. Other champions note.

WANTED, to Sell, a Pair of Boxing Cats. EMSLEY, 18, Chester Street, Kennington Road, S.E. Clarke Laspalle please write.
24/3/1899

AT the Theatre Royal, Glasgow, on Wednesday night, a curious incident occurred. During the performance of *The Broken Melody*, while M. Auguste Van Biene was in the theatre, his old friend, Sandow, who was appearing at the local Empire, came to pay him a visit in his dressing-room. He brought with him his magnificent boarhound, weighing over 15st., who squatted very comfortably in the corner of the dressing-room. Sandow then went round to the front of the house to hear Van Biene play one of his 'cello solos. In due course M. Van Biene's cue was given, and his valet went to his dressing-room to call him, but the huge animal planted himself across the door and defied him to leave the room. The result was a long stage wait, when suddenly Sandow, realising what had happened, rushed round to release M. Van Biene from the predicament in which he was placed. It then transpired that the animal, although the most docile creature in the world, had been trained not to allow anyone to leave the room during his master's absence.

MR JOHN DOUGLASS at half-past two o'clock on Wednesday last became aware that Miss Olive Stettith could not appear at the Surrey Theatre in the role she had played on Monday and Tuesday in *Known to the Police*. The drama having only been represented for two nights, no understudies had been prepared. After numerous cab journeys Miss Stella Leigh, who had played another part in the piece, was found witnessing a matinée performance. By this time it was past four o'clock. A hurried run through of lines and business on the Surrey stage occupied until 5.30, and at a quarter to eight Miss Leigh was on the stage, and went through the part admirably, never once requiring the assistance of the prompter. She was heartily applauded by the audience and warmly congratulated by the company and management.

THE Hammersmith Palace of Varieties, in King Street West, was the scene of an unfortunate incident about ten o'clock on Saturday night. Mr Andrew Wraight was giving an exhibition with a cinematograph, and was throwing a picture of the manager of the hall upon the stage, when the whole of the films became ignited, and there was an instant and startling flare. The exhibitor was enclosed in a box, six feet by four, lined with iron, in accordance with the regulations of the London County Council, while behind him stood a fireman on duty, with hose attached to a hydrant, and wet blankets ready in view of any emergency. Mr Wraight, who was working with one assistant, was enveloped in flames without a moment's notice, but he jumped out of the box into the wet blankets, and the flames which had ignited his clothes were at once subdued. At the same time the fireman turned the hydrant on, and there was an immediate stream of water, which was brought to bear on to the blazing cinematograph apparatus, and, almost before the audience had realised that there was anything wrong, the fire was extinguished. The operator, however, was frightfully burned on the face and hands, and was at once removed to the West London Hospital.
11/3/1899

"WOMAN AND WINE."
TO THE EDITOR OF THE ERA.
Sir, – The following paragraph appeared in the Sunday Chronicle, Feb. 26th, 1899:
"*The Great Ruby* will be played at the Princess's Theatre but a few more nights. On Wednesday, March 8th, *Woman and Wine* will be installed in this theatre. The play achieved a perfectly phenomenal success at the Pavilion Theatre last year. There have been many schemes for its reproduction at the West-end,

but they have all come to naught. It is quite an ordinary melodrama, distinguished by a very realistic fight with daggers between two women stripped to the waist. While we were all reading with interest of the scandal promoted in America by Mr Alfred Aaron's production of a playlet entitled *An Affair of Honour*, and in particular by Miss Cissie Loftus's indignant refusal to appear on a stage so "degraded", it seems to escape notice that the duel which gave rise to the trouble was an almost exact reproduction of that done in *Woman and Wine* without provoking any particular outcry of moral reprobation. There is, in fact, hardly a penny-in-the-slot Cinematograph which does not reproduce the offending incident."

In reply to this I addressed the letter below to the editor of that paper. Your insertion of the paragraph and my reply thereto in the columns of your valuable journal will be esteemed a favour by

Yours faithfully, BEATRICE HOMER.

A Woman of No Importance company, Her Majesty's Theatre, Blackpool, March 8th, 1898.

TO THE EDITOR OF THE SUNDAY CHRONICLE.

Sir, – My attention having been directed to a paragraph by 'Masque', under the heading of 'Plays and Players' in your issue of Sunday, Feb. 26th, I feel it incumbent on me to correct such a glaring mis-statement as is contained therein. As the original La Colombe in the provinces, one of the women mentioned, I give the most indignant denial to this statement, which I can only characterise as a glaring untruth. The artists taking part in the fight referred to were Miss Edith Blande and myself; our dresses consisting of dark skirts and corsets, over which were worn petticoat bodices, which, as a matter of fact, displayed less bust than is usually exposed when wearing ordinary evening dress. For verification of this I refer the writer to the Mutoscope, or, as he designates it, the 'penny-in-the-slot Cinematograph', which, from his paragraph, reproduces the offending incident; and I take most serious exception to his assertion that the artists mentioned were 'stripped to the waist'. Your correspondent's assertion, if uncontradicted, would do an incalculable amount of harm to an honourable profession, already much maligned and misrepresented, and it is questionable if the publication of such a statement is not libellous, as the inference is that any artist appearing on the stage in the semi-nude condition suggested would be entirely void of all womanly modesty.

Yours faithfully, BEATRICE HOMER.

A Woman of No Importance *company, Athenaeum, Lancaster, March 2nd, 1899.*

THE Countess Russell* made her debut at the Theatre Royal, Plymouth, on Monday as Winifred Grey, in *A Runaway Girl*. Lady Scott, the mother of the Countess, and Mrs Dick Russell, her sister, were present. When the lady came on a burst of cheering greeted her. In a sweet voice she sang "The Sly Cigarette", and warm applause followed. The song "I'm Only a Poor Little Singing Girl" and the duet with Guy Stanley, "There's No One in the World Like You", were vociferously redemanded, and the Countess subsequently did a little dance. Quite boldly she sang the topical song, "When the Little Pigs Begin to Fly", introducing quaint little gestures and touches of mimicry that suggested talent. When she becomes more conversant with the details of make-up and stage deportment she may do well.

**The Countess, born Mary Edith Scott, was the wife of the 2nd Earl Russell and sister-in-law of the philosopher Bertrand Russell.*

18/3/1899

NO better proof could be given of the extraordinary changes in our climate that the fact that the majority of the male members of Mr George Edwardes's *A Runaway Girl* company were bathing in the sea every morning last week at 8.30 a.m. at Plymouth. They bathed on Sunday morning, and then left for Birmingham, and woke up in the morning to find three or four inches of snow on the ground.

WANTED, to Sell, Healthy Seal. Wonderful Performer. Guaranteed Quiet. Two Paintings, Tank, Accessories. Price £8 lot. Address, Mr FISH, Post-office, Liverpool.

25/3/1899

MISS ELLEN TERRY was the victim of an unpleasant little incident in the course of the performance of *Robespierre* at the Lyceum Theatre last Saturday. In her scene with Sir Henry Irving in the fourth act a creaky noise, like that of an ill-greased pulley, was heard continuously throughout the dialogue between Robespierre and Clarisse du Malluçon. Miss Terry was evidently much irritated. She looked appealingly at the wings, but in vain; the hideous sound still went on; and finally Miss Terry's nerves were so wrought upon that she had to put her fingers into her ears. We sympathised keenly with the actress in the exquisite annoyance which, in her highly-strung state, she must have suffered on this occasion.

MISS EVA MOORE, who is a staunch bicyclist, is very proud and independent when she is on her machine, and never allows her husband, Mr H.V. Esmond, to assist her in riding up a hill. She has a wholesome contempt for those ladies who get themselves helped along by the aid of a man's strong right arm, and does not think anything would induce her to ride a tandem.

WANTED, First-class Ballet Ladies, to Tour as Lady Cricketers. Those who can Ride a Bicycle. Photo., lowest terms, DOT, Palace, Nelson.
22/4/1899

WANTED, to Sell, Four Real Baby Incubators, by Hearson, of Regent Street (not Potato Cans). Cost Twenty Guineas Each; or would Let for the Season, with or without Babies. Address, JEWELL, Earl's Court Exhibition.
29/4/1899

MR JUSTICE HAWKINS, while on the Bench, used at times to display ignorance of theatrical matters and theatrical people, and his mantle seems to have fallen on Mr Justice Grantham. This learned judge in the course of the action of Macdermott v. the Manchester Palace of Varieties was puzzled on hearing the name of Little Tich. "Little what?" asked he. "Tich, my lord," murmured Mr Marshall Hall. "Trick?" inquired the judge again with a look of perplexity. And then, finally, "Oh, I see, Tick!" It was explained at length that Little Tich was the stage name of Mr Harry Relf, a little gentleman exceedingly eminent as a comedian on both the legitimate and the variety stage, and quite equal to obtaining a salary commensurate with the dignity of a Prime Minister.

EARL POULETT* joins the Canterbury corps of entertainers on Whit Monday, when he will appear in a sketch written by Mr Matthew Monck, entitled *London Streets*. This will be elaborately and carefully mounted, and the production will be under the immediate direction of Mr Fred Holden. The Earl, it appears, will require a large amount of money for legal expenses, hence the reason of his appearance on the stage. He is proud of the fact that the dignity of his birth did not prevent him earning an honest living in the streets with a piano-organ.
**Also known as Viscount Hinton.*
20/5/1899

THE youngest salaried actress in the world is at present appearing at the Theatre Royal, Melbourne, in *Woman and Wine*. She is apparently about two months old, and she was left on the doorstep of Mr Harry Norman, Mr Bland Holt's stage-manager, on a Sunday, and after and having been taken in and cared for with motherly affection by Mrs Harry Norman, was in due course provided with a foster mother and an appointment as a member of Mr Bland Holt's company. She is brought into the theatre at eight o'clock, and is nursed by Mr Bland Holt in his character as Dick Salter through the whole of one scene. When the subject of the baby is first mentioned the supposed widow in the play remarks, "Oh, people are sure to say that it is a foundling." Dick Salter retorts, "Foundling, indeed! With your eyes and my nose and mouth!" Mr Holt is not very experienced with quite young children, and one night his idea of nursing

Norma on stage was to place her in a sitting posture on the palm of his hand. For a moment or so the two-months' old infant made frantic efforts to maintain her equilibrium. Her head wobbled from side to side, and she clutched the air, while Dick Salter went on with his part unconcernedly. A catastrophe was imminent, when an Irish "super" – who is a family man – came to the rescue. "For the love of Hiven, kape a holt on her, guv'nor! Kape a holt!"

AT the West London Theatre this week Mr Walter Melville's company has been playing *The Great World of London*, one scene in which represents the exterior of Liverpool Street railway-station. Newsboys appear displaying their "contents sheets", and the usual bustle of a City terminus is well simulated. On Wednesday the contents sheet of an evening paper read "Eighty, not out," and immediately on its appearance its significance* was greeted by the house with an outburst of applause. The audience rose, raised their hats, and cheered again and again, and it was some minutes before the performance could proceed.
*A reference to Queen Victoria's eightieth birthday.
27/5/1899

MR ARTHUR BOURCHIER'S performance as Jim Blagden in *Wheels Within Wheels*, at the Court Theatre, is, it seems, considered a personal insult to "a gentleman well known in society", and it has been represented by his friends to Messrs Chudleigh and Boucicault that Mr Bourchier should alter his present interpretation. As Mr Bourchier is entirely ignorant who it is whose friends find such a resemblance between him and the brutal and boisterous Blagden, how could the actor change his performance so as to destroy the likeness? Considering, too, the character and demeanour of the personage in the play, the friends of the alleged "double" pay him a very poor compliment by finding similarities; and it would apparently seem simpler and easier, if there be a real living Blagden in society, for him to revise himself in morals and manners, and destroy the resemblance in that way.

DURING the performance of *No Man's Land* at the Grand Theatre, Newcastle, last Monday night, so great an impression was made on at least one of the audience by the brutality of Mat Marsden to the hero, as he lies bound and helpless on the desert island, that, in reply to the hero's exclamation, "Help! Help!" the man immediately started making his way from the pit to the stage. He had already removed his coat in expectation of the coming battle and was climbing over the orchestra, with the cheering words "I'm coming, lad," when some attendants stopped him with some difficulty. The audience enjoyed the interruption thoroughly.
3/6/1899

MISS ILDA ORME, an actress, who was released from a lunatic asylum in England a year ago, publicly horsewhipped Mr Marcus Mayer, Miss Olga Nethersole's manager, on the deck of the American liner *St Paul*, at New York on Wednesday morning. Just before the vessel sailed Mr Mayer was talking with some friends when Miss Orme appeared on deck, made a rush at him, drew a whip, and struck two blows on Mr Mayer's face, raising weals. A policeman was called, but refused to arrest Miss Orme without a warrant, and as Mr Mayer would not delay his voyage in order to obtain one, she was allowed to go unpunished. Miss Orme was under the delusion that Mr Mayer had prevented her from getting theatrical engagements.
10/6/1899

AN inquiry was held at Southwark on Monday into the circumstances attending the death of Charlotte Riley, aged forty-five, lately living at Fulham. The evidence was to the effect that the deceased was originally a gymnast, and eleven years ago, while performing at the Standard Theatre, missed a flying leap on the trapeze. She fell on her face, and as a consequence had to have her nose amputated. For two

years she lay in King's College Hospital, and since her discharge had gained a precarious living as a dressmaker. Recently she got into trouble through pawning some dress material given her to make up, and a summons was issued. She told her sister she would rather die than appear at the court, and subsequently her body was found in the Thames off Jamaica Walk. The jury returned a verdict of "Found drowned".
1/7/1899

WANTED, Coloured Man, Black or Brown, for Savage Show. Must be Sober. Write, FRANK LAND, Post Office, Southend-on-Sea.
15/7/1899

AT the Wandsworth County Court, on Monday last, Sidney Vendome, of 13, Aliwal Road, Clapham Junction, and Miss Grace E. Leslie, an actress, lately performing at the Shakespeare Theatre, Clapham Junction, and now residing at Honor Oak, to recover the sum of 12s. 6d., a week's rent.

Plaintiff said the rooms were engaged for the defendant by her agent. The beds were perfectly clean, and free from vermin, as also was the room. Late one night, soon after occupation, the defendant complained of insects in the bed, and left. Plaintiff never saw anything of the kind.

Defendant said when she went to bed she was bitten on the shoulder by an insect. She got up and lighted the candle, when she found three insects in the bed. She called the landlady, and pointed out the insects to her. The landlady was surprised, and said there was no such thing in the house. She dressed, and left the house that night, the plaintiff calling her a "fussy cat."

The learned Registrar, before whom the case was tried, was not convinced that the insects were pointed out to the plaintiff. Verdict for the plaintiff for the amount claimed and costs.

ON Thursday morning, at the Oxford, a sparrow's nest was discovered carefully built among the gilt letters that are placed over the gallery entrance on the façade of the hall facing Tottenham Court Road. Father and mother were both at home when the nest was found, and five fledglings were enjoying their morning meal from the beaks of their loving parents. Truly plucky birds to brave the noise of large nightly crowds and the glitter and glare of electric light; but, then, the sparrow has always shown an aptitude at adapting himself to the usages and surroundings of modern civilisation.
22/7/1899

DURING a recent performance of *The Man in the Moon*, at the New York Theatre, an actress playing the part of a starving factory-girl raised her right hand and exclaimed bitterly, "My Heaven! Where shall I ever get another meal?" Manager George W. Lederer was astonished to observe that the raised hand had upon it $5,000 worth of diamonds. He immediately went to his office and wrote out this notice, which he posted up in the green-room: "Beginning with this date all members of the *Man in the Moon* company shall refrain from wearing rings or other jewellery upon the stage. A violation of this rule will subject the offender to instant dismissal."

THE English chorus ladies of *The Man in the Moon* company, now at the New York Theatre, and the chorus ladies at the Casino, in the same city, met on Wednesday in the Yorkville Swimming Baths at a game of water polo. There were seventeen players. Miss Irene Cameron scored two goals and secured a victory for the English team.

WANTED, Known, Cliffe Berzac, Owner of the Successful Boxing and Wrestling Pony. Without doubt the most Original Animal Performance on Earth. Last week the Talk of Leicester. Return early next year. Proprietors should Engage this Great Novelty at once. Only few early Dates open. Monday next, Ohmy's Palace, Accrington. All after Toddy (Maude B.).
29/7/1899

A COUPLE of ruffians were sent to trial at Blackburn the other day for robbing a well-known local professional musician named Ernest Storey. Mr Storey was crossing some fields at midnight, when prisoners, who were drunk, met him and compelled him to play a flute solo. After having done so, he raised his hat and said, "Good night, gentlemen, I must be off," but they seized him, rifled his pockets, and, after throwing his instruments away, left him lying in the fields.

AN amusing incident occurred at the Olympian Gardens, Lowestoft, on Wednesday afternoon. Mr Paul Mill, "the penny whistler", on commencing to sing his third song, found that his big black dog had followed him on to the stage, and no inducements could prevail on the animal to leave his master's side, and finally it had to be borne forcibly from the scene.

WANTED, to Let to "Bo-Peep" Pantomime Manager, Two Small, Stage-trained, Pretty Sheep for Run of Pantomime. Not to Travel. ARTHUR GUEST, 300, Essex Road, N.
5/8/1899

MISS LILY MARNEY was concerned in a sensational incident which occurred when she was singing her well-known song, "Arrah, go on", at the Empire, Portsmouth, on Saturday night. A sailor, being apparently under the impression that that he was the individual referred to when this popular artiste says she is "Mashed on a sailor in the gallery", shouted out to Miss Marney, "Have me!" and immediately jumped on to the stage, a distance of over 20ft. Mr Jesse Burton, who was standing in the wings at the time, carried him off the stage, and Miss Marney, with great presence of mind, continued singing the song to the end. Mr Lonsdale then requested Mr Burton to announce to the audience that the man was not seriously hurt, and that Miss Marney, although not recovered from the fright she had sustained, would sing another song. On her reappearance the plucky little lady met with a tremendous reception. A remarkable part of the affair is the fact that the man's comrades coolly retained their seats while the extraordinary leap was taken.

WANTED, a Mechanical Giraffe. Good and Cheap. WILLIAMS, Merrie Men, Rhyl.
19/8/1899

A DETAIL in the new ballet *Napoli*, produced at the Alhambra Theatre last Monday, which evoked universal applause was the dance by little girls attired as street boys, who, holding small plates with pieces of macaroni on them, went through the action of eating it, holding the pliant white pipes in the air, and swallowing them from the lower end. The graceful movements with which this was accomplished, and the neatness and ingenuity with which the dance was arranged, elicited heart-felt admiration.

DURING the performance of *The Swiss Express* by the Brothers Renad and company at the Grand Theatre, Wolverhampton, on Thursday evening, four Wolverhampton detectives entered the gallery and arrested two well-known local men who are alleged to be connected with a big jewel robbery which was done at Cheltenham on Wednesday. The prisoners made desperate attempts to escape from custody, and the audience turned out *en masse* to see the detectives take their prisoners to the police station.
26/8/1899

IN the course of the performance of *The Derby Winner* on Tuesday at the Queen's Theatre, Manchester, Mr Vernon Sansbury, who was playing the leading role, discovered in the course of a soliloquy that the scenery of a large fireplace was on fire. He at once beat the flames out with his hands. His cool-headed

efforts were greatly appreciated by the audience, and it was impossible for him to continue his part for some time, owing to the enthusiastic applause.
2/9/1899

AT the Princess's Theatre, on Wednesday evening, the leader of the pack of hounds that appears in *Going the Pace*, found his way to the Royal box, where he was regaled with chocolate and biscuits. On Thursday, at the close of the hunting scene, the whole pack broke away, and, running up the back staircase leading to the Royal box, burst open the door and rushed in. The occupants were amazed, but the audience, taking the incident to be a part of the performance, greeted it with applause. After an interval of confusion, during which the orchestra struggled in vain to make itself heard whilst the hounds bayed with their forepaws on the front of the box, the huntsmen arrived, and the hounds were prevailed upon to return to the stage.

A NUMBER of remarkable scenes were witnessed at many of the London music halls on Saturday night, when demonstrations of popular feeling in the Dreyfus verdict occurred. In some instances the programme was seriously interrupted. At the Metropolitan Music Hall, Edgeware Road, the audience cheered a topical song alluding to the case, while cries of "Mercier" and "Rouget" were the signal for loud hissing. Cheers were called for Dreyfus, and responded to again and again. A similar scene was witnessed at the Alhambra, where the house was packed from floor to ceiling. In the ballet *A Day Out* one of the tableau scenes represents the Casino Gardens at Boulogne. In it four French recruits were introduced, and immediately the audience burst into a perfect storm of hissing and hooting, interrupted with cries of "Shame!" and "Disgrace!" At the Palace Theatre, where biograph pictures of scenes at Rennes during the trial were being shown, the large audience greeted the representation of Maître Labori with deafening cheers, while the portraits of General Mercier and other members of the General Staff were received with hisses and groans. At the Oxford references to French justice, introduced into Mark Melford's sketch, met last Monday night with a perfect storm of hisses; and at the Tivoli the French flag was received with more than disfavour. A comedian, at the Walworth Palace of Varieties, on Saturday night, sang a song entitled "Dreyfus, victim", and the mention of the name was the signal for a most touching demonstration of sympathy.

WANTED, Engagement, by Young Man of Beautiful Muscular Development. Wishes to join Trio of Athletes. Accustomed to Weight-lifting. HENDERSON, Cook's Circus, Arbroath.
16/9/1899

WANTED, Young Man to Play Poodle in London Pantomime, must have had previous experience. Write, with terms, Box 1,534, "The Era" Office.
23/9/1899

A CURIOUS mistake was made in connection with the production of *The Devil's Disciple* at the Princess's Theatre, Kennington, last Tuesday. A gentleman who knows a good deal of Mr Bernard Shaw's literary and political work, and but little of the modern stage, arrived at the theatre about eight o'clock, a quarter of an hour after the advertised time for the commencement of the new piece, and found the audience screaming with uncontrollable laughter at the absurdities of Scroggins, in *A Cup of Tea*, upon which, instead of on *The Devil's Disciple*, the curtain, in contradiction of advertised announcements, rose at 7.45. Rather scandalised by the freedom of the farce, which he believed to be the first act of Mr Shaw's drama, he strolled out of the theatre, returning just in time to hear General Burgoyne putting the house in a roar with an up-to-date topical allusion to the bad marksmanship of the English infantryman. He left the place in a state of utter bewilderment, and lives lost in wonder at Mr Shaw's extraordinary jocularity.

AT the Shakespeare Theatre, Liverpool, last week, *Why Smith Left Home* attracted a wedding party of thirty people, simply because they belonged to the numerous Smith family, and were anxious to be let into the secret of their namesake's domestic troubles. The tour, which is in the hands of a wealthy City syndicate, is under the able direction of Mr Horace Lingard.

THERE has been some excitement at Ashton-under-Lyne through the escapade of a huge boa constrictor at the Tivoli Theatre. A local conjurer entered the theatre in semi-darkness, and the snake, which had by some means escaped from its case, bounded at him. The man at once shot out of the room, the reptile upsetting chairs, bottles, and glasses in its pursuit. Subsequently the constrictor was secured by its owner, who happened to be at hand. Its conduct is said to have been owing to the fact that its feeding had been overlooked.

WANTED, Known, Arizona Bill, Reptile King, Ventriloquist, Comedian, and Concertina Soloist, just arrived from Arizona with a Large Collection of Venomous Reptiles, including Seven Gila Monsters, Copper Heads, Boa Constrictors, Rattlesnakes, &c. £100 forfeited to anyone who can prove that the Snakes have not their poison fangs and venom intact. A Large Selection of Curiosities, including an Aztec Mummy, in good preservation, supposed to be 2,000 years old. Comedy and Ventriloquial turns taken. Speciality Turn, "Country Boy Musician", with Concertina accompaniment. Open to Juggle in Public any Reptile, however venomous, brought to the show.
For terms apply, permanent address, 33, Park Row, Tredegar.
30/9/1899

MRS LANGTRY, besides the numerous begging letters which she receives, is approached with the most extraordinary propositions. One man has invented an ointment for the improvement of the complexion, for the development of which he requires a "few paltry pounds", for which he will allow her a half interest in the new unguent. Another offers to give her commission on any money he makes out of her tips on the racecourse. One lady has a brother about to embark for South Africa, and says it would be a comfort to all the family if she could take him to see *The Degenerates* before he sails; so may she have two stalls "not too far back in the centre"? Quaintest of all, a young man, in a breezy letter, confesses that he has lost money by betting, and has had to borrow from his employer's till to make it good. He can suggest no other way of replacing it except by the generosity of Mrs Langtry; and proposes to pay interest at the rate of several hundred per cent. per annum, and to employ some of her funds in backing a horse which is a "certainty". He further says that, whilst pondering over how to replace the money, he had a dream, in which he saw "Mr Jersey" standing by his bedside, and this inspired him to make the appeal.
28/10/1899

MISS PIA CAROZZI, the young lady harpist who was shot by her rejected lover in Earl's Court Road on Saturday night last, is still in the West London Hospital. Dr Gask, the house physician, stated yesterday that she was progressing favourably, but although she has regained consciousness, the bullet has not yet been extracted from her cheekbone, and she cannot yet speak. Her brother, who came over specially from Rome, saw her on Thursday at the hospital.
4/11/1899

BY-THE-WAY, directly the first bill of *The Canary* was posted up outside the Prince of Wales's Theatre, a ragged, mangy, disreputable black cat walked in and took possession. This pleased the superstitious in the company – especially when Master Tom walked across the stage during rehearsal. Then, curiously enough on the first night another black cat – a kitten this time – strolled into the house and there established quarters, apparently for the season. And the author opined, when interrogated on the subject, that they both came after the bird.

WANTED, to Sell, Young Baboon. Well Acclimatised. Can Ride Pony. Also Pair Kangaroo Rats. Overstocked. BESSON, Circus, Brede, Sussex.

WANTED, by Mdlle Leodiska, with her New Military Pantomime, "South African War," Performed by a Battalion of Cockatoos. Sure Success. Suitable for Music Hall or Circus. Vacant all December. Address, 56, Campo Lane, Sheffield.
18/11/1899

MRS LANGTRY, when she paid £100 for the right to reproduce "The Absent-Minded Beggar"*, little dreamed of the extra labour and trouble that were involved in her enterprise. The announcement that one of the satin souvenirs would be given to every person at the 100th performance of *The Degenerates* on Friday brought in to her hundreds of applications from all over the country. People sent money for seats in the stall and circle which they said they didn't want, in order that they might obtain a copy; others booked two seats, and asked if, by paying the cost of the satin, they could get six copies; scores of others regretted that they could not come to the theatre, but enclosed postal orders for souvenirs. The poem on satin has cost Mrs Langtry 4s. 2d. a copy, and over 1,250 were printed for presentation at the 100th performance of *The Degenerates* at the Garrick Theatre on Friday.
*A poem by Rudyard Kipling

MANY people imagine that the canary which sings in *The Canary* at the Prince of Wales's Theatre is a mechanical bird. But this is not so. It is a real bird, and we have had the honour of hearing it sing very sweetly at a private performance. It seems to appreciate the footlights, and begins to pipe directly the right time arrives each night.

WANTED, Small Dog (Mongrel), to Walk Well on Hind Legs and Die When Shot. Apply, W.H., 120, Drakefield Road, Upper Tooting, London.
25/11/1899

MISS MARIE TEMPEST is no longer playing in *San Toy* at Daly's Theatre, and her part is being admirably acted and sung by that clever young artist, Miss F. Collingbourne. Mr Percy Anderson designed a very pretty and becoming dress for Miss Tempest, with knickerbockers, which the lady refused to wear. Mr George Edwardes very properly, in a most polite, but firm, manner, desired her to wear the costume; and Miss Tempest, still declining to do so, left the theatre. Mr George Edwardes would find it impossible to carry on Daly's Theatre if each actress were allowed to choose her own dress.
9/12/1899

AN unfortunate accident marked the representation, on Boxing Day, of the comedy-drama *In Old Kentucky*, which formed the Christmas attraction at the Prince's Theatre, Portsmouth. Miss Lilieth Leyton, who has been identified for several years with the part of the gulch heroine, Madge Brierley, has to take a leap in the first act to prevent the explosion of a bomb that threatens to end the life of Madge's lover, Frank Harley. While taking her life-saving swing across the chasm on Tuesday she managed somehow to badly sprain her ankle, and was obliged to desist from playing. Miss Amy Herman Fenton, her understudy, was fortunately ready at a moment's notice, and got through with considerable credit.
30/12/1899

11
1900
THE EXPLOSIVE BOER

THE automatic opera glass boxes at the Theatre Royal, Birmingham, not appearing to yield their due income, Mr Philip Rodway, the acting-manager, became suspicious, and called in the aid of detectives, who secreted themselves in the theatre after the fall of the curtain. The result was that the watchman on night duty, a middle-aged man named Alfred Stokes, was brought before the Birmingham magistrates on a charge of robbery. The detectives gave evidence that they kept watch from 10.30 in the evening until shortly after 6.0 in the morning, when they saw the prisoner go into the circle, shake the opera glass boxes, and put something in his waistcoat pocket. This something is alleged to be one of a number of marked sixpences that were placed in the boxes on the previous afternoon by Mr Rodway and Detective Goldrick. Prisoner elected to take his trial by jury, and was therefore committed to the Sessions, bail being allowed in sums amounting to £40.

AN alarming incident occurred during the performance of *The Geisha* at the Queen's Theatre, Leeds, on Tuesday evening last. Miss Muriel Chester, the Mimosa San, and Mr Harold Thorley, the Reginald Fairfax, had hardly appeared on the balcony of the scenic teahouse when the flooring gave way, precipitating them both on to the stage – a distance of ten or twelve feet. Luckily neither of them was seriously hurt, and Miss Muriel Chester pluckily proceeded with her part.

MR CHARLES FREEMAN, we regret to hear, met with a severe accident on Saturday night last in the prologue of *Current Cash*. The battery used at the end of the Battle scene exploded on being fired, one portion ripping open his boot and disabling his left foot, another striking him on the temple and severely injuring his left eye. He managed, however, after a little delay, to resume his part in the remaining four acts. In these he had to appear in the character of One Eye, which he realised completely.

FRED DONNELLY, music hall artiste, met with a terrible experience on a voyage last Saturday night on the *Mona*, belonging to the Ayr Steam Shipping Company, from Larne, Ireland, to Ayr, Scotland. On leaving Ireland a terrible storm arose, and, failing to get back to the cabin, he was nearly thrown overboard with the rough sea. He was compelled to keep out in the open for six hours, the wind and rain being indescribable. When the boat got near the Ayr Harbour she struck the rocks and smashed into the pier. She was quickly filling with water, when the captain, with great presence of mind, ran her onto a sandbank at 4.0 a.m. Here the shivering passengers could not get any help till 9.30, when a tug came and took them safely to shore. All Mr Donnelly's properties were soaked through, and are absolutely useless. He is very ill over the journey, and could not do his business with the Livermores' Court Minstrels at the Drill Hall, Ayr.

WEST RIDING ASYLUM, MENSTON, NEAR LEEDS. WANTED, Double Bass Player, who will be required to Act as Attendant. Must be able to Read Music at Sight. Salary commences at £30 per year, increasing £2 10s. annually to £55, with Board, Lodging, Washing, and Uniform. Apply to the MEDICAL SUPERINTENDANT OF THE ASYLUM.
6/1/1900

MISS ELLALINE TERRISS'S representation of a tipsy woman in *The Masked Ball* at the Criterion Theatre is certainly one of the most painful and unpleasant exhibitions we have ever seen on the stage. The spectacle of a young wife reeling and drawling out her speeches in imitation of drunkenness is repulsive to every admirer of pure womanhood. Drunkenness amongst females is one of the curses of modern society, and there is nothing that is amusing, but much that is distasteful and distressing, in the sight of a lady pretending to be drunk upon the stage. It is indeed to be deeply regretted that a delightful actress like Miss Terriss should nightly appear in such a painful position.

THE necessity of darkening the house completely during some of the changes of scenery in the production of *A Midsummer Night's Dream* at Her Majesty's on Wednesday, necessitated the fixing of a tiny electric lamp to the top of the baton of Mr Raymond Roze, the conductor, so that the musicians might see his beat. While the theatre was in a gloom, a humourist in the pit, amid a good deal of laughter and cheering, opened a bullseye lantern, apparently with the object of reading his programme; but the intrusive illumination was soon suppressed.

THE Town Council of Aberystwyth having given me the Sole Permit to provide Minstrel Troupe, &c., for Summer Season 1900: WANTED, for Minstrel Troupe, good Tenor, Bass, Male Soprano, good Comedians, with at least Twelve Up-to-Date Clean Songs (published Songs may be Sung here), and good Supply Up-to-Date Gags, not Chestnuts, good Lady Soprano and Contralto for Pierrot Troupes, also Instrumentalists. Twenty Weeks' Engagement to Good People. Amateurs, and Artists Wanting the Earth, or a Seaside Holiday, Save Stamps. Strict Sobriety Essential. Artists please state when and where Engaged, enclosing Day Bill. State lowest terms in first letter, and qualifications.
All Communications, GILBERT ROGERS, "Babes in Wood" pantomime. This Week, Royal Muncaster, Bootle.

WOULD CATHOLIC Artiste or Any Person, obtain (on own conditions) good opening for Young Man on Stage. Advertiser has a really good Singing and Speaking Voice, long Versatile Amateur Experience, was Shakespearian Pupil of Once Famous Tragedian, and had Short Professional Experience, with Excellent Success, but associated with people who could do him no good. Box 1,896, "The Era" Office.

Latest Novelty for Fairs, &c, the "Explosive Boer", large Iron Head. Upon the Nose being hit makes a Loud Report and change of Flags. Full Particulars, STACEY AND CO., Sole Makers, Showman Stores, Settles Street, London, E.
13/1/1900

WANTED, a Man that can and has worked an Untameable Lion. Must understand his business or useless applying. Address, Box 1,002, "The Era" Office.

WANTED, to Sell, Wax Heads of War Generals. Just Modelled. Good Likenesses. Lord Roberts, Kitchener, Methuen, Baden Powell. Best at Lowest Price, 20s. Also Striking War Groups for Window. "His Last Letter", "Dawn at Last", "Good-bye Daddy". STIFF, 181, Goswell Road.

LARGE ELEPHANT, ETHEL. In answer to at least three enquiries, she is now disposed of to Mister Hamilton, of Diorama Fame. This animal is a Lovely Creature. Stands about 6ft. high, and as docile as a sheep, and in show condition. With good training will be worth her weight in Gold. CROSS, Liverpool.

ALMA BEAUMONT, the Celebrated Lady Parachutist, High Diver and Water-Walker, and Troupe of Lady Swimmers, Thirteen Weeks with CIRCUS BUSCH. Vacant April 1st. Address, Circus Busch, Berlin.
20/1/1900

WANTED, for Hancock's Menagerie, Winter Gardens, Plymouth, a Coloured Lady to perform with Snakes and Reptiles; a Man to perform with Bears, Wolves and Hyenas; and a few Useful Inside Men, used to inside of Menagerie; and also a Trombone Player to perform with Organ. Great Success of Cap. Cardeno, the Lion Tamer.

WANTED, Known, Six Nights, Feb. 12th, Clown, Schubert, with his Acrobatic Goats, assisted by Cassidy. Big Success Everywhere. Clean and Funny. Next Week, Transfield's Circus, Lincoln.

WANTED, a Sensible and Trustworthy Lad, or Young Man, to Travel and look after Performing Dogs. Would-be actors or too clever people please save stamps. Address, J. DE VOYE, Town Hall, Newcastle-on-Tyne. No Partner Required.

KLOET, MDLLE. LEAH, in her Classical Picturesque Poses, with Entirely Original Chaste Surroundings and Electrical Effects. Palace, Croydon.

Thrilling Spiral Ascent Surrounded by Fireworks. MINTING The Greatest Gala Attraction on Earth. Ascent and Descent of Spiral, 50ft. High, Surrounded by Coloured Lights and Fireworks, On One Wheel of an Ordinary Bicycle. The feat of a madman. – Lloyd's News. The Rage of London, Paris, Berlin, St Petersburg, &c. Free May 25th, onwards. All letters, Permanent Address, MINTING, Sen., The Hall, Great Yarmouth.
27/1/1900

MRS DUDLEY SMITH, the well-known lady rider, met with a serious accident on Saturday last. While riding along Paradise Street, Birmingham, her horse shied at a motor cycle, and either fell on or else kicked its mistress. Mrs Smith was conveyed in an ambulance to the General Hospital, where it was found that besides breaking a finger and injuries to the forehead, there was also a fracture of the skull. On Monday the lady had sufficiently recovered to allow of her being removed to her home, but is not yet out of danger. The managements of bicycle and motor exhibitions should find more legitimate means of advertising their shows than motor races in the crowded streets of a market town on Saturday afternoon.
3/2/1900

MISS ROSE NORREYS, who was recently removed from Bethlehem Hospital to the City of London Asylum near Dartford, has greatly improved in health, the change from the close and confined surroundings of Lambeth to the uplands of Kent having proved very beneficial. When we visited her one day this week she said she was perfectly happy and comfortable, and that the nurses, who are younger women than those at Bethlehem, were very kind to her indeed. She still suffers from delusions, amongst them being the idea that she is the victim of conspiracies on the part of certain London theatrical managers. Ever since the loss of her reason she has been making her face up daily as if to appear on the stage, but lately her ideas have changed, and she wishes her friends to understand that someone came in the night and bleached her eyebrows, which she now colours white. The pet bird of which she was so fond is dead, but she has in its place a dormouse, to which she is much attached, and which she carries about with her wrapped in a knitted shawl.

MISS MILLIE HYLTON, the popular principal boy of *Goody Two Shoes*, at the Grand Theatre, Leeds, met, we are sorry to hear, with a painful accident on Wednesday night last. In the Court scene Mr Thompson and other members of the company pretend to play croquet, and meanwhile Miss Hylton stands near. Mr Thompson had in his hand a heavy property mallet, and while in the act of raising it to "drive" an imaginary ball he accidentally struck Miss Hylton on the right side of her head. The blow rendered her unconscious, and she had to be carried from the stage. A surgeon who was quickly in attendance found that she had sustained a severe cut on the right ear. She was conveyed home, and has since been confined to her room. She will resume her part in *Goody Two Shoes* as soon as her medical attendant will allow her, and in the meantime it is in the capable hands of Miss Norah Cecil.

SIGNORINA CAROZZI, the Queen's Hall lady harpist who was shot some months ago, on the steps of her house in Kensington, by a French admirer whose attentions were declined, has now completely recovered, and made her reappearance at Mr Albert Chevalier's recitals on Monday last. Her assailant, it will be remembered, turned the pistol upon himself with fatal results.

THE COUNTESS RUSSELL, who has taken counsel of Mr Richard Warner, will make her debut on the lesser stage on the 26th inst. at the Tivoli. We had the Viscountess Dando (Belle Bilton) appearing for a short time at the music halls, but Lady Russell is the first English countess to make the experiment. She is not without experience, having played the part of Winifred Grey in Mr George Edwardes's *Runaway Girl* company on tour. She appeared also in the recent revival of *A Gaiety Girl* at Daly's Theatre.
10/2/1900

A STARTLING but amusing incident occurred at the Grand, Blackpool, on Tuesday, when Mr Wynn Miller's company was playing *Alone in London.* During the Sluice-house scene, in which Richard Redcliffe, played by Mr Eric Blind, ill-treats his wife Nan, a member of the audience of the gentler sex was so overcome by her feelings that, with the exclamation, "You scoundrel, you don't deserve a wife," she threw her shoe at the actor.

WANTED, First-class Assistant to Quick Change Artist. Must be capable of assisting in Sketches. Full control of the Baggage and extensive Stage Apparatus. Must dress well on and off. I bar would-be Comedians who don the silk hat and cigar at right angles whilst the Proprietor cleans the apparatus. Only those who thoroughly understand the term "Behave yourself" need apply. Photo, particulars, BARNEY STUART, Downs View, Bungalow, The Beach, Walmer.

WANTED, Known, "It'll Have to Come Off Tonight" is not a blue song, and must not be sung by anybody. Hands Off. Protected. Written, Composed and Sung by Charles Dixon.
17/2/1900

MISS OLGA NETHERSOLE, Mr Hamilton Revelle, Mr Marcus A. Mayer, Miss Nethersole's manager, and Mr Theodore Moss, lessee of Wallack's Theatre, New York, where *Sapho* is being played, had warrants taken out against them last Wednesday for their arrest on violating Section 365 of the American Criminal Code, relating to public nuisances. The informer, in his complaint, alleges that the theme of the play is the portrayal of the life of a dissolute woman in a way offensive to public morals, and says that in the course of the play Miss Nethersole permits Mr Revelle to carry her up a flight of stairs, in full view of the audience, in an improper manner. Messrs Howe and Hummel, Miss Nethersole's attorneys, promised to produce the defendants in court, and prove the complaint to be

absolutely groundless. Miss Nethersole cannot understand how anyone can see anything improper in *Sapho*.
24/2/1900

DON JUAN'S LAST WAGER at the Prince of Wales's Theatre now finishes at five minutes past eleven. Quite forty minutes has been cut out of the dialogue, and the play goes excellently. The lights in the last act, which failed to act as desired on the first night, are now in perfect order, and the music adds greatly to the success of the play, which is already securing good advance booking. There were two odd incidents in the production of the piece on Tuesday last. One was the spectacle, dimly discerned as the curtain went up on the last scene, of Mr Holbrook Blinn, as the statue of Don Gonzalo, "hurrying up" to take his place on the pedestal. The other proved Mr Martin Harvey's presence of mind, adroitness and personal strength. Mr Herbert Sleath, as Don Luis Mejia, lay a-dying rather too far down the stage, and Mr Harvey, putting Mr Sleath's arm round his – Mr Harvey's – neck, gave the expiring Don a powerful "lift", and while seeming to comfort him moved him bodily to the steps, where he expired correctly and picturesquely.

WANTED, those Kind, Industrious Friends who have copied my Act, Style, Gags, even to my Original Title to Beware Solicitor on Track. Why not come and draw my salary as well? MADGE GRAHAM.

The Marvellous Juggler. FRANCISCO. Acknowledged to be the Greatest Lamp Manipulator Travelling. Audiences held spellbound while lying flat on my back with a Lighted Reading Lamp tilted on my nose, making a Cigarette at the same time. Managers please note the above name. This week, TOWN HALL, PONTYPRIDD. Permanent, 47, Coral Street, Leicester.
3/3/1900

MISS CLO GRAVES, the authoress of *The Bishop's Eye*, is an Irish lady, who was originally trained for an artist's career. She was on the stage for five years. She is an enthusiastic fly-fisher, and rides a tricycle.

MADAME SARAH BERNHARDT has determined not to allow any bonnets to be worn at her theatre for the future, beginning with the first night of *L'Aiglon*, which is due next week. She is also resolved to crush the matinèe hat, which causes so much trouble on both sides of the Channel. Indeed, in London managers are greatly exercised as to how to cope with what has now grown into a nuisance. Of course, the chief offenders are the ladies from the suburbs who come up for a morning's shopping and an afternoon's entertainment. They will not wear the ordinary theatre hat, nor will they wear the pretty toques. "Cartwheels" is what they revel in. Mr Alexander tried to suppress the matinèe hat, but he was vanquished. Now, if Mr Tree, Mr Alexander, Mr Wyndham, Mr Hawtrey, and Messrs Harrison and Maude were to combine and stand by their decision firmly, ladies, finding that the rule of "no hats" existed at every theatre, would soon give in and bow to the inevitable.

AT Penge police Court on Saturday, Charles Edward Darge, aged thirty-five, an employee at Lord George Sanger's Menagerie, which has been stationed at the Crystal Palace for some months past, was charged, on remand, with ill-treating, abusing, and torturing the elephant known as Charlie, which was shot on Feb. 18th, after having killed a man name Baker, alias Chippy Wood. The bench decided that prisoner was guilty of aiding and abetting the deceased man, Baker, in torturing the elephant, and they sentenced him to seven days' imprisonment, the sentence to commence from the 26th ult., the day on which the prisoner was arrested.
10/3/1900

LECOCQ'S opera, *La Belle-au-Bois-Dormant*, if transferred to England is not likely to be done as boldly as in Paris. The scene in the second act, when the Princess and her attendants all undress, is very startling. The ladies first remove their combs and let their hair down. In turn they take off their bodices, petticoats, &c., and stand within a few feet of the footlights with only their very thin chemises and stockings on. They then commence to dress again, putting on their corsets; and, singing all the while, resume their garments one by one.
17/3/1900

THE Alhambra's latest novelty is the motor-car expert Mr Coles, who will make his first appearance on any stage on Monday next. This gentleman holds the 100 miles non-stop club record and two silver medals driving contests. His performance will consist of intricate driving between posts and manipulating his car up and down a flight of stairs.
24/3/1900

AT Lambeth Police Court, on Wednesday, John Williams, who described himself as a newsboy, was charged with assaulting Grace Russell. The prosecutrix, an actress, was walking along St George's Road, Southwark, on Tuesday evening, when the prisoner came up to her, peered into her face, and asked if she was going to treat him. She told him to go away, and he then struck her in the face, causing her nose to bleed profusely. A police-constable stated that in consequence of a complaint which the prosecutrix made at the station, he accompanied her to St George's Road. They found the accused there, in company with four or five other lads. Directly she saw him the prosecutrix pointed out the prisoner as the youth who had assaulted her. Mr Hopkins ordered the prisoner to pay a fine of 20s. or go to prison for fourteen days.
31/3/1900

MISS GRETA WILLIAMS, who was a passenger on the ill-fated *Stella* on March 30th, 1899, and who, after the wreck on the Casquets, cheered the occupants of one of the lifeboats by singing "O, Rest in the Lord", has just had a graceful compliment paid her by the good folk of Guernsey at a benefit concert at which she sang. To show how warmly they admired Miss Williams's pluck in recrossing the Channel in aid of a worthy cause, the Guernsey people presented her with several bouquets and a handsome solid silver vase.

WANTED, Partner. Ella, late of Les Browns, One-Legged Jumpers, Dancers, &c., would like to meet with a Partner. One-legged Ladies only write, with full particulars and photo. ELLA, Freeman Street, Oldham.
7/4/1900

THE anti-*Sapho* crusade, which started in New York and quickly spread to other cities, has been responsible for a number of curious happenings. Some of these are almost tragic, while others border on the ludicrous. A young Chicago actress who had been cast for a minor role in the play, swallowed a dose of carbolic acid. "Prefers death to *Sapho*" was the caption of the newspaper report next day. But the actress lives, and is out of an engagement.

At Kalamazoo, Michigan, a university town, famed for its celery and culture, a performance of *Sapho* was prevented by the chief of police in a novel, but decidedly practical, manner. This functionary, whose weight is stated to be "in the neighbourhood of 300lb.", made a perilous ascent to the flies, and prevented the curtain from rising by sitting on the roller. The audience stood up, sang "There'll be a hot time in the old town tonight", and tried to encourage the company, but the police won, the lights were lowered, money refunded, and *Sapho* was declared "off".
14/4/1900

THE gentleman who manipulates the big drum in the Show scene in *Marsac of Gascony* played with such vigour on Tuesday night last that the drum stick flew out of his hand directly toward Mr J.M. Glover, the conductor, who dodged, as well as did the whole of the orchestra in the adjacent neighbourhood of their worthy chief. Luckily, not even a fiddler was killed, though the house rose most anxiously to see the slaughter.

A CURIOUS coincidence occurred on the first night of *Marsac of Gascony* at Drury Lane Theatre last Saturday. A lady in the upper part of the house gave a loud and shrill sneeze. A few moments afterwards Mr Edward Vroom, as the hero, had to take a pinch of snuff and sneeze after it. The "echo" tickled the audience immensely, and the second sneeze evoked a hearty laugh.

THE Duke and Duchess of York now have an electrophone communication between York House, St James's Palace, and the leading London theatres and concert halls, in order that their Royal Highnesses may listen to the various entertainments, including the opera performances at Covent Garden.

THE case of Ray v. Sillward, an action for breach of contract, came before Judge Lumley-Smith at Westminster on Thursday. In a sketch called *Satan*, run by the defendant, Ray was engaged at £4 10s. a week to play the villain. At first he had no suitable clothing. What was supplied to him made him, so he alleged, feel like a trussed fowl. Instead of rubber shoes he wore heavy boots, and as defendant played with bare feet he had to be very careful. In an exciting struggle between the villain and the defendant, dressed as a baboon, the villain had to hit the baboon with a mantelpiece. But the mantelpiece failed to break until the defendant was severely belaboured with it. Sillward said he had to be struck three times, and had to force his neck into an unnatural position. A verdict was given for the plaintiff for £11, with costs.

MR F. F. PROCTOR has engaged the Earl of Yarmouth as a "top-liner" for his inaugural programme at the Fifth Avenue Theatre, when that house is opened as a "continuous performance" theatre on the 7th prox. He will appear in a one-act comedietta, by Seymour Hicks, which has been successfully tried in England.

WRAY'S PLEASURE GARDENS, ILKLEY, YORKS.
WANTED, a Lady Team of Footballers for Whitsuntide Holidays. Lowest Terms to SECRETARY.
28/4/1900

AT a performance of *The Mysterious Lilith*, by Mr Fred Harcourt, on Saturday evening at the Swansea Empire, a strong-built man about forty, sitting in the balcony, rushed from his seat gesticulating wildly, swearing that he could "see the angels." Outside the building he kept running up and down, with hands distended, body quivering, and an insane stare. He was at last induced to take a seat in the hall of the building, and restoratives were applied, but it was a long time before his excitement subsided. He was pronounced to be quite sober.

ON Monday evening, as Mr George Scott, manager of the Southend Kursaal, stepped out of the coffee-room window of the Royal Hotel, he slipped down and broke his leg. The window is separated from the pavement by a palisade, and the attempt was very hazardous, but Mr Scott was apparently anxious to see a friend, and took what he considered a shorter way than by the hotel entrance. Dr Bridge at once rendered assistance.
12/5/1900

MRS PATRICK CAMPBELL has kindly consented to sell kittens at the Guards' stall of the National Bazaar at the Royal Palace Hotel on Thursday, Friday and Saturday next. Happy kittens! Even to be sold by Mrs Patrick Campbell must be sweet.

JUST as the "second house" audience was assembling at the Haymarket Music Hall, Bean Street, Liverpool, on Monday evening, a youth named John James Walker, sixteen years old, rushed down the steps, over-balanced himself, although there was a strong iron railing, and fell from the gallery to the then empty pit below, a depth of about 26ft. He was shockingly injured, and died before reaching the nearest dispensary, where he was taken at once. On Wednesday the city coroner's jury returned a verdict of accidental death. Mr Fred Willmot, lessee and manager of the hall, will pay the whole of the lad's funeral expenses.

WANTED, Pierrots' Suits to Fit Men 5ft. 10in. Must be Cheap. PERO, 14, Joshua Street, Rochdale.

ALASKA'S Educated SEA LIONS, Seal and Walrus, the First and Only Trained Animal of its kind in existence. Talks and really Blows a Trumpet, &c. Now on Continental Tour. Address, care of Der Artist, Düsseldorf.
19/5/1900

MRS WATKINS, the lady who falsely accused Herr Julius Seeth, the lion tamer at the London Hippodrome, of picking her pocket on a Hammersmith omnibus, has forwarded him, through her solicitor, the following letter: – "Concerning the statement made by Mrs Watkins concerning you on the 15th inst., we now beg to apologise for having accused you of stealing her purse, and sincerely regret that Mrs Watkins ever made such a statement. We appreciate your courtesy in refraining from taking any legal action against us, and herewith hand you a cheque, value £5 5s., being a contribution to the German Hospital, Dalston, and the cost of your solicitor's charge."
2/6/1900

AT half-past one on the afternoon of the 1st inst., Mr Arthur Bertram, Mrs Patrick Campbell's treasurer at the Royalty Theatre, sent Mr Le Butt, a clerk, with a cheque for £130 to Parr's Bank in St Martin's Lane. The cheque was cashed, and the clerk placed the gold and silver into a small brown handbag and, as he thought, properly secured it. He then handed the bag to the fireman regularly employed at the Royalty, and accompanying him to the theatre saw the bag handed to the manager. This was done within half an hour of the cashing of the cheque; but on being opened the bag, instead of containing £130 in gold and silver, was found to contain a dozen pieces of coal. The only explanation offered is that a "double" of the bag had been prepared by a clever gang of thieves, and the changes rung at the counter of the bank.

THE Cheshire Coroner investigated on the 1st inst. the circumstances of a sensational suicide near Chester. James Creighton, a professional musician, well known in London and Brighton, and a member of the Chester Theatre orchestra, had been missing since Wednesday week, when he hired a boat and rowed up the Dee. The boat, containing a pair of eye-glasses and a box of revolver cartridges, was subsequently found, and the body, with a bullet wound in the left breast, was recovered from the river. The evidence showed that deceased had attempted to commit suicide at Brighton by jumping into the sea, and at Chester had once come home wet through, carrying a discharged revolver. He "rambled" in his talk, and composed poetry. A verdict of "Suicide whilst of unsound mind" was returned.

SOCIETY has long since made the theatrical stage a happy hunting-ground for their immature attempts at acting and singing, and of late we have had a peeress or two on the variety boards. The latest development of the craze for "going on" is shortly to be seen at the Empire, where we are to have a bevy

of great ladies appearing in one of the scenes in *On the Beach*, the new ballet. Amongst the crowd on the *plage* will be a dozen or so dames belonging to what Jeames calls the "hupper suckles", and bearing honoured names. They will be paid, and will have to come regularly every night, in order that the grouping of the ballet may not be altered when it once settled. It does not seem to occur to these ladies that the money paid to them would be willingly earned by the numerous "extras" who cannot find employment in the summer, when the pinch of poverty is more or less felt by the theatrical rank and file.
9/6/1900

AT West London Police Court, on Thursday, Frank de Vine, aged thirty, was charged before Mr Lane, Q.C., with committing an unprovoked attack upon a young lady named Maude Wibman, a theatrical artiste. The complainant was saying "Good-night" to a friend in King Street on Wednesday, when the prisoner came up and asked for cigarettes. She told him that she had not any, and that he had better be off. Thinking he had gone, she held out her hand to her friend to shake, when the prisoner knocked it down. He said, "If you will not give me any cigarettes, take that," and struck her in the face. He ran away, but her friend followed him to Jubilee Chambers, where he was arrested. Ivy Smith, the friend in question, gave corroborative evidence. The prisoner said he was very sorry, but Mr Lane sentenced him to be imprisoned for fourteen days with hard labour.
16/6/1900

THE failure on Saturday evening last of the gas supply that works one of the engines at the Belfast Empire Theatre of Varieties was responsible for the omission of Mdlle de Dio's celebrated electrical dances from the programme. Much disappointment was thus felt by a crowded audience at the non-appearance of the graceful danseuse.
23/6/1900

MARY READING, a young woman until lately a housemaid in the service of Mr Otto Goldschmidt, was charged at the West London Police Court, on Tuesday, with stealing a silver medal presented to Mr Goldschmidt's late wife, who as Jenny Lind charmed music-lovers fifty years ago. Reading was sentenced to two months' imprisonment with hard labour.

MR DUNDAS SLATER on Wednesday gave a private press rehearsal at the Alhambra for the purpose of introducing Harry Houdini, who claims to be able to release himself in the space of a few seconds from any handcuffs, manacles or leg-irons yet invented. He has allowed as many as five pairs of handcuffs and irons to be locked on his wrists and legs, whilst he is himself placed in any conceivable position that may be chosen by the audience, and has then almost instantly removed them without any extraneous help whatsoever. Houdini possesses letters from the highest American police officials, endorsing his marvellous abilities in this respect. From handcuffs of different descriptions brought by some of the spectators, Houdini in a very short time on Wednesday effected his release, first beneath the shelter of a moveable tent, and afterwards in a kneeling posture in full view of the audience, his fettered hands being chained to leg-irons, so that he had to grapple with six locks. More telling, from an entertainment aspect, was his swift execution of a transformation box trick.
30/6/1900

AN amusing story comes from Cheltenham, well known as the home of girls' schools. Mr F.R. Benson was playing Hamlet there some little time since, and the theatre was filled to its utmost capacity with a number of the young ladies who were being elevated and amused at the same time. The actor was just in the middle of the ghost scene, the lights were lowered, and the excitement was intense. Suddenly a voice arose from the stage box – "Mr Benson". No answer. "Mr Benson!" Still no answer. "Mr Benson, would you mind having the lights raised? The young ladies can't see to follow their copies!"

AT Marlborough Street Police court on Thursday, Victor Campili, sixteen, of Henry Street, Pentonville, was charged with stealing two gold watches and a pair of field glasses, value £25, the property of Sir Henry Irving; and two gold rings, value 35s., belonging to Miss Cunnington. Mrs Harriet Cunnington, of Stratton Street, Piccadilly, housekeeper to Sir Henry Irving, said that the prisoner had been employed by Sir Henry Irving for about a month as a "house-boy". The watches were missed on Monday from a cabinet in the drawing-room. On the previous Friday the two rings, which belonged to her daughter, were missed from the dresser in the kitchen. She asked him what he had done with the rings, and he denied all knowledge of them. Sir Henry Irving also questioned him about the rings and the missing watches, and the lad replied that he had not seen them. Detective McPherson deposed that he went to Lupus-street, Pimlico, where he saw the prisoner, who ran away. The witness followed him, and on catching him told him that he would be charged with stealing the items mentioned. The prisoner said, on referring to the watch on which were inscribed the words, "John Kemble to Henry Irving", "I broke it up in St James's-park; I broke it into pieces, which I threw into the air. One of the cases I threw across the tent." A piece of the inside of a watch was found in the possession of Campili when searched, and he remarked that it might form a portion of the watch that was broken up. Mr Fenwick remanded the prisoner.

A SAVAGE attack was made one day this week on Mr Dan Leno near a pigsty on the Leno farm by a ferocious chicken. Possibly actuated by a desire to avenge sundry libellous statements on poultry made by the comedian in his song "Our Stores", the bird went for him with beak and claw. Mr Leno, who got caught on a nail, had all his work cut out to protect his face. His principal regret was that he couldn't leave himself there while he fetched someone with a camera to take a snapshot.

WANTED, Rubber Sheet, also Fat Policeman's Dress, for Water Pantomime. Good Condition. Lowest Price. PONGORILA, 3, Market St., Coleshill St., Birmingham.
7/7/1900

AN amusing incident occurred at the Borough Theatre, Stratford, on Monday, during the representation of *The Lights o' London*. In the fourth act the hero and his wife Bess are advised to seek shelter for the night in the "house." The husband's speech concludes with the words, "Is there no other help in this cursed world?" At this a young sailor in the gallery shouted, "Yes, mate, there's something to go on with," and a silver coin was thrown on the stage. Needless to say, this unrehearsed incident created much merriment.

WITHOUT Americans Stratford and Warwick and Leamington and Kenilworth would be sombre and half-deserted, and at Shakespeare's birthplace on Friday and Saturday last were congregated the largest number of Americans citizens that ever collected in an English country town. They came in huge parties. There were 209 in one lot on Friday, and just after them came twenty-six in one party, and forty-four in another. They mostly want to write their names on the wall. At Ann Hathaway's cottage requests come from many Americans to be allowed to lie on Ann Hathaway's rush mattress. Stratford itself has become so American that one of the largest hotels has purchased an American ice-chest, and a local bar sells "cocktails".
14/7/1900

THE Electric Ballet is quite the most novel feature of *The Casino Girl* at the Shaftesbury, and nothing so fascinating or so chaste in the effect of its incandescent beauty has been seen on the regular stage. The eight ballerinas come on in soft light draperies with bodices cut V-shaped, and commence some simple movements. The lights are lowered until the stage is in almost total darkness. Suddenly, the girls' faces are lit up by little electric bulbs hidden in the centre of each low bodice. Next the faces are further illuminated by the glow of lamps set under the hat-brims just over the foreheads. As they wave their draperies, suddenly, under each diaphanous skirt there appears, around the hips, a line of globes of fire. These globes change colour from white to red. Presently each girl's puffed sleeves are full of light. Then a V-shaped decoration of flaming butterflies appears on the front of each corsage, and a tiny line of light encircles each waist. The conclusion is most poetic. When the dancers come out in the darkness to bow a farewell to the applauding audience, the lights in their dresses are suddenly extinguished, and a single flaming butterfly floats over each hat. As they retire nothing can be seen but the flicker of the disappearing butterflies.

THERE was a ceremony of special interest at the popular Hall-by-the-Sea, Margate, on Tuesday, when the stage was occupied during the afternoon performance in connection with the public christening of three of the young lions born in the menagerie. One was christened General Buller, by Mrs Lassam, a visitor from London; another, General Baden-Powell, by Mrs Foxwell, also a visitor from the metropolis; and the third, General French, by Miss Marion Hall, one of the artistes. The cubs went through the ordeal with due decorum, with the exception of one, which did not like the wine used in the ceremony being inadvertently poured into its ear instead of over its head; but its restlessness was soon appeased. The lions, the sponsors, and about 200 of the audience were subsequently photographed in the grounds.

WANTED, Known, Lady Parachutist, with Gas Balloon, open to offers for August Bank Holiday. Address, Lieut LAMPRIERE, Handsworth, Birmingham.
21/7/1900

THERE are two electric light circuits running close together in the Strand – one supplying a neighbouring music hall and the other the Gaiety Theatre and Restaurant. Between these circuits runs a gas main. A "short circuit" between the electric wires fired the gas main on Sunday morning, and was fusing the pipes and cables. From the cavity there ascended a stream of fire ten or twelve feet high, to the effect of which was added rapidly-succeeding explosions. Alarm was immediately given to the fire brigade, and very speedily several engines were on the scene. Their services, however, were of no avail whatever, it being apparent that nothing would serve to abate the danger but cutting the wires. The firemen were thus placed in the singular position of being passive spectators of an outbreak which was beyond their power of dealing with. Electricians were summoned without delay, and the danger of the situation was soon abated.

MR H. GILMAN has added to the many attractions of the Crystal Palace an electric staircase, invented by Mr Reno, an American. It is a clever contrivance, and consists of a continuous moving platform, with a similar continuous moving handrail, both working simultaneously. The passenger steps on the moving incline, resting his hand on the movable handrail, and is carried in an easy and smooth manner to the upper or lower floor at a moderate rate of speed. The motive power is electricity, driven both by belt and cog-wheels. A continuous stream of people can be conveyed at the rate of 3,000 an hour. The moveable staircase has been erected in the south transept in close proximity to the orchestra.

WHILE performing in a marquee at Kirby Muxloe, near Leicester, on Bank Holiday, the Vezzeys met with a disaster. Just as the singing dog was about to appear there arose a gale, and the marquee fell in. Miss Vezzey pulled the concertina dog, with the instrument fastened on him, from under the tent, while Mr Vezzey helped to hold up the canvas. They escaped, luckily, without serious injury; but on their way home across the fields they were overtaken by a bull, which was much attracted by their funny looking Russian poodles. Their instruments were much damaged by rain.

THE chief attraction in the Theatre of the Alexandra Palace, August Bank Holiday and during the week, has undoubtedly been the performances of Charles Judge's clever parrots, cockatoos, &c. The programme of these wonderful birds consists of an artillery attack, cycling, horizontal bar act, several acrobatic tricks, waltzing, and marching correctly to time. A great feature is the cockatoo wedding, in which several of the birds take part. The drive of the bride to church in an elaborate State carriage, attended by coachman and footman, each bird taking its place without hitch or prompting, proves how admirable has been the training of these pets. Nero, the clown bird, afterwards gives an example of serpentine dancing in costume, under coloured lights.
11/8/1900

THE British Consul-General at Havre states in his report on the district for the past year that a certain number of young women and girls of British nationality are employed in the music halls at Havre. These halls depend for their existence in a great measure on the custom they receive from the crews of British ships, and the proprietors therefore endeavour to secure singers and dancers from England. Some are fully aware of the reputation of the music halls before they leave home, but others, who have been engaged in England by agents of the proprietors, only discover after their arrival at Havre the true character of the places where they have accepted employment. The Consul-General arranges, when possible, to send back persons who have been deceived in this respect, and there is no difficulty in doing so when the girls are under age; but he warns British subjects who may seek engagements, either for themselves or their children, in places of public entertainment in Havre that they would do well to communicate with him before signing any agreement.
18/8/1900

RHO–DEER the Charming American Lady Rocket, in the Greatest Sensational Act ever seen. RHO-DEER is fired from a Cannon up in the Air into the Car of a Balloon, terminating her Act by Jumping From the Car to Solid Earth in Three Seconds. The Greatest Draw in the Whole World. Protected by Her Majesty's Royal Letters Patent. Terms, Share or Certainty. Indoors height required, not less than 50ft. Clear. Must be Seen to be Believed. Handsome Apparatus, Splendid Costumes, and a Charming Lady is RHO-DEER, to whom all Communications must be Addressed. 68, Grove Lane, Camberwell, London.
25/8/1900

MR EDITOR. – Sir, in your Portsmouth report last week I was mentioned as comedienne. It should have been "manipulator of musical glass orchestra".
Yours faithfully, MARIE CLIFFORD, Ramsgate, August 28th.

SIR. – As a warning to other professionals I relate a very disagreeable experience of my sister, Miss Edith Stewart. She is now on tour, playing Lucy Pillenger, in *Lady Huntworth's Experiment*; and whilst she was acting at the Theatre Royal, Great Yarmouth, last Saturday, a man in a pretended "railway cart" stopped at her lodgings for a box which he said he had been told to call for. As Miss Stewart's box was ready for removal to Folkestone the landlady let the fellow take it away, but since then it has neither been seen nor heard of. Miss Stewart thus loses nearly all her private wardrobe and most of her jewellery. Other professionals visiting Yarmouth should be on their guard.
Yours faithfully, HERBERT WALTHER, 26, Dancer Road, Fulham, S.W., Aug. 29th, 1900

AT the Theatre Royal, Wigan, on Tuesday, in the course of the production of *The Black Vampire*, a startling accident occurred. In the third act a representation is given of a burning house, and the heroine leaps from the upper room to be caught by the hero, who is hanging head-downward from the telegraph wires. Miss Marie Vaughan failed in her leap, and fell on to the stage, the accident creating great excitement among the audience. She sustained a severe shock.
1/9/1900

DURING the visit of *The Belle of New York* to the Shakespeare, Clapham, the management was inundated with applications for free seats from members of "dramatic clubs". The following is an example: – "We are forming a kind of musical comedy society, and it has occurred to me to ask if you would be so good as to favour me with a couple of seats to see *The Belle of New York*, so that the secretary and myself might study the play officially." – The reply ran: – "As we have not yet succeeded in inducing the railway company to issue complimentary tickets for your use to and from the theatre, would it not be well for you to wait until the play visits a theatre nearer to your residence, so that no expense whatever may be occasioned to you?"

MISS SYLVIA STOREY, who made her first appearance on the stage last November, in *Rip Van Winkle*, is evidently a very "forward" young person, for she suddenly startled her father the other day by asking for an edition of Shakespeare, because she wanted to study the parts of Portia and Juliet. Miss Storey only recently passed her ninth year.

SOME slight commotion was caused at a West End hall on Tuesday night by a man with a step-ladder on his shoulder pushing his way through the grand-circle saloon and jostling the bystanders as he ascended the ladder to examine the electric lamp brackets. Remonstrances turned to shouts of laughter when the culprit was discovered to be Mr Dan Leno.

WANTED, Experienced Lady for Boy Waif and Juvenile Parts. Rehearse at once. Must be petite and capable of extreme pathos. Age, height, references, photos., lowest terms, to GEO. ENCYL LEWIS, Queen's Theatre.
15/9/1900

MR CHARLES WARNER'S appearance for the first time at Mr Robert Arthur's Princess of Wales's Theatre, Kennington, in *Drink*, has been phenomenally successful. The handsome building has been crowded to excess each evening with enthusiastic audiences, and on Saturday last every seat was taken before the doors were opened, the pit stalls, amphitheatre, pit, and dress circle being filled at the early doors. In the great delirium scene, where Coupeau sees rats, snakes, and other horrors, a cat quietly walked on the stage and sat down close to the actor. Such an occurrence ordinarily would have excited roars of laughter; but Mr Warner's intensity held his audience spellbound, and not the slightest titter was heard during the whole scene, though pussy meandered about and played with the flowers at the side of the orchestra. At the conclusion of the scene Mr Warner was called and recalled with acclamation.

THE management of Daly's Theatre have offered a reward for the name of the printer of the bogus programmes of *San Toy* which are sold apparently without let or hindrance outside the theatre. Mr George Edwardes finds he has no easy task before him in trying to get rid of the hawkers who sell these unauthorised programmes. The patrons of the pit and gallery who foolishly part with their money outside are naturally annoyed when they find, after purchasing "playbills" outside, that all programmes are free. To find the printer of these illegal bills is the difficulty. Sir Augustus Harris and Sir Henry Irving had great trouble with these itinerant pests years ago, and were always receiving complaints, especially from country playgoers.

THE "Lancashire Giant", Thomas Hopkinson, has just sued J.W. Delmar, of the Bijou Theatre, Llandudno, for wrongful dismissal. Part of the giant's work was to shout outside the theatre to attract visitors. The defendant asserted that the giant made insufficient noise, but Hopkinson declared he could be heard across the street, and if he shouted louder he would be stopped as a nuisance. The giant recovered £6 10s. by way of damages.

WANTED to Sell, Troupe of Performing Cats, with all Properties. They do Everything. Can be seen in London. Address, ROSIE MEERS, 32, Gerrard Street, London.
22/9/1900

AT Clerkenwell Police Court, on Tuesday, George Oliver Miller, forty-three, a compositor, of 2, Elms Villa, Isabella Road, Homerton, was charged, before Mr Bros, with threatening to shoot Charles Miller, his brother, of Sadler's Wells Theatre. Mr Weaver Burnard prosecuted. The prosecutor said that for some time past the prisoner had called at the theatre and annoyed him, demanding money. On Friday last the prisoner made a request, which was refused, and he then threatened to shoot his brother. The prisoner told the magistrate that that he carried the revolver merely for the purpose of frightening his brother. When he bought the weapon he had no intention of shooting his brother, and did not buy any cartridges. He would now undertake not to speak to his brother again, and would accept an offer he had of a situation in Johannesburg. Mr Bros remanded the accused, allowing bail.
6/10/1900

TIGHTS, SKINS, PADDINGS. – Mr and Mrs MAYERS, the Great Leg Padding Makers. Bad-shaped or Thin Legs made Perfect. Quite Imperceptible. Woven Cats', Monkeys', Poodles', Bears', Harlequins' Dresses. Only Stock in London. Tights in Silk, Cotton, or Wool. Worsted Tights, 7s. 6d. Established 1871. 21, SHEPPERTON ROAD, ESSEX ROAD, ISLINGTON, LONDON, N.

SCROGGS, the King Charles spaniel which used to appear in *Sweet Nell* at the Haymarket Theatre, has been causing some anxiety. The Board of Agriculture feared that that he might possibly, on his return from Ireland – which the company will visit during its tour – import rabies into England, and Scroggs has been the subject of much correspondence between the Board and Mr Fred Terry. Mr Long's officials have now agreed to allow Scroggs to proceed to Dublin and to return to this country provided that on his return he wears a "wire cage muzzle", except at such times as he may be engaged in his stage performance.

WANTED, Showmen to Know, Paul Kruger, Metal Figure, 5ft. high; you Drop Penny in his Hat, Pull his Nose, and from under his Vest Drops a Box of Sweets. Great Attraction, £3 each. Boxes, 1s. Gross. List Free. INTERCHANGEABLE AUTOMATIC COMPANY, Limited, 327, Upper Street, London, N.
20/10/1900

MR COLERIDGE TAYLOR, the composer of the music to *Herod*, has just christened his new little baby boy after his already famous cantata, based on Longfellow's beautiful legend, "Hiawatha". Mr Taylor, whose father was an African and his mother an Englishwoman, has lived nearly all his life in England, and began to compose when quite a child – he is only twenty-six now. He introduces a curious tone into his melodies always reminiscent of the forest and the wild country, as witness his oddly named "Four Waltzes", published by Novellos.

MISS RICHARDSON, daughter of the Mayor of Mafeking, in her recent lecture, at the Croydon Town Hall, on the siege, said she would show a picture of the effects of a Boer shell. Just as she spoke the words a large portion of the ceiling fell with a loud crash on the stage. The audience at first thought the "effect" was intended, but when they discovered its accidental nature they dispersed, fearing that the whole of the ceiling would come down.
2/11/1900

THERE is at least one man alive who saw Napoleon in the flesh, and that man an actor – the oldest in the world, we believe – Mr James Doel. It was immediately after the fall of the great French general, when,

of course, he was conveyed to Plymouth in the *Bellerophon*. The warship was surrounded by hundreds of boats, whose passengers were eager to get a good glimpse of the Emperor. Among these was the present Nestor of the English stage, Mr James Doel, who then, as now, lived at Plymouth. Mr Doel saw Napoleon, "a short, active man," as he describes him, "with a good breadth across the chest," pace the deck.
10/11/1900

A LAD of fourteen, named Trifitt, has recovered seven guineas and costs from Mrs Proctor, the proprietress of a travelling circus, under somewhat unusual circumstances. The boy attended one of the circus performances, and he alleged that a clown forcibly drew him from the audience for the purpose of performing somersaults over him, and when he objected he tripped him up in the ring, dislocating his shoulder. He also said that the clown put him in a row with four other boys, but instead of throwing a somersault, he pushed the lads over and trod upon the plaintiff's arm. His honour, Judge Raikes, held that Mrs Proctor was responsible, because her son was in the ring at the time of the occurrence and did not interfere.
17/11/1900

AN amusing embarrassment in the performance of Mrs Oscar Beringer's play, *The Plot of His Story*, at the St James's Theatre, on Thursday last, was caused presumably by the dampness of the matches placed on the table in the scene of the author's study. Mr Irving and Mr Elwood made five or six attempts to get a light for the latter gentleman's cigar, but in vain. The match went out every time, and the gloomy Lothario, who was meditating an elopement with his friend's wife, had to do without his smoke.

EASTBOURNE audiences evidently prefer their entertainments cast in a more serious form than is usually presented at the Devonshire Park Theatre. Many theatrical companies have failed to be attractive at ordinary prices – owing to the fact that the auditorium is nothing much better than a large room, which sadly wants decoration and is without even a private box – whereas Mr Winston Churchill on Monday afternoon packed the theatre from floor to ceiling at nearly double charges for admission. The audience was fashionably passive, and listened with sedate attention to the distinguished lecturer. Mr Churchill is not an orator, and he has a slight lisp, but his voice is clear and carrying. In his views on the war he blames no-one, and apportions praise only here and there; in fact, criticism is carefully avoided.
24/11/1900

IT is curious and significant that when a clergyman attacks the drama it generally turns out that he is quite unacquainted with it, and that he never goes to a theatre. Archbishop Walsh, referring to the condition of the Dublin stage, at St Margaret's Church, Dublin, last Sunday, in a sermon in which he alluded to plays, "the evil suggestiveness of which," he said, "is intensified at times by a variety of devices that would not be tolerated even in London," confessed that he had no direct personal knowledge of what went on at the local theatres, and was dependent for his information on "hearsay evidence". Why did not the Archbishop go and see for himself what was the state of the drama in Dublin?

THERE is at least one anachronism in *The Swashbuckler* at the Duke of York's Theatre, where Mr N.L. Parker's piece is running gaily. In the second act Miss Evelyn Millard uses a three-pronged fork when eating the hedgehog. The two-pronged fork did not come into general use until the close of the seventeenth century, while the three-pronged was almost unknown until the beginning of the present one.

ZANETTO and LORENE, the Lion-jawed Athletes and Human Cranes. Zanetto Lifts a Grand Piano With His Teeth. Lorene Lifts and Holds with her Hair a 4½in. Howitzer Field Gun, while Fired. At Liberty after Seventy Weeks with Horace Parri, Esq. Address Letters, John A. Walmsley, Variety Artiste Agent, 2, King Street, Accrington.

WANTED, to Sell, Yarmouth Murder. Correct Model of the Accused, from life; also of the Dead Woman, just as the body was found; also of the child, Ruby, and Alice Meadows, and boy. We have the identical photos taken of the dead woman in the mortuary, the authentic one. A good draw for the Horrors. STIFF, 181, Goswell Road.
1/12/1900

WHEN Mr H.E. Moss announced that Cinderella's slipper was to cost over £100, much speculation was aroused as to the cost of the whole production at the London Hippodrome. Here are some interesting items: – Cinderella's coach, which is built of glass, covered with myriads of tiny electric lights, will be worthy of a place in the British Museum. As a novelty from a spectacular point, nothing has been seen like it; as a valuable property, it would tax the exchequer of a millionaire to purchase such another. It is shaped exactly like the Lord Mayor's State carriage, and will be drawn by six black ponies, caparisoned in red morocco and gilt harness, and attended by twelve flunkeys and outriders in costumes costing £63 each. The coach itself has cost £1,000. The whole of the arena will be turned into a gigantic ball-room, and Mr Moss promises the most remarkable electrical effects that have ever been conceived. Altogether 400 persons will appear in *Cinderella*.

MR WALTER STANTON, the man of feathers, has just returned from the land of stars and stripes. Since his two years' absence he has given his giant rooster performance for five months at the New York Theatre, in *The Man in the Moon*, under Mr George W. Lederer. Mr Stanton has given Americans an opportunity of witnessing his latest novelty, *The Cockatoo*. Any manager who is playing Robinson Crusoe would find this novelty an excellent introduction for pantomime. The make-up is life-like, and when the big bird is seen flying about the stage chased by a mischievous monkey, who eventually succeeds in plucking the feathers till the bird is considerably bared, the contagion of laughter infects the whole of the audience.
15/12/1900

CONSIDERABLE excitement was caused recently close to the Strand by a cabhorse coming to grief, and an elderly person, dressed half as man and half as woman, and of a ghastly complexion, running to hold its head. He was assaulted by the cabman, and arrested by a constable on the reasonable suspicion of being a lunatic. He turned out to be one of our most famous music-hall singers, who had half done a quick change in the cab, and the cabman had thus not recognised the young lady who had got in as the old gentleman who had rushed out when the horse fell.
22/12/1900

A KEEPER at Lord George Sanger's circus at Mill Hill left his post office bank book, his pipe and tobacco, some coppers, and various small articles in the pockets of his coat, which he hung up within reach of the elephant he was in charge of. He returned just in time to see the last of these things disappear into the elephant's mouth. The loss of the bank book was serious, as he had saved much money. So he went to a member of the Finchley District Council for advice. The post office authorities were consulted, and they promised the keeper he would not lose his money. The elephant is still alive.

EMMA PLANT, the wife of a circus proprietor, was on Tuesday looking after a glass bottle shooting-range on a piece of waste ground in Bow Common Lane. She left the range in the charge of her

daughter, a little girl of ten, while she went into the caravan which stood behind the range to "turn the meat". A boy of about eleven came up and paid a penny for a shot. The girl loaded the rifle, and the boy fired. At that moment Mrs Plant was coming down the steps of the caravan, and the bullet struck her in the throat, inflicting a wound from which she died the next morning. The boy ran away. At the inquest in Poplar on Thursday the husband stated that the end of the range was protected by steel plates, and that to hit the caravan the aim must have been very wide. The Coroner remarked that the shot might have hit any passer-by; while a juror thought it was exceedingly dangerous to allow little boys to go shooting without the slightest idea of what they were likely to hit. "Death from misadventure" was the verdict, the coroner being requested to draw the attention of the Borough Council to the matter.
29/12/1900

INDEX

ABERYSTWYTH: strict sobriety essential in, 126

ACTOR: accidentally poisons self with cleaning fluid, 29; accidentally reveals identity of villain, 28; arrested at behest of suspected poisoner, 90; assaulted with coal hammer, 79; characterization enhanced by eye injury, 125; dies too far downstage, 129; extinguishes fire with tails of frock-coat, 59; fake telegram trick discovered, 40; fatally stabbed during performance, 82; found sleeping in dusthole, 55; gets lost between dressing-room and stage, 30; goes mad on stage, 92; impaled on dulcimer, 75; injured in sledgehammer fight, 94; insulted by newspaper-reader, 12, 114; invited to join criminal enterprise, 106; loses track of time, 26; mistaken for quack doctor, 62; nose almost severed in melodrama, 49; shoots self in hand, 39; shot at by discarded mistress, 26; stalked by fan, 63; sucked down by small waterspout, 33

ACTORS: deluged with pop, 97; ejected by Sabbatarian landlady, 36; mistaken for bank robbers, 76; narrowly escape shipwreck, 52; pass through solid walls, 51, 60; pelted with mud, 70; quarrel over money prevents performance, 33; stranded by train derailment, 54

ACTRESS: climbs Mount Etna, 113; delusional, 119, 127; dies during Boxing Day pantomime, 57; falls from crane onto stage, 28; feathered headdress catches fire, 102; husband tweaks cab driver's nose, 102; impersonated by high-kicking fruit-picker, 30; impersonated by servant, 11; must have good natural scream, 105; mysterious disappearance of, 60; receives curious marriage proposal from stranger, 51; struck by mallet, 128; threatened by unhinged admirer, 23; thrown into orchestra by curtain, 91; vermin found in bed of, 120; youngest in world, 118

ACROBAT: cuts throat in Birmingham, 65

ACROBATS: destructive, 92

AMAZON WARRIORS: overcrowding of in Sunderland, 48

ASHLEY, Mr and Mrs (actors): deaths from influenza, 20

ANGLO-FRENCH TELEPHONE LINE: opera broadcast from Paris, 12

ARISTOCRATS, thespian: Countess Russell, 26, 117; Duke of Manchester, 113; Earl of Ellesmere's daughters, 51; Earl of Yarmouth, 58, 131; Lord Rosslyn, 102, 105; Lord Sholto Douglas, 65, 72; Viscount Hinton, 114, 118

ARIZONA BILL: reptile-juggler and concertina soloist, 123

AUDIENCE PARTICIPATION: 22, 54, 67, 80, 83, 101, 111, 112, 113, 119, 121, 126, 128, 134

AUSTRALIA: actors do not visit to improve themselves, 32

AUTOMATIC OPERA GLASS BOXES: robbed by night-watchman, 125

BABOON: hit with mantelpiece, 131

BABY INCUBATORS: not potato cans, 118

BALUSTRADE: acting manager chucked over, 85

BANJO: errand boy assaulted with, 7

BARRETT, Wilson (actor): showered with gifts during performance of *Hamlet*, 42

BARRIE, J M: falls off stage, 98

BAT: wreaks havoc in music hall, 54

BEHAVE YOURSELF: assistant must understand this term, 128

BELGIAN GIRLS: forced to pull canal barges, 93

BELL-RINGERS: attempt to gain free entrance to theatre, 36

BERNHARDT, Sarah (actress): protected by limelight man, 107; refuses to climb stairs in Portsmouth, 95; resolves to crush matinée hat nuisance, 129

BERRY, James (ex-hangman): has weirdest show extant, 28; lantern used in lecture contributes to fire, 25

BILLIARD BALL: mistaken for bomb, 49

BOER: explosive, 126

BOURCHIER, Arthur (actor): performance is insult to unnamed society gentleman, 119; trapped overnight in Criterion Theatre, 10

BOX-OFFICE: mistaken for railway ticket-office, 35
BROWN POTTER, Mrs (actress): accidentally stabs Mr Kyrle Bellew, 63; bitten by vampire bat, 60; castigated by American preacher, 52
CAMEL: christened by Mayoress, 104
CAMPBELL, Mrs Patrick (actress): sells kittens at bazaar, 132
CANARY: given to actress in bouquet, 111
CAT: as dramatic critic, 35; chases mouse on tin ceiling, 57; eats theatre's ornamental goldfish, 39; fails to wreck gripping scene, 137; squashed in music hall, 73; strikes solemn chord, 30
CATS: boxing, 116; lucky black, 123; performing, 61, 108, 138
CEILING COLLAPSE: perfectly timed, 138
CHARACTERS KILLED IN PLAY: appear before curtain to remove unpleasant impressions, 112
CHESTNUTS, antediluvian: Henri's Boss Musical Act free from, 104
CHURCHILL, Winston: not an orator, 139
CIGARETTES: souvenir recipients disgusted by lack of gold tips, 88; theatre's stock used up in third act of *Lady Windermere's Fan*, 28
CINEMATOGRAPH: film catches fire, 116; films exchanged for torture paintings, 105
CLOG: agent threatened with, 22
CLOG-DANCE CONTEST: absence of causes riot, 17
CLOG DANCER: thief elopes with, 4
CLOWN: violent, 139
COCAINE: accidentally administered by artiste's mother, 65; as substitute for tea, 107
COCKATOOS: re-enact South African war, 124; wedding of, 136
COMEDIAN: assaulted by American vocalist, 34; cuts throat, 107; expectorating, 10
COMMERCIAL TRAVELLER: threatens to kill theatre manager, 63
CONFECTIONERY, lump of: thrown at actor by blackguard, 77
CONJUROR: finds painter's card in wife's stocking, 14; menaced by boa constrictor, 123; pebbles removed from stomach of, 115
CORNET SOLOIST, one-armed: carried across high wire, 37
COW: invades orchestra pit, 91
CROSSING LEGS: English actors partial to, 4
DACRE, Mr and Mrs Arthur (actors): murder/suicide pact, 70
DADDY WOULDN'T BUY ME A BOW-WOW (song): not appreciated in Denmark, 43
DANCER: falls through glass roof, 53; hurled off stage by centrifugal force, 3; knocked into orchestra by falling scenery, 36; seeks separation from brutal glass-beveller, 92
DE BENSAUDE, Mrs: well rid of Mr De Bensaude, 93
DEVIL'S DISCIPLE, THE (play): mistaken for farce, 122
DOCTOR'S SURGERY: mistaken for music hall, 21
DODDIE and CONQUEROR, unresolved drama of: 17, 19, 21
DOG: disguised as panther, 74; dismayed by stage suicide, 66; hysterical, 107; incendiary, 81; leaps from moving train, 6; makes surprise stage appearance, 95; must die when shot, 124; partially blinded by policeman, 103; sings 'Annie Rooney', 86; stuffed, 53, 59
DOGS: as society entertainers, 95; boxing, 87; invade royal box, 122; performing, 111, 135; save lives at Brighton, 79; should travel by weight if professional performers, 88; worrying, 75
DOVE: sex not enquired into, 42; steals £4 ring, 81
DRESSER: makes surprise stage appearance, 30
DRESSING-ROOMS: ceiling collapses, 97; damp and malodorous, 17; reached by almost perpendicular ladder, 9
DREYFUS, Alfred: audience sympathy for, 122
DUCHESS OF YORK: alleged skill on banjo, 86
EGYPTIAN MUMMY: contains valuable diamond jewellery, 41
ELECTRIC LIGHTS: on costumes, 32, 33, 134; on jewellery, 35
ELECTRIC SHOCK: discourages supers from blocking prompt entrance, 75
ELECTRIC STAIRCASE: instructions for use of, 135
ELECTROPHONE: early attempt to broadcast from theatres, 41
ELEN, Gus: receives begging letter, 56
ELEPHANT: gets stuck in pub, 105; loveliness of Ethel, 127; partner sought to purchase two, 106; post office book eaten by, 140; remains unobserved in house, 31; wrecks milkman's cart, 92
ELK: high-diving, 106
EPILEPTIC FITS: suffered by actor and flautist, 8
FALSE TEETH: dislodged by abandonment to mirth, 14

FISHER, Scott (actor): suicide of, 109
FISHING: on horseback, 96
FITZGEORGE, Mrs (former actress): death of, 3
FLAUTIST: assaulted in field, 121
FOUR-EYED KITTEN: worth same as small barrel organ, 69
FOX, C H (wig-maker): suicide of, 39
FUSE: inadvisibility of holding up to gas light, 66
GALLERY: collapses at Maidenhead theatre, 105
GIANT: stentorian, 137
GLOBE-RUNNER: causes congestion in Strand, 40
GREAT WHEEL: people trapped on overnight, 80
GYMNAST: nose amputated, 119
HEDGEHOG: eaten with anachronistic fork, 139
HICKS, Seymour (actor): age underestimated, 3
HILL, Jenny (singer): not responsible for exploding bouquet, 5
HINCKLEY: inhabited by ignorant bigots, 86
HORSE: acts as motor, 93; does own stunts, 112; drives pony in perambulator, 69; indeterminate sex of, 10; precipitated into cellar, 24
HOUDINI, Harry (escapologist/magician): escapes from handcuffs, 133
HOUSEMAID: attempts to poison employer's family, 49
IBSEN, Henrik: hair is irresistible to imitators, 100; keeps looking-glass in hat, 50
ILFRACOMBE-BUXTON JOURNEY: takes thirty hours, 95
INATTENTIVENESS: rife in Manchester, 94
INDECENT PLACARDS: discovered to be adverts for temperance drink, 56
IRVING, Henry: pet dog falls through trap door, 100; poorly impersonated, 104; robbed by houseboy, 134; shortened by optical illusion, 92
JACKSON, Peter: ambition to play Othello, 49; plays Uncle Tom, 45
JOHANNESBURG: musicians demand exorbitant salaries, 41
JONES, Sissieretta (the Black Patti): does not like to be known as the Black Patti, 62
KALAMAZOO: performance of *Sapho* prevented in by portly police chief, 130
KANGAROO, boxing: widowed at sea, 31
KINDRED SOULS (play): absence of violent deaths deters playgoers, 32
KORRIE, Nellie (child pianist): beats off juvenile footpads, 22
KRUGER, Paul: dispenses sweets from under vest, 138
LAMB: undergoes mock operation on stage, 91
LANGTRY, Edward: dies in lunatic asylum, 99
LANGTRY, Lily: lack of forethought regarding souvenir poem, 124; receives odd business propositions, 123
LENO, Dan: attacked by chicken, 134; mistaken for electrician, 137
LEVEL-CROSSING GATES: demolished by theatre company's train, 69
LIMELIGHT MAN: cries of pain drowned by Ghost in *Hamlet*, 13
LION CUBS: christened with wine, 135
LION TAMER: unjustly accused of picking pocket, 132
MACARONI: incorporated into choreography, 121
MARYLEBONE THEATRE: patron defrauded by former Colney Hatch inmate, 19
MATINEE HATS: combined with fan, 112; removed at Lyceum Theatre, 112
MECHANICAL LEGS: only one set available in each town, 45
MEDICAL STUDENTS: disruptive behaviour of, 59, 100
MOCK FUNERAL: closely followed by real one, 12
MONKEY: declines to bite people, 68
MOONEY, Loretta (vaudeville artiste): marries Lord Sholto Douglas, 65
MOTOR CAR: actress' fans impressed by, 96
MOTOR CAR, prop: collides with prop eagle, 90
MYSTERIOUS CROWLEY (female impersonator): no longer mysterious, 22
NANKI-POO, female: not acceptable to Sir Arthur Sullivan, 45
NETHERSOLE, Olga (actress): carried upstairs in improper manner, 128; theft of jewels foiled by maid, 67
NEW YORKER: hauls London solicitor out of theatre seat, 68
OLD KENT ROAD: thought to be in Scotland, 25
ONE-LEGGED LADY: seeks one-legged partner, 130

OPERA SINGER: falls through floor of cab, 49; saved from shipwreck, 111; struck by dead rabbit, 50; sues "Fairy" for breach of promise, 37; suffers wardrobe malfunction, 50
OSCULATION, mock: causes abandonment of play in Motherwell, 16
OSTRICH: runs amok in Lancaster, 108
PENNY-IN-THE-SLOT GAS METER: theatre illuminated by, 96
PHONOGRAPH: uncanny, 8
PHYSIOGNOMIST: gives rash advice, 43
PIANIST: plays rubbish whilst drunk, 31
PIPE, lit: rashness of leaving in coat pocket, 78
PRIMA-DONNA, pea-shelling: truth behind story of, 66
PROPERTY MAN: led astray by cheap fiction, 51
QUEEN VICTORIA: heroine of Siamese play, 82
RACING MEN: mimic child actress, 9
ROYAL ACADEMY STUDENTS' DRAMATIC CLUB: dire performance by, 64
RUNCORN: fear of, 13
RUSSELL, Ada (singer): brings about redemption of awful scamp, 28
SAUSAGE NIGHT: 27th anniversary of, 76
SCHOOLMASTER, Welsh: conned by bogus agent, 21
SCENERY: blown off train, 7; catches fire, 121; falls on opera singers, 28
SCENIC TEAHOUSE: instability of, 125
SECOND MRS TANQUERAY, THE (play): mistaken for comedy in Birmingham, 115
SERPENTINE DANCE: performed by cockatoo in costume, 136; performer falls over footlights, 32
SHAKESPEARE, alleged descendant of: ejected from bus, 86
SHAKESPEARE'S BIRTHPLACE: American tourists want to write names on wall of, 134
SHEEP: pretty, 121
SHOWMAN, negro: wife attacked by lover in Glasgow, 15
SIDE-COMBS: found in schoolboy's hair, 92
SNAKE: bejewelled, 26; revitalizes listless super, 84
SPARROW: evolution of: 120
SPIRITUAL DIFFICULTIES: attended to in Marylebone, 86
STAG HUNT: splendid novelty for any pantomime, 17
STAGE EXPLOSION: mistaken for Anarchist outrage, 49
STAMPEDE: causes disaster in Gateshead theatre, 18
STEAM, clouds of: enhances dance in pantomime, 36
STOCK: actors must know meaning of word, 77
STRIPTEASE: in French opera, 130; prior to equestrian act, 111; prior to trapeze act, 108
STUFFED BABIES: sat on by pantomime star, 44
SUN BLIND: vandalized during hours of darkness, 68
SWORD: blade flies into audience, 41
TAIL: patent pneumatic, 113; wagged by string, 67
TALKING: during performance: 8, 84
TA-RA-RA BOOM-DE-AY: as accompaniment to vandalism, 27; dance performed by horse, 34
TATTOOED MAN: mistaken for bridegroom in Wales, 11
TEMPEST, Marie (actress): refuses to wear knickerbockers, 124
TERRISS, Ellaline (actress): distasteful representation of tipsy young wife, 126
TERRISS, William (actor): murder, 101; stage deaths, 8
TERRY, Ellen: covets milkman's smock, 97; disputed birthplace of, 110; tormented by creaky noise, 118
THEATRICAL AGENT: fraudulent, 46
THOMAS, Brandon (author and actor): eats mysterious cake, 43
TIPS: resented by music hall artiste, 97
TOPLESS KNIFE FIGHT: indignantly refuted, 116
TRAIN, profile: effect of ruined by small girl, 16; pushed aside by actor with comic effect, 97
TREE, Herbert Beerbohm (actor): extinguishes fire as Hamlet, 23; prize-winning teeth of infant, 67; robbed by visitor, 78
TRICYCLE: bulletproof, 76; elephantine, 26; involved in child actor's disappearance, 103; owned by unlucky Mr McAnney, 61; ridden by Irish lady playwright, 129
TROMBONE: played underwater, 45
TURNIP: thrown from bridge and caught on fork, 76
VAN BIENE, Auguste (actor and musician): dislikes 'music dragged in by the hair', 98; not a professional beauty, 89; trapped in dressing-room by boarhound, 116

VENTRILOQUIST'S DUMMY: receives valuable gift from Alfred Rothschild, 91
VICTORINA (strong lady): carries pony off stage, 32; seeks club-swinging cleaning lady, 13
WATER COOLER: inadequate substitute for funerary urn, 90
WEBBER, Hannah (male impersonator): works passage to England disguised as cattleman, 97
WOODEN LEG: used to conceal rifle in proposed drama, 25
WOODEN THEATRE: ideal for peeping Toms, 57
X-RAYS: grand side show, 110
YODELLERS: German sopranos preferred, 35
YORICK'S SKULL: christened in champagne, 49
ZALESKA, Wanda (theatre lessee): fires shots at ruffians, 22; takes charge of bear at railway station, 42

ABOUT THE AUTHOR

Julia D Atkinson was born in Bradford, West Yorkshire, in 1960. She was formerly a critic for the British Theatre Guide. Her ground-breaking article *A name not just now familiar to ears polite:* The Importance of Being Earnest *and* Lady Windermere's Fan *on tour, 1895-1900*, was published in the July 2015 issue of *The Wildean: a Journal of Oscar Wilde Studies*. She now lives in York.

From the same author in this series:
A Complete Somersault into the Orchestra: Comic and Curious Clippings from the Legendary Theatrical Paper The Era, *1870-1880*
Please Throw Two Carrots at Your Mother: Comic and Curious Clippings from the Legendary Theatrical Paper The Era, *1880-1890*
Crocodiles in the Green Room: Comic and Curious Clippings from the Legendary Theatrical Paper The Era, *1900-1910*

FAIRIES IN CABS

www.ingramcontent.com/pod-product-compliance
Lightning Source LLC
Chambersburg PA
CBHW081449070526
44586CB00019B/2276